best of the best

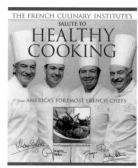

LOBSTER
AT HOME

JASPER WHITE
WINNER OF THE JAMES BEARD AWARD

THE FRENCH CULINARY INSTITUTE'S
SALUTE TO
HEALTHY
COOKING

from AMERICA'S FOREMOST FRENCH CHEFS

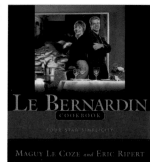

Le Bernardin
COOKBOOK

FOUR-STAR SIMPLICITY

MAGUY LE COZE and ERIC RIPERT

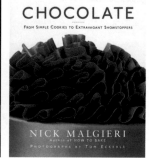

CHOCOLATE
FROM SIMPLE COOKIES TO EXTRAVAGANT SHOWSTOPPERS

NICK MALGIERI
Author of HOW TO BAKE
PHOTOGRAPHS BY TOM ECKERLE

JEAN-GEORGE
Cooking at Home with a Four-Star Ch

JEAN-GEORGES VONGERICHTE
AND MARK BITTMAN

best ^{of} the
best

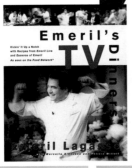

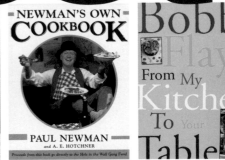

THE BEST RECIPES
FROM THE 35 BEST COOKBOOKS
OF THE YEAR

American Express Publishing Corporation
New York

FOOD & WINE BOOKS

Editor in Chief **Judith Hill**

Art Director **Perri DeFino**

Managing Editor **Terri Mauro**

Consulting Editor **Dana Speers**

Designer **Leslie Andersen**

Production Editor **Amy Schuler**

Copy Editor **Barbara A. Mateer**

Editorial Assistant **Colleen McKinney**

Production Coordinator **Catherine DeAngelis**

Vice President, Consumer Marketing **Mark V. Stanich**

Director, Brand Development **David Geller**

Director, Retail Sales **Marshall Corey**

Marketing Manager **Johanna Morelli**

Operations Manager **Doreen Camardi**

Business Manager **Joanne Ragazzo**

ISBN: 0-916103-53-6   ISSN: 1524-2862

contents

best of the best defined

what's in this book

Hundreds of cookbooks come out each year. We read them, we test and taste recipes, we check sales statistics. Eventually, we winnow the field to those that we, the editors of FOOD & WINE Books, consider to be the most deserving and the most popular cookbooks of the year. At the same time, we're on the lookout for the most interesting, tastiest recipes. This volume recognizes the 115 best recipes from the 35 best cookbooks published this year—the best of the best.

We print each recipe exactly as it appears in its own book, and, so that you can really get the feeling of each cookbook, we duplicate as closely as possible the layout and design. An explanation of why we selected it, some highlights from the book, and its cover precede each selection of recipes.

The organization into categories is dictated by the best books themselves, and these divisions change each year depending on the subjects of the cookbooks honored. This year, for instance, there aren't enough noteworthy vegetarian and healthy books to fill a chapter; whereas restaurant-chefs' cookbooks are still going strong and so form their own category this year as they did last.

what's not

- Culinary reference books or textbooks
- Books published solely as paperbacks
- Books only published outside the U.S.

Judith Hill

JUDITH HILL, *Editor in Chief*,
FOOD & WINE Books

if we could buy only 4 cookbooks this year, they'd be

LOBSTER AT HOME
by Jasper White

MEDITERRANEAN GRAINS AND GREENS
by Paula Wolfert

MY MOTHER'S SOUTHERN DESSERTS
by James Villas and Martha Pearl Villas

SEDUCTIONS OF RICE
by Jeffrey Alford and Naomi Duguid

editor's choice awards

Editor's Choice Award
best of the best

As we perused and read and tested all the cookbooks published this year, favorites emerged, even among our chosen Best of the Best. We are pleased to present here our Editor's Choice Awards—the crème de la crème.

best book of the year

MEDITERRANEAN GRAINS AND GREENS

BY PAULA WOLFERT

PAGE 96

HARPERCOLLINS PUBLISHERS, INC.

most delectable recipe

SAVORY

RISOTTO WITH LOBSTER

PAGE 20

from **LOBSTER AT HOME**

BY JASPER WHITE

SCRIBNER

most fascinating to read

SEDUCTIONS OF RICE

BY JEFFREY ALFORD AND NAOMI DUGUID

PAGE 186

ARTISAN

SWEET

SNOWFLAKE COCONUT CAKE WITH

SEVEN-MINUTE FROSTING

PAGE 245

from **MY MOTHER'S SOUTHERN DESSERTS**

BY JAMES VILLAS AND MARTHA PEARL VILLAS

WILLIAM MORROW AND COMPANY, INC.

best looking

THE CAFE COOK BOOK

BY ROSE GRAY AND RUTH ROGERS

PAGE 44

BROADWAY BOOKS

category **1**

restaurant

Chefs market themselves just like any other celebrities. Their faces appear on magazine covers, on television, and, of course, on book jackets. When the first star-chef books appeared over a decade ago, many of the recipes were unrealistically complicated. The genre therefore waned, but it's back and more vital than ever because today's chefs are savvier about what sells. Now we benefit as much as they do. Their books are crammed with dishes that, besides being impressive, stylish, and delectable, are entirely possible—even easy—to make at home.

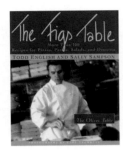
chefs

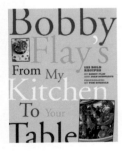

lobster demystified and cooked to perfection

author

New England seafood authority Jasper White, formerly chef/owner of Jasper's in Boston

why he wrote it

"This book is the result of what I've learned so far about lobster. Too often we reserve it for eating in a restaurant or pass over it in the market in favor of what we think of as more easily prepared food. In this book I hope to show you how easy and rewarding it can be to cook lobster at home."

why it made our list

We'd love this book for nothing more than its dead-on accurate instructions for steaming lobster; one taste of the succulent meat right out of the steamer convinced us to use his method forevermore. And his lobster broth just slurped up with a spoon is heaven. But why stop there when White offers so many excellent ways to use these two basics, from the classic Lobster Thermidor and Lobster Newburg to the innovative Lobster Pizza and Lobster-Papaya Quesadillas with Mango Cream? With helpful diagrams and detailed instructions, White makes dealing with a lobster easy, even for first-time lobster cooks.

chapters

The Lobster Primer • Basic Cooking Techniques • Soups, Broths, Chowders and a Bisque • Hot Appetizers and Small Dishes • Lobster Salads, Sandwiches, Cold Plates and Composed Salads • Classic Main Courses • Great Lobsters from Great Chefs

previous books

White is the author of *Jasper White's Cooking from New England*.

specifics

255 pages, 114 recipes, 8 color photographs, $30. Published by Scribner.

from the book

"In addition to checking the lobster for general appearance, hardness of shell, length of antennae, and weight (in relation to size), I also look for a lively disposition. A freshly caught, healthy lobster should swing its claws at you like a prizefighter."

LOBSTER
AT HOME

JASPER WHITE
WINNER OF THE JAMES BEARD AWARD

STEAMING LOBSTERS

Steaming lobsters has several advantages over boiling. Steaming cooks lobsters more slowly than boiling, producing meat that is tenderer, especially with larger lobsters. Steaming is more forgiving than boiling, making overcooking less of a risk and allowing for the inevitable lag time between cooking and serving. It is also safer and cleaner than boiling because there is no spillover or gallons of near-boiling water to dispose of. Last and most important, steam does not penetrate the way water can and therefore preserves the true flavor of the lobster.

There are several methods for steaming lobster: on the grill wrapped in foil, in the oven and even in the microwave (opposite page). The most common method, however, is to steam the lobsters in a pot on the stove. Any pot can be transformed into a steamer, although the ideal pot for steaming is the same as for boiling: tall and somewhat narrow but large enough to allow the steam to circulate around the lobsters. The lobsters must be suspended far enough above the water so that when they release liquid during steaming, they do not end up sitting in it. If you do not own one of those venerable three-piece black steamers with a spigot on the bottom sold in New England hardware stores, seafood markets and cookware stores, there are several ways to improvise a rack. A colander placed upside down works well. Rockweed, when available, makes a great "rack" and adds the smell of the ocean to the steamer. Simply place 8 to 10 inches of rockweed on the bottom of the pot with just enough water to get things started (½ inch).

The ratio of lobsters to the pot is similar to that for boiling. A 4- to 5-gallon pot is ideal for steaming a total of 6 to 8 pounds of lobster. That means the pot will comfortably hold six 1-pound (chicken) lobsters, four 1½- to 2-pound (select) lobsters or two 2½- to 3-pound (jumbo) lobsters. Plan accordingly. Use more than one pot if necessary. If the lobsters do not fit comfortably in the pot and if you cannot see the bottom of the pot, it is overcrowded.

The procedure for steaming is simple: Fill the steamer pot with 1 inch of salt water, either ocean water or fresh water with salt added. Set up the steaming rack inside the pot. Turn the heat to high and cover the steamer. The water will boil quickly. When it does, place the lobsters in the pot and cover tightly. Use the chart on the opposite page to time the lobsters. Rearrange the lobsters halfway through the steaming. Be careful when removing the lid—the steam is very hot. Using long tongs, move the lobsters around. Work quickly and cover the pot again as soon as possible. When the lobsters have cooked for the recommended time, remove one and break it open where the carapace meets the tail. The tail meat should be creamy white with no translucency, and the roe, if there is any, should be bright red. If not, allow the lobsters to steam for a few minutes more. When they are ready, turn off the steamer and serve as soon as possible.

STEAMING CHART FOR LOBSTER

Time the lobsters from the moment they are added to the pot. Times are based on the lobster-to-pot ratio recommended on page 12. Cover the steamer tightly immediately after adding the lobsters.

1 pound	10 minutes
1¼ pounds	12 minutes
1½ pounds	14 minutes
1¾ pounds	16 minutes
2 pounds	18 minutes
2½ pounds	22 minutes
3 pounds	25 to 30 minutes
5 pounds	40 to 45 minutes

STEAMING LOBSTER IN A MICROWAVE

There are several good reasons to steam lobster in a microwave oven. The combination of direct cooking from the microwaves and steaming produces an evenly cooked, tender lobster. Using this technique is slightly faster than steaming on the stovetop in a pot. And best of all, there is no pot to be cleaned and no hot water to dispose of. The biggest drawback is that you can cook only one lobster at a time, but if you want to cook up a couple of lobsters for salad or another cold preparation, that is no problem.

To steam lobster in a microwave, you will need a 1-gallon plastic zippered freezer bag. Cut a lemon in half. Spear one lemon half on the head of the lobster (the rostrum will stick right in the lemon). The lemon flavors the steam and at the same time covers the rostrum, thus preventing it from ripping a hole in the bag. Carefully place the lobster in the freezer bag, add a few pieces of rockweed, seal the bag and place on a plate in the microwave. Cook at the highest setting. The water sacs in the rockweed will burst and release steam, like a miniature lobster bake. If no rockweed is available, add ¼ cup of water instead. Follow the chart below for recommended cooking times.

MICROWAVE STEAMING CHART FOR LOBSTER

For lobsters over 2 pounds, you will need a 2-gallon freezer bag. Since every microwave oven is a little different, you may need to adjust your cooking time accordingly.

1 pound	6 minutes
1¼ pounds	7 minutes
1½ pounds	8 minutes
1¾ pounds	9 minutes

Removing Steamed Lobster (page 12)

Avocado & Lobster Salad with Toasted Almonds (page 16)

Avocado & Lobster Salad with Toasted Almonds

The pairing of chilled lobster and avocado seems at first to be light and refreshing, but in fact it is luscious and special—a perfect marriage of creamy texture and rich flavors. I like to use crunchy garnishes—romaine, carrots, bean sprouts and almonds, which contrast nicely with the soft avocado. To ensure that your avocados are perfectly ripe, purchase them a few days in advance. Refrigerate only after they have ripened. I prefer this dish as a main course; it is a little too rich for an appetizer.

ingredients for 1 batch Traditional Lobster Salad (page 18)

¼ cup sliced blanched almonds

kosher or sea salt

1 head romaine lettuce

2 ounces soybean sprouts

½ medium carrot (2 ounces), peeled, grated or very thinly slivered (julienne)

3 scallions (white and some green parts), very thinly sliced on a diagonal

¼ cup peanut, avocado or almond oil

2 tablespoons white wine or champagne vinegar

1 teaspoon sugar

freshly ground black pepper

½ pint cherry or pear tomatoes, red and/or yellow

6 fresh basil leaves, coarsely chopped

2 ripe large avocados

1. Prepare the lobster salad. Cover and chill for at least 30 minutes. Chill the plates you will be using as well.

2. Preheat the oven to 300°F. Spread the almonds on a small baking sheet and toast for about 20 minutes until they begin to turn golden. Remove from the oven and immediately sprinkle generously with salt. Let cool, then wrap tightly in plastic wrap. This can be done several hours in advance.

3. Remove the dark, tough outer lettuce leaves and discard. Choose 8 beautiful yellow leaves from the heart. Rinse, drain, cover and refrigerate. Rinse and dry the remaining lettuce and cut into thin strips about ¼ inch wide (chiffonade). Mix with the bean sprouts, carrot and scallions. Cover and refrigerate until ready to use.

4. Combine the oil, vinegar and sugar to make a vinaigrette. Season to taste with salt and pepper. Halve the tomatoes and combine with the basil and 2 tablespoons of the vinaigrette in a bowl. Let stand while you prepare the salads.

5. Halve the avocados and carefully remove the pits. Using a large serving spoon, scoop the avocado out of its skin. Keep the spoon pressed against the skin so that you do not mar the avocado halves. This job can also be done by simply peeling the skin off with your fingers.

6. Place 2 lettuce leaves on each of 4 plates so that they stick up slightly over the lip of the plate, looking like a pair of rabbit ears. Drizzle a few drops of vinaigrette on each leaf. Combine the lettuce mixture with the remaining vinaigrette and spread it around each plate, leaving a little nest in the center. Place an avocado half in the center and fill with lobster salad. Try not to be perfect; the salad looks better when the lobster salad spills over a little, leaving some of the avocado showing. Spoon the tomatoes around the avocado and sprinkle with toasted almonds.

Serves 4 as a main course

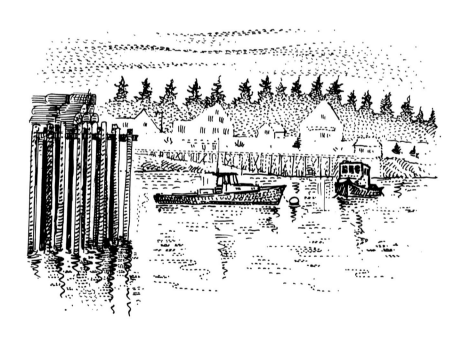

Traditional Lobster Salad

This classic mayonnaise-based lobster salad reminds me of Fourth of July picnics on the Maine coast. Its beautiful colors and rich taste, as well as the many ways it can be presented—set it out at a family-style buffet or use it for sandwiches—make it a favorite with my family. My recipe strays from the standard by substituting cucumber and scallion for the usual chopped celery and onion. I like the crunch of the cucumber, and the scallions don't leave the bitter taste that raw onion can. The recipe gives you the option of using bottled mayonnaise or making Special Tarragon Mayonnaise, which is also excellent for other cold seafood salads such as crab, salmon and tuna.

Fresh tarragon melds beautifully with sumptuous lobster meat but should not be overdone—do not use more than the recommended amount. If fresh tarragon is unavailable, omit it; dried tarragon is a poor substitute. This salad is best eaten a few hours after it is made, but it will keep, covered and refrigerated, for up to 2 days.

1 pound fully cooked lobster meat, or 5 pounds live lobsters

1 medium cucumber (5 to 6 ounces), peeled, seeded and finely diced

½ cup Special Tarragon Mayonnaise (recipe follows) or bottled mayonnaise

3 small scallions (white and most of the green parts), thinly sliced

kosher or sea salt

freshly ground black pepper

1. If using live lobsters, steam or boil them. Let cool at room temperature. Use a cleaver to crack and remove the meat from the claws, knuckles and tails. Remove the cartilage from the claws and the intestine from the tails of the cooked meat. Cut the meat into ½-inch dice. You may pick all the meat from the carcass and add it to the meat or freeze the carcass for soup or broth.

2. Place the cucumber in a colander for at least 5 minutes to drain the excess liquid.

3. Combine the lobster, cucumber and mayonnaise. If the salad is to be served within the hour, add the scallions. If not, add them 30 minutes before serving. Season with salt if needed and pepper. Cover with plastic wrap and chill for at least 30 minutes before serving.

Serves 6 for sandwiches or as a light entrée

Special Tarragon Mayonnaise

Covered and refrigerated, this mayonnaise will keep for up to three days.

1 large egg yolk

1 tablespoon Dijon mustard

2 teaspoons chopped fresh tarragon leaves

1 cup salad oil, such as safflower, sunflower or peanut (avoid full-flavored oil)

juice of ½ large lemon

1 tablespoon ice water

kosher or sea salt

freshly ground black pepper

cayenne pepper or Tabasco sauce

By Hand

1. Place a stainless-steel mixing bowl on a damp cloth to keep the bowl from sliding around. Add the egg yolk, mustard and tarragon to the bowl and whisk until blended.

2. Drizzle the oil into the bowl while whisking constantly. Be sure that the mixture is smooth and well blended at all times. Stop adding the oil periodically to allow yourself time to catch up; when there is no oil visible, continue adding and whisking. When half the oil is added, add 1 teaspoon of the lemon juice. Alternate between the remaining oil and lemon juice, whisking all the while, until both are incorporated.

3. Whisk in the ice water. (The water stabilizes the mayonnaise, which prevents separating, a common flaw of homemade mayonnaise.) Season to taste with salt, pepper and cayenne. Whisk. Store in a small container, covered and refrigerated, until needed.

Using a Food Processor

1. Place the egg yolk, mustard and tarragon in the bowl of a food processor. Put the lid on and pulse the machine for a few seconds to blend the ingredients.

2. With the machine on, add half the oil by pouring it in at a slow but steady speed. Alternate the last half of the oil with the lemon juice until both are incorporated.

3. Add the ice water and pulse for a few seconds. Season to taste with salt, pepper and cayenne. Pulse. Store in a small container, covered and refrigerated, until needed.

Makes 1 cup

COOK'S NOTE: *To make this a sauce for chilled lobster, add 2 tablespoons water or 3 tablespoons heavy cream for each ½ cup mayonnaise. Even better, add chopped cooked roe (2 tablespoons per ½ cup), finely diced tomato (4 tablespoons per ½ cup) or chopped hard-boiled egg (1 egg per ½ cup). One tablespoon freshly chopped Italian parsley tastes good with any of the added ingredients.*

most delectable savory recipe

Risotto with Lobster

Risotto, a creamy dish of rice cooked in broth and finished with butter and cheese, is a gem of Northern Italian cuisine. It is made with highly glutinous arborio rice, available in most supermarkets. The rice is first sautéed in butter and olive oil, and then hot broth is added to it in small amounts. The rice is stirred continuously during the cooking, and more broth is added only after all the previous broth has been absorbed. After the rice is cooked al dente—firm to the bite—it is removed from the heat and finished by stirring in butter and cheese, though cheese is not always used. The cooking time from start to finish is about seventeen minutes.

The broth, which is usually chicken, plays an important role in the final taste of risotto, serving as the canvas on which all the other flavors are blended. When made with lobster, the broth moves a step ahead, becoming the defining characteristic of the dish. Lobster broth produces such exquisitely flavored rice that even lobster meat as a garnish is optional.

I have created a master recipe for making risotto with lobster broth; it is purposely simple, intended to feature the flavorful Savory Lobster Broth without such competing flavors as cheese, mushrooms or vegetables. The variations following the recipe demonstrate the broth's ability to integrate beautifully with other ingredients.

Equipment: You will need a heavy 2-quart saucepan, a small pot to heat up 2 cups broth, a ladle and a wooden spoon. The 2-quart pot allows for fast and even cooking and gives you plenty of room to stir the rice. The wooden spoon prevents the rice from absorbing any metallic flavor.

4 ounces fully cooked lobster meat, or
1 live 1¼-pound lobster
2 cups Savory Lobster Broth (page 22)
2 tablespoons olive oil
2 tablespoons unsalted butter

1 small onion (3 ounces), finely diced
1 cup Arborio rice
kosher or sea salt
freshly ground black pepper

1. If using live lobster, boil or steam it. Let cool at room temperature. Use a cleaver to crack and remove the meat from the claws, knuckles and tail. Remove the cartilage from the claws and the intestine from the tail of the cooked meat. Cut the lobster meat into chunks about ½ to ¾ inch thick. Cover and refrigerate until you are ready to cook the risotto.

2. Heat the lobster broth in a small pot and keep hot but not boiling.

3. Before making the risotto, remove the lobster meat from the refrigerator and let stand at room temperature. Preheat the oven to 200°F to warm the serving platter or plates.

4. Heat the olive oil and 1 tablespoon of the butter in a heavy 2-quart saucepan over medium heat until the butter is melted. Add the onion and cook gently for 4 to 5 minutes until golden. Add the rice and stir continuously, using a wooden spoon, for 1 minute. Ladle in about ⅓ cup hot broth. Stir constantly and gently until the broth is absorbed. Add another ladleful of broth and stir constantly until the broth is absorbed; repeat until the rice is cooked al dente. Stir in the lobster meat and remove from the heat. Season with salt and pepper. It should require very little seasoning because the lobster broth is already highly seasoned. Stir in the remaining butter and spoon the risotto onto the warmed platter or individual plates. Serve at once.

Serves 4 as a first course

COOK'S NOTE: *You can transform Risotto with Lobster into spectacular variations by simply adding one or two ingredients to the original recipe.*

Risotto with Lobster & Parmigiano-Reggiano

Add to the fully cooked risotto ¼ cup grated Parmigiano-Reggiano cheese along with the last tablespoon butter.

Risotto with Lobster & Fresh Peas

Cook ½ cup shucked fresh peas in a small pot of boiling salted water until tender (8 ounces fresh garden peas will make about ½ cup shucked). Remove the peas from the boiling water and submerge in ice water immediately to stop the cooking. Drain and reserve. Before you add the last ladleful of lobster broth to the risotto, combine 1 tablespoon lobster broth with the last tablespoon butter and the blanched peas in a small skillet (6 inches). Warm the peas over medium heat. Gently stir the peas with the buttery sauce into the fully cooked risotto.

Savory Lobster Broth

A RECIPE OF MAJOR IMPORTANCE

The exquisite flavor and fragrant aroma of this broth comes from roasting lobster carcasses and simmering them with caramelized vegetables, wine, tomatoes, herbs and spices. The flavor is slightly reminiscent of the classic French fish soup soupe de poissons *but has a more pronounced lobster taste and is not as thick. Powerful on the first sip, it gradually softens with lingering layers of complex flavors. Like raw oysters, this broth enlivens the palate and gives you a surge of energy. It serves as the base for many other dishes made with fish and shellfish; it can make a quick sauce for pasta; and it is the foundation for more serious sauces such as Lobster Thermidor.*

For the home cook, this broth takes more time than effort. Like other stocks and broths, once you put it together, it is simply a matter of being at home while it cooks. This recipe makes approximately 5 quarts; you may halve the recipe if desired, but it will reduce faster and yield a little less broth.

This recipe can be made with the carcasses from lobsters weighing 1 to 3 pounds. Carcasses from larger lobsters will take longer to cook in order to extract their full flavor, but the flavors will be the same whatever the size you use.

Equipment: You will need a medium Chinese cleaver or large chef's knife, a large stockpot (at least 12 quarts), a roasting pan or baking sheet and a china cap or strainer.

8 small or 4 to 6 medium lobster carcasses, 2½ to 3 pounds total

2 tablespoons plus ¼ cup olive oil (not extra-virgin)

8 to 10 cloves garlic, sliced

3 or 4 medium onions (1½ pounds), coarsely chopped

3 or 4 medium carrots (8 ounces), peeled and coarsely chopped

1 small bulb fennel (8 ounces), coarsely chopped (*optional;* not available in early summer)

5 quarts water, plus a little more for deglazing

1 bottle (750 milliliters) dry white wine

3 or 4 ribs celery (8 ounces), coarsely chopped

1 can (28 ounces) good-quality Italian plum tomatoes

2 tablespoons whole black peppercorns

1 teaspoon Spanish saffron threads

½ to 1 teaspoon dried red pepper flakes

2 bay leaves

4 sprigs fresh thyme

6 sprigs fresh tarragon

kosher or sea salt

freshly ground black pepper

1. Preheat the oven to 400°F.

2. With a cleaver or chef's knife, split the lobster carcasses in half lengthwise and remove the head sacs and half of the tomalley. If using the carcasses of large lobsters, split them again to quarter them. Place the carcasses, shell side up, in a large roasting pan or on a baking sheet and drizzle 2 tablespoons olive oil over all. Place in the oven and roast for about 45 minutes, turning the pieces over halfway through the roasting. The roasted carcasses will be brittle and slightly browned (even a little charred) and will release a heavy, sweet smell.

3. Pour the remaining ¼ cup olive oil in a 12-inch sauté pan over medium heat. Add the garlic, onions, carrots and fennel to the pan and cook without stirring for 5 minutes. Then stir every 3 or 4 minutes to prevent sticking for about 20 minutes until the vegetables are well browned. Place in the stockpot. Deglaze the pan with a little water and add to the pot as well.

4. Combine the 5 quarts water and the wine in the pot with the browned vegetables. Add the celery. Break the tomatoes into pieces using your hands or a fork and add to the pot. Bring to a boil, then reduce the heat for a steady simmer.

5. Add the roasted lobster carcasses to the pot. Deglaze the roasting pan with a little water, scraping the little browned bits from the bottom of the pan. Add to the pot.

6. Skim the foam from the top of the broth if necessary and add the peppercorns, saffron threads, red pepper, bay leaves, thyme and tarragon. Lobster broth should not simmer as slowly as chicken stock. Look for a steady bubbling but not a rolling boil. It takes this more aggressive simmer to extract the full flavor of the broth. Simmer for 1½ to 2 hours, stirring occasionally. After 1 hour, lightly salt the broth and begin periodic tastings at intervals of 10 minutes. It should taste rich and savory with a distinct flavor of lobster and subtle underlying flavors of the other ingredients.

7. Strain the broth and season to taste with salt and pepper. Use a ladle to remove some of the oil that settles on top, but do not remove all of it because it has great flavor and character. Cover and chill the broth until needed. Refrigerated, it will keep well for 2 to 3 days. It can be frozen for up to 4 weeks.

Makes 5 quarts

from a restaurant
that's unlike any other

authors

The powers that be at Le Bernardin, New York's celebrated seafood restaurant: Maguy Le Coze, who opened the restaurant in 1986 with her late brother Gilbert, and Eric Ripert, the young chef who worked with the brother-and-sister team and eventually took over the kitchen when Gilbert passed away

why they wrote it

According to Le Coze, "This book is about the spirit of Le Bernardin, the lives of Gilbert, Eric, and myself. It's about dedication and joy and hard work, and the true art of Gilbert Le Coze, which was not just food but life itself."

why it made our list

Le Coze's introduction, about herself and her brother and the struggles and experiences that led to the opening of their restaurant, is a real page-turner; we couldn't stop reading it. The recipes that make up the rest of the book are no less compelling. Famous for impeccable, lean and clean fish dishes, Le Bernardin is arguably the best fish restaurant in the United States, and now its famous preparations are accessible to everyone, in clear and concise recipes that make the most of each fish variety. "Every fish gets treated according to its personality," explains Ripert. "What I do is look for the right sauce and the right vegetable for each fish. That way, everything goes together, and the fish is the star of the plate."

chapters

Basics • Raw Fish • Salads • Appetizers • Poached and Steamed Fish • Sautéed Fish • Roasted Fish • Grilled Fish • Shellfish • Big Parties • Desserts

specifics

384 pages, 133 recipes, 18 color photographs, 18 black-and-white photographs, $35. Published by Doubleday.

from the book

"Gilbert's idea to serve raw fish actually came from our uncle Corentin, a fisherman in Port Navalo. In those days, fishermen used to go out on boats for a month, to Terre Neuve, to catch cod. When uncle got hungry, he'd take a cod, skin it, slice it, add salt and pepper, and eat it with bread."

Le Bernardin

COOKBOOK

FOUR-STAR SIMPLICITY

MAGUY LE COZE *and* ERIC RIPERT

Herb Salad with Thyme-Crusted Tuna

Makes 4 servings

Eric: *Joel Robuchon inspired this salad—he used to serve a similar one in Paris—and I could eat it every day. To make it even better, toss in truffle shavings and barbecue the tuna.*

Maguy: *Barbecue Tuna? Oooh-la-la. I guess you'd say this is our tribute to American salads. Thank goodness we shave truffles on top to make the salad really French.*

4 cups mesclun (baby greens)

4 teaspoons fresh chervil leaves

12 small fresh basil leaves

20 fresh tarragon leaves

8 fresh mint leaves

2 (1-inch-thick) tuna steaks (about 10 ounces each)

4 teaspoons barely chopped fresh thyme leaves

$^1\!/_2$ teaspoon coarse sea salt

$^1\!/_2$ teaspoon freshly ground white pepper

$^1\!/_2$ cup extra-virgin olive oil

$^1\!/_2$ cup vinaigrette (opposite page)

Balsamic vinegar, for garnish

SPECIAL EQUIPMENT:

Two 10-inch nonstick skillets

1 In a bowl, toss the mesclun with the chervil, basil, tarragon, and mint. Set aside.

2 Trim off and discard the dark blood section of the tuna. Sprinkle one side of each tuna steak with a teaspoon of thyme, a pinch of salt, and a pinch of

pepper. Drizzle 1 tablespoon of olive oil over each steak and rub it into the tuna. Turn the steaks over and repeat on the other side.

3   Heat two 10-inch nonstick skillets over high heat until just smoking. Add 1 tuna steak to each skillet and sear until the tuna is browned on the outside and rare, but warm in the center, about 1½ minutes per side. Cut the tuna on the diagonal into ½-inch-wide slices.

4   Toss the mesclun mixture with the vinaigrette. Divide the salad among 4 dinner plates, mounding it to the side of the plate. Fan the tuna slices in a half-circle around the salad. Drizzle 1 tablespoon of olive oil on each plate, making an arc in front of the tuna. Drizzle a few drops of balsamic vinegar into the olive oil and serve immediately.

Vinaigrette

Makes 1¹/₃ cups

2 teaspoons Dijon mustard

1 teaspoon fine sea salt

2 pinches freshly ground white pepper

3 tablespoons red wine vinegar

3 tablespoons sherry vinegar

½ cup plus 1 tablespoon olive oil

½ cup plus 1 tablespoon corn oil

In a mixing bowl, whisk together the mustard, salt, pepper, and vinegars. Whisking constantly, very slowly drizzle in the olive oil and then the corn oil. Store, tightly covered, in the refrigerator for up to 1 week.

Black Bass Seviche

Makes 4 servings

Eric: *Gilbert invented this dish with classical seviche in mind, but he made it his own with a well-timed, last-minute squeeze of lemon juice. The result is a tangier, fresher seviche. Just make sure the fish dice is small enough, otherwise the lemon juice won't "cook" the black bass.*

Maguy: *When Eric makes this seviche, he chops the black bass very fine. When I make it, I like the pieces chunkier, so you can feel the fish in your mouth. And since I'm not diet-conscious, I always add extra olive oil.*

2 (6-ounce) black bass fillets

1 teaspoon seeded and very finely diced jalapeño

$\frac{1}{2}$ ripe tomato, peeled, seeded, and cut into $\frac{1}{8}$-inch dice (opposite page)

1 teaspoon thinly sliced fresh mint leaves

1 teaspoon thinly sliced fresh coriander leaves

Fine sea salt, to taste

Freshly ground white pepper, to taste

6 tablespoons extra-virgin olive oil

Juice of 1 lime

Juice of 1 lemon

4 slices toasted country-style bread, quartered

1   Skin the fillets and trim off any blood or white parts left from the skin. Cut the bass into tiny dice (no larger than $\frac{1}{8}$ inch). Divide it among four 8-inch salad plates. Use a fork to gently spread the bass into a flat, even layer, covering the surface of the plates up to the rim. Cover the plates with plastic and refrigerate each one as you finish.

2   Sprinkle the jalapeño, then the tomato, mint, and coriander over each plate. *(The recipe can be made to this point up to 5 hours ahead; cover the plates with plastic and refrigerate.)*

3   To serve, hold your fingers several inches above the plates and sprinkle with salt and pepper. Drizzle 1½ tablespoons of olive oil over each plate, making sure all of the fish is coated with oil. Still working well above the fish, sprinkle it with the lime juice and then the lemon juice.

4   Taste a little of the seviche and season with more salt and lemon juice if needed. Serve immediately, passing the toast separately.

Dicing Tomatoes

1   Bring a medium-size saucepan of water to a boil. Core each tomato and cut a small X across the bottom. Blanch in the boiling water to just loosen the skin but not cook the tomato, about 5 seconds. Immediately dip the tomato into a bowl of ice water until cold.

2   Peel and quarter each tomato. Use a paring knife to scrape out all the seeds and pulp, leaving only the firm, outer shell of the tomato. Cut into very neat dice, as called for in the recipe.

Chocolate Mille-Feuille

Left: Black Bass Seviche

CHOCOLATE MILLE-FEUILLE

Makes 8 servings

Eric: *I don't know what inspiration moved Hervé, our pastry chef, and his then sous chef Paul, to make chocolate mille-feuille, but it must have been divine. The dessert certainly is.*

¹/₂ cup plus 6 tablespoons unsalted butter

¹/₄ cup unsweetened cocoa powder, plus more for garnish

5 sheets frozen phyllo dough, defrosted

5 scant tablespoons sugar

1 recipe Pastry Cream (page 34)

1 recipe Espresso-Chocolate Ganache (page 35)

1 cup heavy cream

SPECIAL EQUIPMENT:

Parchment paper

Pastry brush

1   Cut a sheet of parchment paper slightly larger than the phyllo and place it on a work surface. Heat the butter in a small saucepan until the butter melts but is not hot. Stir in the cocoa powder.

2   Lay 1 sheet of phyllo over the parchment paper (keep the other sheets covered with a damp cloth). Brush the phyllo sheet with the butter mixture until the pastry is well coated. Sprinkle it with 1 tablespoon of sugar. Cover it with another sheet of phyllo dough, pressing it firmly over the bottom one. Brush with the butter to coat lightly and sprinkle with 1 scant tablespoon of sugar. Repeat with the remaining phyllo, butter, and sugar. Cover with another sheet of parchment paper, pressing it firmly over the phyllo.

3   Use scissors to cut the parchment paper and phyllo layers in half crosswise.

Slide each of the pieces onto separate baking sheets and refrigerate until cold. *(The recipe can be made to this point up to 1 day ahead.)*

4   Preheat the oven to 350 degrees. Place a baking sheet on top of each of the baking sheets with the phyllo, to weight the pastry as it bakes (if you do not have 4 baking sheets, bake the pastry in 2 batches). Bake until the phyllo is browned and crisp all over, 25 to 30 minutes, rotating the pans in the oven halfway through the cooking time. Remove the top baking sheets and let the pastry cool. *(The recipe can be made to this point up to 1 hour ahead.)*

5   To serve, place the pastry cream over a pan of hot water to warm it slightly. Whisk until the cream is smooth, then add the ganache and whisk until well combined. Whip the heavy cream until it barely holds soft peaks. Remove the paper from both sides of the pastry and break it into irregular, angular pieces, 3 to 4 inches across; you will need 32 pieces.

6   Spoon a dab of the chocolate cream in the center of 8 dessert plates and cover it with 1 piece of pastry. Top with a rounded tablespoon of chocolate cream. Lay another piece of the pastry over the filling, arranging it over the first so that the angles do not match. Top with a rounded tablespoon of chocolate cream. Cover with another piece of pastry, with opposing angles as before. Top with a rounded tablespoon of the chocolate cream and then a dollop of the whipped cream. Cover with another piece of pastry. Sift a little cocoa around the plate and serve immediately.

PASTRY CREAM

Makes 1¹/₄ cups

3 egg yolks

¹/₄ cup sugar

2¹/₂ tablespoons cornstarch

1 cup whole milk

1 (2-inch) piece of vanilla bean, split lengthwise

3 tablespoons unsalted butter

1   In a mixing bowl, whisk together the egg yolks, sugar, and cornstarch until well combined. Whisk in 2 tablespoons of milk. Place the remaining milk and the vanilla bean in a medium saucepan. Bring the milk to a boil and whisk it into the yolk mixture.

2   Pour the mixture into the saucepan and bring it to a boil over medium heat, whisking constantly. Remove from the heat and whisk in the butter. Line a baking sheet with plastic wrap and spread the pastry cream over the plastic to cool it as quickly as possible. Cover with plastic wrap and refrigerate it until cold. *(The recipe can be made up to 2 days ahead.)*

Espresso-Chocolate Ganache

Makes 1 1/4 cups

4 ounces extra-bittersweet chocolate, chopped

2 egg yolks

1/4 cup sugar

1 cup half and half

2 teaspoons brewed espresso

1   Bring a pan of water to a simmer. Place the chocolate in a metal bowl and set it over the pan of barely simmering water. Stir occasionally until melted.

2   In a mixing bowl, whisk together the egg yolks and sugar. Place the half and half in a medium saucepan and bring it to a boil. Whisk half into the yolk mixture, then whisk the yolk mixture into the remaining half and half. Place over medium heat and stir constantly for 5 to 7 minutes, until the custard is thick enough to coat the back of a spoon; do not let it come to a simmer.

3   Pour the custard over the chocolate and stir until smooth. Stir in the espresso. Cover and refrigerate overnight. *(The recipe can be made up to 2 days ahead.)*

signature dishes, surprising in their simplicity

authors

Four-star chef Jean-Georges Vongerichten, owner of Jean Georges, Vong, and Jojo in New York City (and other Vongs around the world), in collaboration with cookbook writer and *New York Times* food columnist Mark Bittman

why they wrote it

"Because, although he has reached the top level of his profession, Jean-Georges is a home cook at heart," writes Bittman. "Like any busy cook, he looks for shortcuts, and he finds them. He is full of delightful surprises, and, regardless of whether you are familiar with his cooking, you will find those surprises throughout the book. . . . In short, this is one chef's book that should delight rather than frustrate you. I intend to continue to cook from it for years to come."

why it made our list

Vongerichten's dishes are famous for their simplicity, and that means his recipes needed little or no tinkering to become easy enough for a nonprofessional to prepare. You'll find no long ingredient lists or endless numbers of steps here—but lots of intense flavors and intriguing combinations. Writes Bittman, "I soon came to learn that 'that's it' was a signature phrase for Jean-Georges; when other chefs would just be gearing up, his dishes were already done. They not only sound simple . . . they are simple." And simply irresistible.

chapters

First Courses • Soups • Salads • Fish and Shellfish • Chicken and Other Poultry • Meat • Vegetables • Pasta, Grains, and Rice • Desserts

other books

This is Vongerichten's first book. Bittman is the author of another of this year's *Best of the Best* books, *How to Cook Everything* (page 144).

specifics

238 pages, 164 recipes,
22 color photographs,
93 black-and-white photographs
$35. Published by Broadway Books.

from the book

"In the past, I've found many chefs who claim they produce accessible recipes, but when it comes right down to it, they say things like, 'You can't possibly make this sauce without foie gras,' or 'This dish isn't worth eating unless you use crème fraîche.'"

JEAN-GEORGES

Cooking at Home with a Four-Star Chef

JEAN-GEORGES VONGERICHTEN

AND MARK BITTMAN

This velvety soup is quite sweet, but cayenne lends a little bite; its bright orange color and creamy texture make it a real crowd pleaser. You can prepare the soup with any winter squash, such as acorn or even pumpkin. Early in the season, before the squash is fully ripe, you may need to add a little sugar to the liquid. But as summer turns to fall, there will be enough natural sweetness in the vegetable, and you can eliminate the sugar altogether.

MAKES 4 SERVINGS

Serve it garnished, if you like, with shrimp or mushrooms, sautéed in butter or grilled with a little olive oil.

CREAMY BUTTERNUT SQUASH SOUP

2 pounds butternut squash, peeled and cut into chunks

4 cups Rich Chicken Stock (opposite page) or other stock

1¼ cups sour cream, crème fraîche, or heavy cream

2 tablespoons butter

Salt and freshly ground black pepper

¼ teaspoon cayenne, or to taste

About 1 tablespoon sugar (optional)

Sautéed or grilled shrimp or mushrooms, optional

Several chives, cut into 1-inch pieces

1 Combine the squash and stock in a saucepan and bring to a boil over high heat. Reduce the heat to medium and simmer for about 20 minutes, or until the squash is very tender.

2 Cool a bit for safety's sake, then puree the mixture in a blender. (You may prepare the recipe in advance up to this point; refrigerate in a covered container for up to 2 days.)

3 Return the puree to the saucepan and turn the heat to medium-low. Stir in the sour cream, crème fraîche, or cream, along with the butter, salt and pepper to taste, and the cayenne. Cook, stirring, until heated through (do not boil), then taste and add sugar and more seasoning, if necessary. Keep warm over low heat.

4 Serve the soup with a few cooked shrimp or mushrooms if you like, and the chives.

A stock in which nothing is chopped or browned. This has the mild but rich flavor of chicken and vegetables, but none of the dark, roasted complexity of dark chicken stock.

MAKES ABOUT 8 CUPS

RICH CHICKEN STOCK

1 medium onion, peeled

6 cloves

3 garlic cloves, cut in half

2 pounds chicken wings

1 carrot, peeled

1 bay leaf

1 celery stalk

3 or 4 thyme sprigs

1 leek, trimmed and washed

1 Stud the onion with the cloves, then combine all the ingredients in a large saucepan or small stockpot with 10 cups water. Turn the heat to medium-high and bring to a boil. As soon as bubbles start coming to the surface, adjust the heat so that the mixture cooks at a steady simmer, but not a rapid boil.

2 Cook for about 1½ hours, stirring occasionally. Cool slightly, then strain, pressing lightly on the solids to extract some of their liquid (don't press too hard or you will cloud the mixture unnecessarily). Use immediately, or refrigerate for up to 3 days, or freeze for up to 3 months.

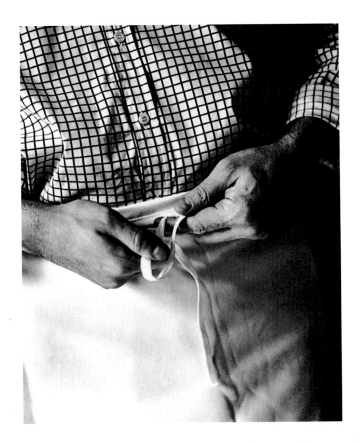

This unique combination of flavors has been on the menu at Restaurant Jean Georges since its opening, and it continues to draw raves. The form of the layered scallops and cauliflower is basic but lovely, and the dark green sauce has a mysterious, mustardy flavor; few people could guess what is in it, and almost no one could imagine how simple it is.

MAKES 4 SERVINGS Choose a rich starter for a pleasant contrast.

SCALLOPS AND CAULIFLOWER WITH CAPER-RAISIN SAUCE

1/3 cup capers, drained of all but 1 tablespoon of their liquid

1/3 cup golden raisins

8 to 12 cauliflower florets

4 tablespoons (1/2 stick) butter

4 tablespoons canola, grapeseed, or other neutral-flavored oil

Salt and freshly ground black pepper

2 tablespoons minced parsley leaves

12 large sea scallops (at least 1 pound), cut in half through their equators

1/4 teaspoon freshly grated nutmeg, plus a little more

1 tablespoon sherry vinegar

1 Preheat the oven to 250°F. Combine the capers and raisins in a small saucepan and add 3/4 cup water; simmer gently until the raisins are plump, about 10 minutes. Do not cook rapidly; you don't want to reduce the liquid. Let the mixture cool for a couple of minutes, then puree it in a blender. Return it to the saucepan.

2 Meanwhile, use a sharp knife or mandoline to cut the cauliflower florets into 1/4-inch-thick slices; you will need a total of 24 slices. Place 1 tablespoon each butter and oil in a large skillet and sauté the cauliflower over medium-high heat; do this in 2 or more batches to avoid crowding (add another tablespoon of butter or oil when necessary). Season it with salt and pepper as it cooks. Don't turn it too often; you want it to brown nicely. Total cooking time will be about 10 minutes, after which the cauliflower should be brown and crisp-tender. Remove and keep warm in a bowl in the oven.

3 Deglaze the pan by heating 1/4 cup water in it and stirring and scraping the bottom over high heat for a minute or two. Add the parsley and pour this juice over the cauliflower; gently stir and return the cauliflower to the oven while you cook the scallops.

4 Place 1 tablespoon each butter and oil in another large ovenproof skillet and turn the heat to medium-high. When the butter foams, add the scallops and cook on one side only until nicely browned, 2 to 3

minutes. Again, do this in batches to avoid crowding (adding another tablespoon of butter or oil when necessary). Remove the scallops from the pan as they brown and season with salt and pepper; keep them warm in the oven.

5 Reheat the sauce, then add the nutmeg, vinegar, and pepper and salt, if needed. Taste and adjust seasoning.

6 Spoon a little of the sauce onto each of 4 serving plates. Place 6 scallop pieces, browned side up, on each plate; top each scallop with a piece of cauliflower. Finish with a tiny grating of nutmeg.

A striking-looking dish, especially with rare-cooked lamb, which makes it red, black, and green. If time allows, the mushroom flavor will be even more pronounced if the mushroom-crusted lamb sits in the refrigerator for about 2 hours before cooking. Any butcher, including those in supermarkets, can provide you with boned racks of lamb, although it is among the easiest boning jobs to do yourself.

Serve this, if you like, with a beet salad or a warm French potato salad.

MAKES 4 SERVINGS

BONELESS LAMB WITH MUSHROOM CRUST AND LEEK PUREE

2 leeks, trimmed of hard green parts, split in half, well washed, and roughly chopped

1 tablespoon butter

Salt and freshly ground black pepper

2 ounces dried black trumpet or other dried mushrooms

1 egg, beaten with a little salt and pepper

Flour for dredging

2 racks of lamb, boned

4 tablespoons extra virgin olive oil

4 ounces shiitake or other mushrooms, trimmed and cut into chunks

2 garlic cloves, lightly smashed

2 thyme sprigs

Coarse salt

1 Cook the leeks in boiling salted water until tender, about 4 minutes. Drain and transfer to a blender with the butter and salt and pepper to taste. Puree and keep warm.

2 Place the dried mushrooms in a spice or coffee grinder and grind to the consistency of coffee. Place them on a plate. Beat the egg in a bowl and place the flour on a plate. Dip the lamb very lightly in the flour, shaking off the excess, then dip it in the egg, then into the mushrooms. Pat the mushrooms to adhere; you want to coat the lamb heavily. Refrigerate for up to 2 hours, if time allows. Preheat the oven to 500°F.

3 Heat 2 tablespoons olive oil in a 10-inch skillet and add the shiitake mushrooms, garlic, and thyme. Cook, stirring occasionally, until the mushrooms are tender, about 10 minutes.

4 Meanwhile, place the remaining 2 tablespoons oil in an ovenproof skillet and turn the heat to medium-high. A minute later, add the lamb; cook for 2 minutes on one side, then turn over the lamb and place the skillet in the oven for 3 to 4 minutes for rare meat, a little longer if you like it more done.

5 Let the lamb rest for a minute, then cut it into ½-inch-thick slices. Place a dollop of leek puree on each plate, top with a portion of mushrooms, then place the lamb on top. Sprinkle with a little coarse salt and serve.

traditional cuisine meets cutting-edge cooking

authors

Rose Gray and Ruth Rogers, founders of London's Italian-food mecca, The River Cafe

why they wrote it

"On recent trips to Italy we visited the wine and olive estates at Felsina and Selvapiana to select olive oil. We also went to the regions of Puglia and Sicily, where talking to cooks and producers we learned about their vegetables—cima di rape, ceci, and cicoria—spices, and the semolina bread called pagnotta. The recipes in this, our second cookbook, have been stimulated by all these experiences and reflect the food we love to cook and eat at The River Cafe."

why it made our list

Gray and Rogers have built their reputations on successfully and interestingly adapting traditional Italian cuisine to modern tastes. This book is a guide to what Rogers and Gray are cooking now. And also how they're cooking—a wood-burning oven has become a fixture at the restaurant, and slow-roasting a few select ingredients yields particularly flavorful dishes. Don't have a wood-burning oven in *your* kitchen? Don't fret: The chefs have developed strategies for reproducing the same effect in your home oven.

chapters

Drinks • Salads, Mozzarella, Frittata • Pasta, Polenta • Risotto • Soups, Stocks • Wood-Roasted Vegetables • Vegetables in Padella • Fish, Shellfish • Pork, Chicken, Duck, Game • Bread, Pizza, Bruschetta • Sauces • Cream, Tortes, Fruit, Ice Cream

previous books

Gray and Rogers also collaborated on the *Rogers Gray Italian Country Cookbook*.

specifics

352 pages, 204 recipes,
96 color photographs,
30 black-and-white photographs
$35. Published by Broadway Books.

from the book

"**Organic eggs with a dated laying stamp are the best to use, especially for ice cream. They also carry a stamp showing that they are approved by an organic certifying body. If eggs are not date-stamped, test for freshness by breaking an egg open on a flat plate. The yolk should remain ovoid and the white should be thick, jelly-like, and hold its shape.**"

THE CAFE COOK BOOK

Rose Gray and Ruth Rogers

Italian Recipes from London's River Cafe

Editor's Choice Award

best
looking
book

Spaghetti con cozze delle marche
Spaghetti with mussels

For 6 as a starter

6 pounds mussels, cleaned
1/4 cup olive oil
3 garlic cloves, peeled and chopped
1 small dried red chile, crumbled
2 tablespoons chopped fresh oregano
1/2 cup white wine (Verdicchio Classico)
2 pounds ripe tomatoes, skinned, seeded, and chopped
coarse sea salt and freshly ground black pepper
3 tablespoons chopped fresh flat-leaf parsley
1 pound spaghetti
extra virgin olive oil

In a large heavy saucepan with a tight-fitting lid, heat half the olive oil. Add the mussels, cover, and cook briefly over a high heat until all open, about 5 minutes. Discard any still closed. Drain, retaining the liquid. When the mussels are cool remove from their shells and chop. Reduce the liquid by half, strain, and add to the mussels.

In a separate large pan heat the remainder of the oil, add the garlic, chile, and oregano, and cook briefly until the garlic begins to color. Add the wine, reduce for a minute, then add the tomatoes. Cook, stirring to prevent sticking, for 15 minutes until reduced. Add the mussels, juice, seasoning, and parsley. Heat up the sauce.

Cook the spaghetti in a generous amount of boiling salted water, then drain. Add to the sauce. To serve, pour over extra virgin olive oil.

Patate e acciughe al forno
Potato and anchovy gratin

For 6

2 pounds Yukon Gold potatoes

2 tablespoons olive oil

2 tablespoons unsalted butter

6 garlic cloves, peeled and sliced

20 salted anchovy fillets, prepared (see page 51)

1 teaspoon finely chopped fresh rosemary

2 dried red chiles, crumbled

1/2 cup freshly grated Parmesan

1 cup cream

coarse sea salt and freshly ground black pepper

3 tablespoons chopped flat-leaf parsley

Preheat the oven to 375° F. Peel the potatoes and cut lengthways into 1/4-in-thick slices. Put into cold water to soak off the starch for 5 minutes.

Heat the oil and butter in a small saucepan. Add the garlic and gently fry for 2 minutes then add the anchovy fillets. Break up and melt the anchovies into a sauce. Add the rosemary and chile. Stir to combine, then remove the pan from the heat.

Drain the potatoes, spread out on a towel, and pat dry. Place in a large bowl and add the anchovy sauce, three-quarters of the Parmesan, and the cream. Season and toss together. Put in a baking dish, cover with foil, and bake in the preheated oven for 25 minutes. Remove the foil, gently turn the potatoes over, then add the parsley. Test for seasoning, then scatter over the remaining Parmesan. Continue to bake for a further 15 minutes. The potatoes should be lightly browned and crisp.

Porri e carciofi brasate
Braised leeks and artichokes

For 6

3 pounds leeks
6 small or 3 large artichokes
1 lemon, halved
2 tablespoons olive oil
3 garlic cloves, peeled and finely sliced
2 tablespoons chopped fresh mint leaves
coarse sea salt and freshly ground black pepper
1/2 cup white wine
2-3 tablespoons roughly chopped fresh flat-leaf parsley

Peel the outer leaves from the leeks, and trim the roots and the larger tough green parts. Wash thoroughly and shake dry. Cut the leeks in diagonal dice about 1/2 in thick. Trim the artichokes, until you are left with the pale tender heart. Peel the fiber from the stalks of smaller artichokes; discard the stalks of larger artichokes, as they are too tough. Cut each artichoke heart in eighths and scrape away any choke or prickly violet leaves. Place in a bowl of water with the lemon halves as you cut, then drain and dry.

Heat the oil in a large heavy saucepan with a lid. When hot add the artichoke slices and cook quickly until lightly colored, then add the leeks. Stir-fry together for 5 minutes then add the garlic, mint, salt, and pepper. When the garlic has softened, add the wine and stir to scrape up any artichoke and leek stuck on the bottom. Cover with a lid and cook until the wine has evaporated, about 10-15 minutes. Add the parsley, taste for seasoning, and serve.

from
Notes on ingredients

Anchovies The best salted anchovies come from Spain, from the fishing ports of Omdarroa and Zumai on the Bay of Biscay. The season lasts from April to June. The fish are caught, sold, graded, salted, and packed all on the same day. First the anchovies are graded by size, the largest and most perfect being called "bar 1." These are always packed in 22-pound cans. 35-pounds of fresh anchovies are carefully layered with coarse sea salt in and on top of the cans, using a collar, then pressed with cement blocks over a period of three months until they fit into the can. Anchovies graded "bar 2" are salted and packed in the same way in 22-pound and 11-pound cans. Anchovies graded "bar 3" and "bar 4" are the smaller fish. They are selected, salted, and packed into large barrels and pressed in the same way for three months, then washed, filleted, and preserved in olive oil. Spanish salted anchovies from 22-pound cans are sold all over Italy, usually by the gram. Stalls selling just salted fish can be found in many markets.

To prepare salted anchovies taken dry from the can, rinse under a slow-running cold tap to wash off any salt and carefully pull each fillet off the bone. Pat dry and use immediately or cover with extra virgin olive oil.

Olive oil The kind of extra virgin olive oil we use for cooking is different from the estate-bottled oils we use for pouring over bruschetta and adding to soups. The cooking oil is a blend of several extra virgin olive oils from all over Italy, produced from olives that are pressed when they are fully ripe and have dropped from the trees. Ripe olives produce more oil when pressed and have a higher acidity. The resulting oil has little flavor or aroma but is much cheaper and is fine for general cooking.

Estate-bottled cold-pressed extra virgin olive oils have very distinctive characteristics and flavors. We go to Italy every November to coincide with the olive

harvest and choose oils to use in the restaurant in the coming year. Tuscan oils, which are thick, green, and fruity, have always been our favorite. We choose two that complement each other from different estates and our current extra virgin olive oils are from Selvapiana and Felsina.

The oil from the Selvapiana estate is pressed from the "Frantoio" variety. The olive trees grow alongside the famous vineyards in the cooler Chianti Ruffina zone northeast of Florence. The olives are picked early, when green, and pressed in a modern cold press, producing the greenest and most intensely spicy oil. The new oil is bottled immediately and arrives in the restaurant by December, where our customers enjoy Bruschetta al'olio nuovo – a joy that excites us all.

At the Felsina estate in Castelnuovo Baradenga, on the southernmost borders of Chianti Classico, the olives are pressed in the old traditional way. The estate's mill at Farnetella has been run by the same man for the last 45 years. A manual process results in 4 gallons of oil from 220 pounds of olives. The olives are the "Corriegiolo" variety, the greenest of all olives. They are hand-picked and crushed the same day, producing an incredibly fresh, green smooth oil that we have chosen for its long life, low acidity, and subtle pepperiness. We use this oil for salads and blanched vegetables throughout the year.

Salt Sea salt is pure flaky crystals free from all additives, a completely natural product with a better flavor than table salt and rich in natural minerals. Because of its intense flavor, you use less.

Natural coarse sea salt comes mostly from Spain and France. The grains are slightly smaller than young peas and contain desirable trace elements and minerals. The salt is unrefined and is sometimes gray in color. Use this for salting fish, chicken, and pasta water.

pizza with panache
and other italian fare

author

Renowned Boston pizza maker Todd English, chef and owner of Olives, his first restaurant, and four Figs restaurants, writing with cookbook author Sally Sampson

why he wrote it

"Because cookbooks are modern grandmas that teach us old and new ways of cooking. I actually learn things in the process. Just the fact that I can now write a recipe seems amazing. It seems that any time you try to teach something you learn more in the process."

why it made our list

Figs' pizzas aren't the thick-crusted, over-sauced variety you'd pick up at your local pizzeria (unless you live in Boston, and Figs *is* your local pizzeria). The crust is crisp and paper-thin, the sauce is applied with a delicate hand, and the toppings are carefully chosen to complete the delicious effect. English is known for producing irresistible Mediterranean-inspired food, and that goes beyond pizzas; the book also contains one of the best risotto recipes we've tested all year. If it's English's pizza you want, though, you'll have to get some special equipment—a pizza stone at the least. You'll also need, says English, "a strong mind and a strong will. You have to be hardheaded and brave. Your tendency will always be to put more on top than you should." The stout of heart will find that pizza making has never been more rewarding.

chapters

Basics • Starters • Salad Dressings and Sauces • Soups • Basic Sauces for Pizza, Pasta, and Polenta • Pasta • Polenta and Risotto • Pizza • Autostrada Panini, Burgers, and Olivia's Crunchy Chicken • Desserts

previous books

The Olives Table, with recipes from English's *other* Boston area restaurant, was also written with Sampson.

specifics

238 pages, more than 100 recipes, 67 color photographs, $25. Published by Simon & Schuster.

from the book

"**If the dough is made right, the pizza will never be perfectly round. Our dough should be very wet and free-form: I might go so far as to say that the dough has a mind of its own. The dough determines what you do, not the other way around.**"

The Figs Table

More Than 100
Recipes for Pizzas, Pastas, Salads, and Desserts

TODD ENGLISH AND SALLY SAMPSON

authors of
The Olives Table

PHOTOGRAPHS BY CARL TREMBLAY

Portobello Mushrooms, Mushroom Purée, and Fontina Cheese Pizza

*T*his is Sally's favorite. When I took it off the menu, she ordered it anyway. And now that she's convinced me to put it back on, I'm discovering I should never have taken it off.

MAKES 2 PIZZAS

2 pizza rounds (page 56)
Cornmeal for sprinkling
2 teaspoons olive oil
½ teaspoon minced garlic
2 pinches kosher salt
2 pinches black pepper
6 ounces Italian Fontina cheese, thinly sliced
1 cup Portobello, Porcini, and Button Mushroom Purée (page 59)
2 portobello mushroom caps, trimmed and thinly sliced on the bias
2 tablespoons freshly grated Parmesan cheese
2 pinches black pepper, for garnish
Tiny drizzle truffle oil (optional), for garnish

One hour prior to cooking, place a baking stone in the oven and preheat it to 500 degrees.

Roll out 1 pizza dough as thinly as possible. Place it on a pizza peel sprinkled with cornmeal. Cover the surface with 1 teaspoon oil, ¼ teaspoon minced garlic, and 1 pinch each salt and pepper. Be sure to leave an outer lip of 1 inch all the way around.

Evenly distribute 3 ounces Fontina cheese on the pizza. Top with ½ cup Portobello, Porcini, and Button Mushroom Purée and 1 mushroom cap and sprinkle with 1½ teaspoons Parmesan cheese.

Shake the paddle lightly and slide the pizza onto the baking stone. Bake until browned, about 6 to 7 minutes. Transfer to a firm surface and cut into slices.

Serve immediately, garnished with 1½ teaspoons Parmesan cheese and 1 pinch black pepper. Drizzle with truffle oil, if desired.

Repeat with the remaining dough.

Figs Pizza Dough

With a little bit of time and effort, Figs pizza dough can easily be mastered. However, if you don't have the time or are intimidated by working with yeast, call your local pizza place and see if they'll sell you some of their dough. In some areas you can buy refrigerated dough (*not* the kind in a tube); this would also work well. If you use a heavy, bready, prebaked, vacuum-packed pizza crust, it just won't be the same.

Our dough is far wetter than you'd ever believe; it makes a light, crisp crust. It may take you a few tries before you get it right. Be patient and err on the side of underworking the dough; if you overwork it, the crust will be tough and dry.

This recipe makes four rounds of pizza, though the topping recipes make two pizzas. We figure that this way you only have to make the dough every other time. Simply wrap the remaining two balls of dough in plastic wrap and freeze for up to two weeks.

MAKES FOUR 8- TO 10-INCH PIZZAS
(SERVES 1 TO 2 PEOPLE PER PIZZA)

¼ cup whole-wheat flour
3½ cups all-purpose flour, plus additional for rolling
2 teaspoons (¼ ounce) fresh yeast
2 teaspoons kosher salt
2 teaspoons sugar
2 teaspoons olive oil
1⅔ cups lukewarm water

Place the whole-wheat flour, all-purpose flour, yeast, salt, and sugar in a mixer fitted with a dough hook. While the mixer is running, gradually add the oil and water. Knead on low speed until the dough is firm and smooth, about 10 minutes.

Divide the dough into four balls, about 7½ ounces each. Line two cookie sheets with parchment paper. Place two balls on a sheet and cover with a damp towel. Let them rise in a warm spot until they have doubled in bulk, about 2 hours.

To roll out the dough: Dab your fingers in flour and then place 1 ball on a generously floured work surface and press down in the center with the tips of your fingers, spreading the dough with your hand. When the dough has doubled in width, use a floured rolling pin and roll out until it is very thin, like flatbread. The outer border should be a little thicker than the inner circle. Pick the dough up with a spatula or the back of a knife, allowing it to fold up almost like an umbrella and transfer it to a paddle. Do not worry that the pizza is not round, you are looking for an 8- to 10-inch shape, a cross between an oval and a rectangle. If you get a hole, simply pinch the edges back together. Repeat with the remaining balls.

Portobello, Porcini, and Button Mushroom Purée

*E*arthy, rich, and intense, this purée is great to keep around to swirl into risotto, toss with spaghetti, or serve under a roasted chicken breast or a grilled steak.

Don't omit the porcini mushrooms. Most specialty stores sell them dried.

MAKES ABOUT 1 CUP

1 tablespoon olive oil
2 teaspoons chopped garlic
½ cup sliced Spanish onion
¼ cup red wine
4 portobello mushroom caps, trimmed and coarsely chopped
    (about 1½ cups)
¼ cup dried or frozen porcini mushrooms, coarsely chopped (soaked
    and strained, if dried)
½ cup button mushrooms, trimmed and coarsely chopped
¼ to ½ teaspoon kosher salt
1 teaspoon chopped fresh rosemary leaves
¼ to ½ cup heavy cream

Place a large skillet over medium heat and, when it is hot, add the oil. Add the garlic and onion and cook until translucent, about 3 to 5 minutes. Add the wine to deglaze the skillet.

Add the mushrooms and cook until soft, about 8 to 10 minutes. Add the salt, rosemary, and cream and cook until slightly reduced, about 3 to 4 minutes. Transfer to a food processor fitted with a steel blade and pulse until it has the consistency of thick mud.

Serve immediately, or cover and refrigerate up to one week.

Asparagus Butter Risotto with Shrimp

The first time I had this dish it was made with wild asparagus, which, although not essential, is even more intense in flavor.

Whipping the asparagus into the butter seems to amplify the flavor of the asparagus. The asparagus butter can be served alone on pasta, polenta, or grilled fish. Keep a stick in your freezer.

You can substitute artichoke bottoms or hearts for the asparagus.

SERVES 4

3 tablespoons unsalted butter, at room temperature
*¾ pound asparagus, stems peeled, chopped, and blanched, tips set
    aside*
½ cup chopped fresh basil leaves
3 garlic cloves, chopped
1 leek, well washed and chopped
1 cup arborio rice
½ cup white wine
*4 to 4½ cups homemade chicken broth or canned low-sodium
    chicken broth*
16 large shrimp, cleaned, deveined, and roughly chopped
1 cup freshly grated Parmesan cheese
½ to 1 teaspoon kosher salt
½ teaspoon black pepper
4 rosemary sprigs, for garnish

To make the asparagus butter: Place 2 tablespoons butter, the asparagus stems, and the basil in a food processor fitted with a steel blade and purée. Set aside.

To make the risotto: Place a large, straight-sided, nonreactive stainless steel, nonstick, or lined copper saucepan over medium-high heat and, when it is hot, add the remaining 1 tablespoon butter. Add the garlic and leek and cook until they are transparent and soft, about 7 to 10 minutes. Add the rice and stir until it is well coated.

Add the wine and cook until it has been absorbed. Add 2 cups chicken broth, 1 cup at a time, stirring with each addition, until all the liquid has been absorbed, about 10 minutes. Add the asparagus tips, shrimp, and remaining 2 cups chicken broth and cook until all the liquid has been absorbed.

Add the asparagus butter, Parmesan cheese, salt, and pepper, stirring well after each addition, and cook for 1 to 2 minutes.

Divide the risotto among 4 shallow bowls and serve immediately, garnished with the rosemary sprigs.

an artful way to serve a quartet of dishes

authors

New York City chefs Ellen Greaves, of the Tea Box at Takashimaya, and Wayne Nish, co-owner of March

why they wrote it

"Creating a meal in a bento box is a unique culinary experience, offering pleasure on many levels: in cooking, in visual design, in service, and, of course, in eating. We have written this book to bring these pleasures to anyone who loves delicious food beautifully served, whatever your level of kitchen expertise. Guided by the menus, recipes, and pictures you will find in these pages, you can easily create a bento meal—one with a flavor and a look that is distinctly your own."

why it made our list

Here you'll find east-west cooking presented in a refreshingly different way. Each of the twelve menus in this lovely little book is designed to be served in a bento box, a lacquered, lidded container with four compartments that's commonly used in Japan. All the components of the meal—usually small servings of meat, fish, rice or potatoes, and a vegetable or salad—are of equal importance and balanced in appearance as well as flavor. And though the final effect is stunning, the individual recipes are exceedingly easy. It's an interesting, artfully simple way to serve food.

chapters

Spring • Summer • Fall • Winter

specifics

168 pages, 48 recipes, 49 color photographs, $25. Published by William Morrow and Company, Inc.

from the book

"Pay attention to the food: That is every cook and chef's silent wish. Without diminishing the spontaneity of the occasion or distracting the course of conversation, we all want our guests to *notice* what we serve them."

Seasonal American Meals and Japanese Presentations

Simple Menus for the Bento Box

Ellen Greaves & Wayne Nish

Curried Basmati Rice with Raisins
Braised Leeks with Pecorino Cheese
Salt-Cured Salmon with Fennel Salad
Rack of Lamb with Sweet Mustard Glaze

An elegant presentation, the curve of a lamb bone dramatically sweeping out of the frame, declares this bento to be a special occasion dinner. The home-cured salmon and flash-roasted rack of New Zealand lamb are rare treats (in two senses of the term). Both have a richness of flavor and sensual texture that belie their astonishing ease of preparation.

The salt cure for the salmon, which you will learn here (and nowhere else!), is a marvelous method of transforming raw fish into a succulent delicacy. It rivals fine gravlax and smoked salmons, like Nova—at a fraction of the expense and effort. You will bury a salmon fillet in kosher salt with aromatic spices. Six hours later it will be cured and ready to serve, sublimely perfumed with coriander and chives, sliced thinly, and arranged over a pile of lightly dressed fennel slivers, as we do in this bento.

The small New Zealand racks of lamb (now widely available in the United States) yield delicate portions of meat that fit wonderfully into a bento box—both in physical and aesthetic terms. It is important that the rack be well trimmed by your butcher: "Frenched to the eye," as we say, with its insulating cap of fat completely removed. For the bento, it is coated with a simple mix of Dijon mustard and sugar and roasted for just 10 minutes. The intense richness of the small chop is cut by the sweet and spicy glaze.

Accompanying these extravagant dishes are two distinctive preparations. Sweet leeks, braised in chicken stock and butter, enjoy an unusual and salty accent from sheep's milk pecorino cheese. Curried rice is a natural and traditional companion for lamb. We add several layers of flavor, from the nutty quality of aromatic basmati rice and from raisins plumped in Earl Grey tea, which passes along its elusive nuance of bergamot oil.

Setting up our bento, we opposed round and square, flat and concave vessels. And we ranged widely in our selection of dishes, finding an alabaster-like bowl that echoed the translucence of leeks and cheese shavings, a pressed wooden bowl for the grainy rice, a snowy platform of heavily glazed ceramic for the salmon, and a stark slab of travertine—an elegant platform to show off the lamb chop.

Curried Basmati Rice with Raisins

Makes 4 bento servings

2 cups basmati rice

2 cups water

2 teaspoons loose Earl Grey tea (or 1 Earl Grey tea bag)

¼ cup dark raisins

1 tablespoon butter

2 tablespoons mild curry powder

1½ teaspoons kosher salt

Freshly ground black pepper

Wash the rice until the water runs clear. Let the rice soak in the 2 cups of water for 30 minutes.

Make the Earl Grey tea with 1 cup of barely boiling water and let it brew for 4 minutes. Strain the tea onto the raisins in a bowl and let them plump up for 15 minutes.

Melt the butter in a small saucepan with a lid over medium heat and stir in the curry powder. Stir the curry for a few seconds until it starts to color. Stop the curry from cooking by pouring in the rice and water and then add the raisins and salt.

Bring the rice to a boil and stir well. Cover the pot and simmer over low heat for 11 minutes. Remove the pot from the heat and let sit for 5 minutes. Fluff the rice with a fork and season with salt and freshly ground pepper to taste.

Braised Leeks with Pecorino Cheese

1 bunch leeks (4 thick leeks or 6 thin ones), white part and pale green part only

1 tablespoon sweet butter

1 cup chicken stock

Salt and freshly ground black pepper

1 ounce pecorino Romano cheese, shaved in curls from a large piece using a vegetable peeler

Cut the leeks into 1-inch pieces on an angle. Wash the leeks very well, taking care to rid them of any sand. Drain well.

Heat the butter in a small saucepan over medium heat. When the butter is melted, stir in the leeks. Add the chicken stock, season with salt and pepper, and bring to a simmer. Cover the leeks and turn the heat down to low. Cook the leeks at a simmer for 10 minutes, then check for doneness. They should be still firm but not crisp. Let the leeks cool to room temperature in the cooking liquid, then drain well. Serve and garnish with the cheese curls.

Salt-Cured Salmon with Fennel Salad

Makes 4 bento servings

1 pound kosher salt

⅓ cup whole black peppercorns, cracked in a blender

⅓ cup coriander seeds, cracked in a blender

2 ounces chives, finely sliced

12 ounces salmon fillet cut from the thick part of the fish

1 bulb young fennel

1 tablespoon extra-virgin olive oil

½ tablespoon champagne vinegar or good-quality white wine vinegar

Salt and freshly ground black pepper

In a bowl, mix together the kosher salt, peppercorns, coriander seeds, and chives. Place half of this in a stainless steel, ceramic, or glass baking dish, add the salmon, and cover with the rest of the mixture. Tightly cover the dish with plastic wrap. Let the salmon cure in the refrigerator for 6 hours, then thoroughly brush off the salt and seeds. Slice the salmon very thinly with a clean, sharp, wet knife.

Using a mandoline or sharp knife, slice the fennel very thinly across the grain. Toss the fennel with the olive oil and vinegar and season to taste with salt and pepper. Serve slices of the cured salmon on the fennel salad and garnish with fennel sprigs.

Rack of Lamb with
Sweet Mustard Glaze

Makes 4 bento servings

2 tablespoons sugar

3 tablespoons Dijon mustard

½ New Zealand rack of lamb, with 8 bones, in one piece (have your butcher French
the bones for you)

Salt and freshly ground black pepper

Preheat the oven to 475°F. In a bowl, mix the sugar with the mustard.

Bring the lamb rack to room temperature, leaving it out for up to 1 hour. Season the
rack with salt and pepper and spread the mustard and sugar mix on the surface. Roast the
rack in the hot oven for 10 minutes, remove from the heat, and let rest for 10 minutes. Carve
the rack into 8 chops and serve 2 chops per person.

simple, exuberant dishes
make entertaining easy

author

New York restaurateur Bobby Flay, proprietor of Mesa Grill and Bolo and also host of food shows on Lifetime and the Food Network, writing with cookbook author Joan Schwartz

why he wrote it

"In your home, exciting dishes like these will bring people together and set the stage for informal good times. I will tell you how to prepare them so that you, your family, and your friends all can share them around your own table. This book is about enjoying good company and wonderful food, and, perhaps the most important, it's all about flavor!"

why it made our list

When it comes to full-flavored food, Bobby Flay has the recipe. The Spanish-style dishes he serves at Bolo are the inspiration for this book, although Italian, Mexican, and Cuban influences are obvious as well. Flay doesn't shy away from strong flavors, whether putting together his signature relishes—sweet, hot, or sour—or deciding on seasoning. "When you use an ingredient," he advises, "you want to taste it, so don't sprinkle on a bit of oregano, or cilantro, or ancho chile powder—throw in a lot! Let spicy, salty, sweet, and sour flavors jump out at you from dishes accented with chile peppers, capers, fruits, herbs, and vinegars." You'll love the benefits of being bold.

chapters

From the Oven • From the Grill • From the Stovetop • Rice • Cool Platters • Vinaigrettes, Oils, Sauces, and Relishes • Desserts and Drinks

previous books

Flay and Schwartz also worked together on *Bobby Flay's Bold American Food.*

specifics

256 pages, 125 recipes,
40 color photographs,
30 black-and-white photographs,
$32.50. Published by
Clarkson N. Potter Publishers.

from the book

"Keep tasting food as you prepare it and taste the finished dish one last time before you put it on the plate. If you're not chewing, you're not cooking."

Bobby Flay's

From My Kitchen To Your Table

125 BOLD RECIPES

BY BOBBY FLAY
AND JOAN SCHWARTZ

PHOTOGRAPHS
BY TOM ECKERLE

Potato-Horseradish — Crusted Red Snapper with Roasted Pepper Relish

MAKES 8 SERVINGS

At Bolo, my Spanish restaurant in New York, we wrap red snapper in a crust of crisp potatoes and pungent horseradish. Horseradish is a great but generally underutilized flavor. It electrifies this dish and melds perfectly with the flavors in the Roasted Pepper Relish.

8 red snapper fillets, 5 to 6 ounces each
   Salt and pepper
1 large potato, peeled and finely grated
½ cup prepared horseradish, drained
4 tablespoons pure olive oil
   Roasted Pepper Relish (opposite page)

Preheat the oven to 350° F.

Season each fillet to taste with salt and pepper. Combine the potato and horseradish and spread the mixture over the top of each fillet, pressing down so it will adhere.

Heat the oil in a large sauté pan over medium heat until almost smoking. Sear each fillet potato-side down until a crust forms, about 3 minutes. Turn the fillets over and finish cooking in the oven until done, about 5 minutes for medium. Place on a large serving platter and top each fillet with some relish. Serve any remaining relish on the side.

Roasted Pepper Relish

MAKES 3 CUPS

This is a sparkling combination of sweet and hot peppers. Roasting takes away their raw flavor and softens them, as well as making them easy to peel.

Serve with Potato-Horseradish–Crusted Red Snapper (opposite page) or any poultry or fish.

2	red bell peppers, roasted, peeled, seeded, and diced
2	yellow bell peppers, roasted, peeled, seeded, and diced
½	cup chopped black olives
1	tablespoon crushed red pepper flakes
2	tablespoons minced garlic
2	tablespoons fresh thyme leaves
½	cup chopped parsley
¼	cup sherry vinegar
2	tablespoons honey
6	tablespoons pure olive oil
	Salt and pepper

In a mixing bowl, combine the bell peppers, olives, pepper flakes, garlic, thyme, parsley, vinegar, honey, and oil. Season to taste with salt and pepper. May be refrigerated up to 1 day. Serve at room temperature.

Garlic and Oregano–Marinated Grilled Chicken with Grilled Pepper and Black Olive Relish

MAKES 8 SERVINGS

Marinate this chicken with tons of garlic and lots of fresh oregano (fresh is really the best, but if you can't find it, dried is acceptable). Then grill it like any ordinary chicken. The result (see photo, page 79) will be far from ordinary—it will be full of great flavor.

FOR THE GARLIC AND FRESH OREGANO MARINADE

2 tablespoons sherry vinegar (I prefer Spanish)
2 tablespoons fresh lemon juice
2 tablespoons fresh lime juice
2 tablespoons honey
1 tablespoon ancho chile powder (available at Hispanic or specialty markets)
12 garlic cloves, coarsely chopped
½ cup fresh oregano leaves
2 cups pure olive oil
Salt and pepper

In a blender, combine the vinegar, lemon juice, lime juice, honey, ancho chile powder, garlic, and oregano and blend 30 seconds. With the motor running, slowly add the olive oil until emulsified. Season to taste with salt and pepper. Makes about 3 cups.

FOR THE CHICKEN	**4 chickens, 2½ pounds each, cut into quarters** **Salt and pepper** **Garlic and Fresh Oregano Marinade** **Grilled Pepper and Black Olive Relish (page 78)**

Season the chicken quarters with salt and pepper to taste and marinate in the garlic and fresh oregano marinade 2 hours, refrigerated.

Prepare a grill.

Remove the chicken quarters from the marinade and shake off any excess. Grill until done, about 10 minutes on each side, and place on a serving platter, surrounded by the relish.

Grilled Pepper and Black Olive Relish

MAKES 3 CUPS

Lots of Spanish flavors are joined in this dish, starting with roasted red peppers in combination with black olives. Serve with Garlic and Oregano–Marinated Grilled Chicken (page 76) or any grilled chicken or fish.

2 grilled red bell peppers, peeled, seeded, and diced
2 grilled yellow bell peppers, peeled, seeded, and diced
1 cup pitted and coarsely chopped niçoise olives
2 tablespoons minced garlic
¼ cup fresh thyme leaves
½ cup coarsely chopped parsley
¼ cup sherry vinegar (I prefer Spanish)
2 tablespoons honey
Salt and pepper

Combine the peppers, olives, garlic, thyme, parsley, vinegar, and honey in a mixing bowl. Season to taste with salt and pepper. May be refrigerated up to 1 day. Use at room temperature.

bam!

need we say more?

author

Ubiquitous TV chef Emeril Lagasse, chef/owner of Emeril's, NOLA, and Delmonico Restaurant and Bar in New Orleans and Emeril's New Orleans Fish House in Las Vegas, with Felicia Willett, who coordinates food production for *Emeril Live*, and cookbook author Marcelle Bienvenu

why he wrote it

"This is only a cookbook. It's not a bible of cooking according to Emeril, it's only a compilation of some of the dishes I've demonstrated on television and in particular those I've had fun doing. I want to share them with you and perhaps you will learn a few tricks here and there that will make cooking and entertaining as much fun for you as it is for me."

why it made our list

Like having a backstage pass to *Emeril Live* or *Essence of Emeril*, this book offers behind-the-scenes glimpses and favorite dishes from Lagasse's popular Food Network programs. The recipes are quick and easy with a minimum of fuss and liberal doses of the chef's favorite seasonings as well as his food philosophies. "I've said it many times before," declares Lagasse, "and I'll say it again—we're not building any rocket ships, we're cooking, plain and simple."

chapters

Back to the Basics • Fall River Memories • Louisiana Specialties • Southern Favorites • Emerilized Starters • Salad Sensations • Vegetable World • Emeril's Fish Market • Know Your Birds • Pork Fat Rules • Where's the Meat? Vegetarians Beware! • Creole Jazz Brunch • Swingin' Sweets

previous books

Lagasse is the author of *Emeril's New New Orleans Cooking, Louisiana Real and Rustic,* and *Emeril's Creole Christmas,* one of last year's *Best of the Best.*

specifics

288 pages, 172 recipes, 139 black-and-white photographs, $25. Published by William Morrow and Company, Inc.

from the book

"I love all the things that can be made with pork—bacon, sausages, pork patties, barbecue—full fat flavor! Wow! Yeah, yeah, yeah, the food police go crazy with all that, but take the advice of my good friend Julia Child and eat everything in moderation."

Emeril's TV Dinners

**Kickin' It Up a Notch
with Recipes from *Emeril Live*
and *Essence of Emeril***

As seen on the Food Network®

Emeril Lagasse

with Marcelle Bienvenu and Felicia Willett

Truffle Chips

Makes 4 to 6 servings

In New Orleans we have Zapp's potato chips, made in nearby Gramercy, located on the mighty Mississippi River, which come in many different flavors, and I love them all. What makes them so good is that whatever flavor you try, your mouth is bammed with taste—my kind of chip. I decided to make my own and kick them up with a little truffle oil. Yeah, babe!

If you have one, use a mandoline to slice the potatoes paper-thin. Soak the slices in cool water for 30 minutes and drain. Pat dry completely with paper towels.

In a large, heavy, deep pot or electric fryer, heat 4 inches of vegetable oil to 360°F. Deep-fry the potatoes until golden brown, 3 to 5 minutes. Drain on paper towels. Season with salt and pepper.

Transfer the potatoes to a large mixing bowl and toss with the truffle oil and cheese. Serve immediately.

2 pounds new or small red potatoes, scrubbed
Vegetable oil for deep-frying
Salt and freshly ground black pepper to taste
1 tablespoon white truffle oil (available in specialty food stores)
1 cup freshly grated Parmigiano-Reggiano cheese

General manager Tony Lott inspecting the waiters at Emeril's Restaurant before service

Pan-Roasted Filet Mignon Stuffed with English Stilton and Walnuts

Makes 4 servings

Give me some good blue cheese and I'm a happy, happy man! Stilton cheese is probably the king of English cheeses. Made with whole cow's milk and allowed to ripen for 4 to 6 months while being skewered numerous times to create the blue veins, it is rich and creamy, but slightly crumbly. When stuffed into a filet mignon that's cooked to a turn, it's a meal fit for, what else?, a king, and hey, we all want to be kings, right?

1 pound new or small red potatoes, quartered

1 tablespoon dried thyme

2 tablespoons olive oil

Salt and cracked black peppercorns to taste

1 cup Veal Reduction (opposite page)

3 ounces sliced bacon, chopped

2 tablespoons chopped shallots

1 teaspoon chopped garlic

½ cup walnut pieces

4 filet mignons (about 8 ounces each)

Freshly ground black pepper to taste

1 cup crumbled Stilton cheese

½ cup port wine

1 cup vegetable oil

4 shallots, thinly sliced and separated into rings

¼ cup bleached all-purpose flour

1 tablespoon chopped fresh parsley leaves

Preheat the oven to 400°F.

In a medium-size mixing bowl, toss the potatoes with the thyme and 1 tablespoon of the olive oil. Season with salt and cracked peppercorns. Put the potatoes in a large ovenproof sauté pan. Roast until golden brown, about 20 minutes. Remove from the oven and transfer back to the mixing bowl.

Place the sauté pan over medium-high heat, add the veal reduction, and deglaze the pan, scraping the bottom to get any browned bits. Reduce the heat to medium and cook for 1 minute. Set aside and keep warm.

In a medium-size sauté pan over medium heat, fry the bacon until crispy, stirring occasionally, about 8 minutes. Add the chopped shallots, garlic, and walnuts and cook, stirring, for 2 minutes. Remove from the heat.

In the mixing bowl, toss the potatoes with the bacon mixture. Set aside and keep warm.

Using a sharp knife, cut a pocket about 2 inches long along the side of each filet. Season the inside of the pocket with salt and pepper. Stuff each pocket with 2 tablespoons of the cheese. Season the filets with salt and more cracked pepper.

Heat the remaining tablespoon olive oil in a large ovenproof sauté pan over medium-high heat. Sear the filets for 2 minutes on each side. Transfer the pan to the oven and roast for 6 to 8 minutes for medium-rare, 130° to 140°F; 10 minutes for medium, 145° to 150°F; and 12 minutes for well done, 155° to 165°F. Remove the filets from the pan, set aside and keep warm.

Return the sauté pan to the stove over medium-high heat. Add the port and deglaze the pan, scraping the browned bits off the bottom. Reduce the wine by half, cooking about 5 minutes.

Pour the vegetable oil into a deep, heavy saucepan and heat to 360°F. Season the shallot rings with salt and pepper. Put the flour in a shallow bowl and season with salt and pepper. Dredge the shallot rings in the flour and coat evenly, tapping off any excess. Fry them until golden brown, about 2 minutes. Drain on paper towels, then season with salt.

To serve, divide the potatoes into 4 equal portions and mound in the center of each plate. Lay a filet on top of the potatoes. Spoon the veal reduction over each filet. Drizzle each plate with the port wine reduction. Garnish with the remaining ½ cup Stilton cheese, the fried shallots, and the parsley.

Veal Reduction

Makes 1 cup

1 quart veal stock

¼ teaspoon salt

Bring the stock seasoned with the salt to a boil in a medium-size saucepan over high heat. Reduce the heat to medium and simmer until it reduces by three-fourths, about 1 hour.

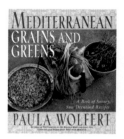

category 2

specific

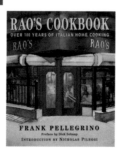

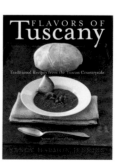

*M*editerranean, and especially Italian, cooking has had a long run as America's darling. Hence, countless Italian cookbooks—once again this year, we were flooded with them. The culinary riches of the Mediterranean are virtually inexhaustible, so the long-lasting popularity is understandable and the books on this region dominate their category justifiably. They are accompanied only by lone representatives of Mexican and English food. (You'll find French cuisine, America's former favorite, in the Restaurant Chefs, General Interest, and Desserts sections.)

cuisines

traditional mexican dishes
from a true expert

author

Cookbook writer and Mexican-food authority Diana Kennedy

why she wrote it

"I am constantly asked: What is this one about? And how does it differ from the other books? You could say that this one is a natural extension of the others because I learn something every time I travel, talk to cooks, and even cook with them. . . . I have included some recipes that have never (to my knowledge) been written down, others that appeared in books published a century or more ago and have now been largely forgotten. . . . So this book offers a deeper and more personal look into the foods of this complex and fascinating country."

why it made our list

With over forty years of experience cooking Mexican food, Kennedy knows her stuff. Forget about nachos and burritos; the dishes here are truly authentic. Kennedy seasons the book with tales of her travels—"for those who read my cookbooks (so they tell me) like novels"—and explanations of the traditions that influenced the food, and vice versa. Some of the ingredients and equipment may be hard to find, but if you can get your hands on them, you'll be able to savor a taste of real Mexican cooking.

chapters

The Western Center and its Pacific Coast • A Journey North: The Bajío to the Northern Plains • The Central Hub • The Gulf Coast • The Southern Pacific Coast • A Miscellany of Culinary Experiences

previous books

Kennedy's five earlier books include *The Cuisines of Mexico* and *The Art of Mexican Cooking*.

specifics

560 pages, more than 300 recipes, 77 color photographs, $32.50. Published by Clarkson N. Potter Publishers.

from the book

"Zitácuaro is known for its hearty eating. As you stroll thorough the market any morning of the year, the small stands offer steaming *menudo* from large *cazuelas*. Don Lacho, who has a monopoly on heads of the slaughtered cattle from the *rastro*, offers you a sample of his succulent barbecued meat (*el rostro* as it is known locally) prized from the cheek. If you feel squeamish, just shut your eyes and eat."

MY MEXICO

A CULINARY ODYSSEY
WITH MORE THAN
300 RECIPES

DIANA KENNEDY

ASADO DE BODAS ESTILO PARRAS

PARRAS PORK AND CHILE WEDDING STEW

[SERVES 6]

THIS VERSION OF *ASADO DE BODAS*, AS IT IS PREPARED IN PARRAS, IS SO DIF-FERENT FROM THE OTHERS; IT IS A STRONGLY FLAVORED STEW OF PORK popularly served for weddings and other family and ceremonial occasions. It is often accompanied by flour tortillas (or even whole-wheat flour tortillas) and beans that resemble American pintos in color and flavor.

Rubbing the spices into the meat and setting it aside to season gives it a very good flavor. Particularly noticeable is the flavor of the local oregano that grows wild in the arid hills around.

The dish can be prepared ahead so that the sauce matures in flavor. In any case it is best to let it cool off before serving, to skim off the excess fat that rises to the surface. Then it can be reheated and served.

2¼ pounds (1 generous kg) stewing pork with some fat,
cut into ¾-inch (2-cm) cubes

1¼ tablespoons dried oregano

1 tablespoon cumin seeds

2 bay leaves, crumbled

2 cloves

5 garlic cloves, peeled

1 tablespoon salt or to taste

1 tablespoon mild vinegar

3 ancho chiles, veins and seeds removed

3 guajillo chiles, veins and seeds removed

approximately 3 cups (750 ml) water

3 tablespoons pork lard or vegetable oil

1 tablespoon sugar

½ orange, cut into slices

Put the meat into a bowl. Grind the oregano, cumin seeds, bay leaves, and cloves together to make a powder. Crush the garlic together with the salt and vinegar. Add the powdered herbs, mixing to a thick paste. Rub the paste into the meat with your hands and set aside to season —at least 1 hour or overnight in the refrigerator.

Cover the chiles with hot water and soak for about 20 minutes or until softened and reconstituted (do not leave too long in the water or they will lose their flavor). Drain, discarding the water. Transfer to a blender with 1½ cups (375 ml) of the water and blend as smoothly as possible.

In a heavy heatproof casserole, heat the lard, add the seasoned meat, and fry over medium heat until the meat is just starting to brown (take care: if the heat is too high, the spices will burn).

Add the blended chiles to the pan, pressing them through a fine strainer to remove the tough pieces of guajillo skin that stubbornly remain despite the blending. Fry the sauce for about 5 minutes, stirring and scraping the bottom of the pan to prevent sticking.

Add the remaining 1½ cups (375 ml) water, cover the pan, and cook over medium heat, stirring from time to time, for about 15 minutes. Add the sugar and orange and continue cooking until the meat is tender. Add a little more water if necessary to thin the sauce to medium consistency so it coats the back of a wooden spoon.

TOSTONES DE PLÁTANO

PLANTAIN TOSTADAS

Restaurant Los Tulipanes, Villahermosa

[MAKES 6 5-INCH (13-CM) TOSTONES]

THERE ARE TWO TRADITIONAL, AND RELATED, RESTAURANTS IN VILLAHER-MOSA, THE CAPITAL OF THE STATE OF TABASCO, THAT SERVE THE BEST OF regional foods with a menu that helpfully provides a glossary of the indigenous names: Los Tulipanes and El Guaraguao.

One of the most impressive dishes is a fish salad made of the very white flesh of the *peje lagarto* (a gar), served in the hollowed shell of the fish, with the pointed head still attached.

Instead of bread, a basket of *tostones de plátano*, 7-inch (18-cm) disks of flattened plantain, crisp-fried and slightly sweet, appears on the table—they are addictive. To make them at home I use a normal-sized tortilla press with a 6-inch (15-cm) plate, but if you have a larger press you can make more impressive *tostones* that resemble those of Tabasco.

It is very important, when choosing the plantains, that while the skins are still green the flesh inside is just beginning to ripen and has a sweet flavor. The totally green ones are more starchy and bland.

Some cooks will dip the uncooked *tostones* into salted water before frying. But this breaks your oil down fast, so I have opted for the method used in Los Tulipanes' kitchen: salt is sprinkled on the plantain just after pressing down to flatten it.

Your press should be lined with pieces of heavy plastic—not those light ones recommended for making tortillas. I find a wok useful for the frying process; you can get the depth of oil without using too much of it.

You can reheat the *tostones* and make them crisp again by placing them on brown paper-lined trays in a 400°F (205°C) oven. The paper will absorb a lot of the excess oil. (I recommend the same method for *chiles rellenos*.)

2½ pounds (1.125 kg) plantains (see note opposite),
peeled weight about 1½ pounds (675 g)
vegetable oil for frying
salt to taste

Cut the peeled plantains into lengths of 2½ inches (6.5 cm). Heat the oil—which should be at least 1½ inches (4 cm) deep in the pan—and add a few of the plantain pieces; be careful not to crowd the pan. Fry over medium heat, turning them over from time to time until they are an even golden brown, about 10 minutes. Remove and drain.

Place a piece of the plastic on each of the plates of the tortilla press. Put one length of the fried plantain upright on the bottom plate and smash it down with your hand to flatten slightly. Close the press and flatten the plantain out, turning the plastic around (because the plates are not always even) until you have an almost transparent even disk of about 5 inches (13 cm). The edge will not be perfectly even, but don't worry. Peel back the top plastic and sprinkle the plantain with salt; carefully transfer to the hot oil. Fry on both sides until crisp and a deep golden brown. Drain on brown paper and serve immediately.

1. FRESH CHILES COSTEÑOS. JAMILTEPEC, OAXACA. 2. DRYING CHILES COSTEÑOS. PINOTEPA NACIONAL. 3. FRESH CHILES FROM CAMPECHE MARKET. X-CAT-IK, CHILE DE CUBA (EGGPLANT-COLORED HABANERO), HABANEROS IN VARIOUS STAGES OF RIPENESS, FRESH CHILE VERDE AND DRIED, WHEN IT IS KNOWN AS CHILE SECO. IN CENTER, CHILE DULCE, FRESH AND VERY RIPE. 4. FRESH CHILES CRILLOS. TEHUANTEPEC, OAXACA. 5. CHILES GUAJILLOS (DRIED). JEREZ MARKET 6. TWO VARIETIES OF FRESH CHILES GÜEROS.

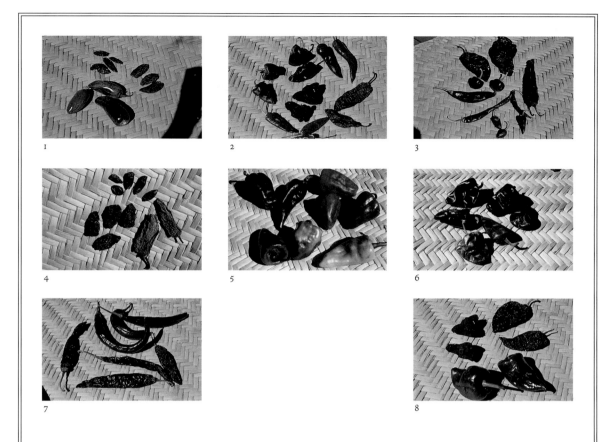

1. JALAPEÑOS FRESH AND DRIED, CHILE MORA, CHILE MORITA (DRIED SERRANO, LAST PICKING).

2. VARIOUS DRIED OAXACAN CHILES: CHILHAUCLE RED AND BLACK, CHILCOSTLE, COSTEÑO, PASILLA OAXAQUEÑA, OR CHILE MIJE (IN MIDDLE CHILE PASADO, NOT FROM OAXACA). 3. CORNER: PULLA, GUAJILLO, CASCABEL, ANCHO, MULATO, PASILLA, CATARINO OR CORA WITH CHILE DE ÁRBOL IN THE MIDDLE.

4. CHILPOCLES: MORA, MORITA, AND MECO. 5. FRESH CHILHUACLES: NEGRO, ROJO, AMARILLO (BLACK, RED, AND YELLOW) IN VARIOUS STAGES OF RIPENESS 6. CHILHAUCLES DRIED: BLACK, RED, AND YELLOW.

7. CHILACA FRESH, PASILLA DRIED. 8. CHILE POBLANO, DRIED AS ANCHO, PEELED AND DRIED AS POSADO.

from one of our most important cookbook authors

author

Mediterranean traveler and award-winning food writer Paula Wolfert

why she wrote it

"In every recipe there's a little something that makes it special, and, hopefully, better. It's these secrets . . . that I try to search out, then pass on in my classes and books to my students and readers. . . . Throughout this book I've tried to present the great and true tastes of Mediterranean grains and greens dishes in recipes updated for the modern kitchen."

why it made our list

It was a joy preparing recipes from this book. Delicious and far from run-of-the-mill, they come originally from Mediterranean home cooks whom Wolfert has met during her years of travel and research in her favorite area of the world. The absolute accuracy of these recipes shows that she painstakingly tested and improved and retested them all. For ingredients that aren't always readily available, she offers substitutions; for recipes that might seem complicated, she offers such clear step-by-step instructions that they become easy. When a book is a labor of love, it shows—and makes us love it, too.

chapters

A Bowl of Leafy Greens • Breads and Pastries • Soups • Appetizers • Salads • Light Meals • Main Course Dishes • Side Dishes • Sweet Greens and Grains • Sauces, Condiments, and Seasonings

previous books

Wolfert is the author of five other cookbooks, including *Couscous and Other Good Food from Morocco* and *The Cooking of Southwest France*.

specifics

384 pages, 182 recipes, $27.50.
Published by HarperCollins Publishers, Inc.

from the book

"Everywhere around the Mediter-ranean, there are women who spe-cialize in foraging. They call it 'apron cooking' because of the aprons they wear, usually homemade with three pockets: one for bitter greens, one for sweet, and the third for roots or mushrooms."

MEDITERRANEAN
GRAINS AND
GREENS

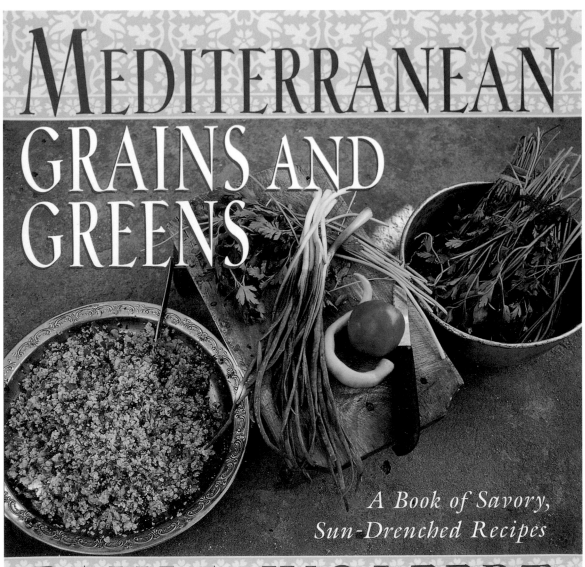

A Book of Savory,
Sun-Drenched Recipes

PAULA WOLFERT

AUTHOR OF *THE COOKING OF THE EASTERN MEDITERRANEAN* AND
COUSCOUS AND OTHER GOOD FOOD FROM MOROCCO

Editor's Choice Award

best
book of
the year

FARRO, LEAFY GREENS, AND POTATO SOUP AS PREPARED IN THE MARCHES (*Italy*)

❧

Serves 3 or 4

On a spring trip to the Marches (on the Adriatic coast of central Italy) I met a marvelous white-haired forager-chef-restaurateur, Felice Orazi, famous for his spring soup made with a local wild green called *bubbolino*, farro, and freshly dug potatoes.

Felice's wife, Rosalba, also uses *bubbolino* in her equally famous risottos and frittatas. Felice's restaurant, Le Copertelle, is nestled on the side of a mountain. He starts picking *bubbolino* in March, when this marvelous pealike green is barely an inch out of the ground. It's then, he says, that the plant is at its tender best. On the April day when I visited he looked out the window just before going out to forage. "Hmmm . . . the weather's weird today," he said. "I think I'll find some mushrooms, too." Then he smiled. "It's going to be a good lunch."

He returned with *bubbolino* and mushrooms, and the lunch, as promised, was good—in fact, out of this world! He told me that as spring progresses into summer he must go out earlier each day in order to climb higher up the mountain, since at lower levels the plants have matured and are too bitter for cooking.

Bladder campion (as *bubbolino* is called in English) tastes like a cross between asparagus and sweet peas—which is how I've simulated its taste in the following recipe, also adding a little arugula for texture.

When I first started searching for wild greens, I thought bladder campion would be hard to find. In fact, I found it right in the middle of my daylily patch in front of my summer home on Martha's Vineyard. Unfortunately, it was too mature to use.

If you do decide to go for the real thing, be sure to consult a reliable book on wild edible plants in your area. Otherwise you may make a mistake and cook an inedible look-alike.

½ cup farro

3 tablespoons olive oil plus more for garnish

½ cup chopped flat-leaf parsley

½ teaspoon red pepper flakes (without seeds) or more to taste

4 cloves garlic, peeled and sliced

½ pound boiling potatoes, peeled and chopped

¼ pound arugula leaves, stemmed and finely shredded

1 cup shelled peas

3 fresh asparagus spears, sliced very thin crosswise (optional)

Salt

Freshly ground black pepper

3 cups vegetable, meat, or poultry stock, simmering

Freshly grated pecorino Romano or Parmigiano-Reggiano

1. Pick over and rinse the farro and soak in tepid water overnight.

2. Drain the farro, cover with fresh cold water, and cook, covered, until tender, 45 minutes or longer, depending upon the age of the grain.

3. Meanwhile, in a heavy-bottomed bean or soup pot, heat the oil; add the parsley, red pepper, garlic, and potatoes; and sauté until soft and golden brown, about 15 minutes, mashing the potatoes in the pot, so that they begin to stick to the bottom of the pan and create caramelized areas here and there—but avoid burning.

4. Add the arugula, peas, and asparagus, if using, and stir-fry for a few minutes. Season with salt and pepper. Add the fully cooked farro and 3 cups simmering stock and bring back to a boil. Cook at the simmer for 30 minutes to cook the vegetables and blend flavors.

5. Adjust the seasoning with salt and pepper. Remove from the heat and let stand 5 minutes before serving. Serve with a drizzle of fresh olive oil and a small spoonful of cheese.

Swiss Chard

❀

Recently I asked a number of American friends which leafy green they thought was most popular around the Mediterranean. Almost everyone chose spinach. In fact, the answer is Swiss chard, possibly because it's gentler, softer, and can resist more heat, an important factor in warm Mediterranean countries. Also, of course, it's easy to clean and one of the best greens to use as a base for an intriguing greens mixture, as well as being excellent when served alone.

There are two primary types of Swiss chard: the big crinkly kind with thick crunchy stalks, and the finer kind with small smooth-textured leaves sprouting from thin stems. If you have a kitchen garden, you can get excellent Swiss chard seeds, including those for a tasty French variety called Paros, which bears delicious stalks and leaves.

Green Dumplings Tossed with Diced Tomato, Toasted Walnuts, and Fresh Herbs (*Italy*)

❀

Serves 2 or 3 as a first course or lunch

These delicious, light, easy-to-make dumplings are flatter than most gnocchi and fluffier, too, because they use very little flour. But lightness and fluffiness can be a two-edged sword: Unless properly handled these gnocchi can fall apart when they hit boiling water. It's best to roll them the day before, then chill them overnight.

Various sauces can be used to top these light delicious dumplings. Try a lightly herbed tomato sauce or this Ligurian-inspired version made with chopped walnuts, tomatoes, and fresh herbs.

¾ pound young "sweet" leafy greens such as stemmed spinach, lamb's-quarters, beet greens, chard, or a mixture of the above plus a few borage leaves

Fine sea salt

1 tablespoon unsalted butter

¼ teaspoon freshly ground black pepper

Grated nutmeg

½ cup ricotta cheese

6 tablespoons freshly and finely grated Parmigiano-Reggiano

1 egg plus 1 egg yolk

All-purpose flour

SAUCE

5 tablespoons unsalted butter, melted and clarified to make 3 tablespoons

3 tablespoons chopped fresh walnuts

4 tablespoons coarsely chopped fresh tomatoes

2 to 3 tablespoons chopped mixed herbs: parsley, marjoram, and dill

1½ tablespoons freshly and finely grated Parmigiano-Reggiano

1. Wash and cook the greens with a pinch of salt for 3 to 4 minutes in a boiling salted water; drain well. Chop them very fine and squeeze to remove excess moisture. In a large skillet, heat the butter and fry the greens until glossy but dry. Season with ½ teaspoon salt, pepper, and a pinch of grated nutmeg.

2. Push the ricotta cheese through a sieve; pour off any liquid. In a medium-large bowl combine the greens, ricotta, cheese, egg, and egg yolk, mixing well with a wooden spoon until well combined. Add just enough flour to hold the mixture together, about 3 tablespoons. Correct the seasoning. If the mixture is sticky and difficult to handle, chill it before continuing.

3. With well-floured hands pinch off a tablespoon of dough and place on a well-floured cloth spread over a baking sheet. Repeat until all the mixture is used up. Gently indent each piece with a floured thumb. Leave to dry, uncovered, at room temperature for 1 hour before cooking. Or refrigerate, uncovered, until ready to cook. Makes about 2 dozen dumplings. This recipe can be prepared one day in advance up to this point. Cover and refrigerate.

4. About 20 minutes before serving, preheat the oven to 325 degrees.

5. Bring a wide pan of water to a boil. Add salt to the boiling water and slide in half the dumplings. Cook until they rise to the surface, about 1 minute. Let them boil another 30 seconds, then remove with a slotted spoon to a buttered, shallow baking dish. Keep warm in the oven. Repeat with remaining dumplings.

6. Spoon the warmed butter over the dumplings and scatter the walnuts, tomatoes, and herbs on top. Return to the oven for a minute or two. Serve with a small sprinkling of grated cheese.

CHICKEN CAMARGUE–STYLE WITH RICE AND BLACK AND GREEN OLIVES (*France*)

❊

Serves 4

*I*t was probably in the fifteenth century that men first planted rice in the marshy wilderness south of Arles, the area known today as the Camargue. Because of the high salt content of the water this early attempt at growing rice was not a success. It wasn't until after World War II that there was a revival of interest in rice growing in the region. New paddies were created, irrigation programs were instituted, and now Camargue rice is big business. Unlike their Italian and Spanish neighbors, who produce short-grain rice for their risottos and *arroces*, the French planted long-grain Carolina rice, which they prefer.

A dozen or so years ago, they started planting a rice hybrid developed from an indigenous red wild grass, producing a delicious, nutty, very light rice called "red rice," much prized by French and British chefs.

This rice, chicken, and olive dish reflects the recent impact of North African gastronomy upon southern French cooking. It is made in a completely different way from the vast array of North African chicken and olive dishes, but matches such dishes in intensity of flavor. Chicken skin is always a problem when cooking with rice and vegetables. To maintain an attractive skin, I wash and dry the chicken early in the day, then leave the legs and thighs, skin side up, on paper toweling to thoroughly dry out. This seems to encourage the skin to crisp when browning and to keep a good appearance even after being cooked in a closed pan.

2 pounds chicken, legs and thighs (4 of each)

Salt

Freshly ground black pepper

2 tablespoons olive oil

1½ cups chopped onions

1 tablespoon chopped garlic

1 large green bell pepper, cored, seeded, and finely diced (1½ cups)

2 ripe tomatoes, seeded and pressed through a sieve or puréed (1 cup)

½ cup blanched slivered almonds

½ cup black raisins

1 teaspoon ground ginger

1 teaspoon ground coriander

Pinch of red pepper flakes without seeds

1 cup medium- or long-grain rice

½ cup French black olives, preferably Nyons, rinsed and pitted

½ cup green olives, rinsed and pitted

2 tablespoons chopped flat-leaf parsley

1. Season the chicken with salt and pepper.

2. Heat the oil in a 10- or 12-inch straight-sided, heavy-bottomed skillet and in it place the chicken, skin side down. Brown over high heat for 7 minutes. Lower the heat, turn the chicken, and continue browning for another 3 minutes. Remove from the skillet.

3. Pour off all but 2 tablespoons fat from the skillet and add the onion. Cook, stirring, 3 to 4 minutes. Stir in the garlic, bell pepper, tomatoes, almonds, raisins, and spices. Cook over medium-low heat, stirring often, for 10 minutes. Return the chicken to the skillet, skin side up, cover, and cook for 10 minutes more. Carefully remove the chicken to a side dish.

4. Stir up the caramelized vegetables and their juices in the skillet. Add 1½ cups water and bring to a boil. Sprinkle the rice in an even layer over the vegetables, then top with the chicken, skin side up. Cover tightly and continue cooking until the rice and chicken are tender, 18 minutes. Five minutes before serving, stir in the olives and correct the seasoning. Sprinkle with the parsley just before serving.

CRETAN MIXED GREENS AND TOMATOES WITH BLACK-EYED PEAS (*Greece*)

Serves 6 to 8

On the island of Crete, March and April are the best months to pick wild edible greens for making pies. Also in spring, in the markets of Heraklion, you'll find neatly tied-up bunches of aromatic greens called *yahnera*: a few shoots of wild fennel bunched with salsify tops, leaves of young corn poppy, Roman pimpernel, shepherd's purse, wild carrot, edible chrysanthemum, and a thick furry thistle called *eryngo*—all sweet fragrant greens nearly impossible to put together outside Crete.

The dominant flavor of a *yahnera* bunch, wild fennel, is hard to find. In spring, it grows rampantly in California; elsewhere combine supermarket fennel and some crushed fennel seeds. To simulate the other greens, I make up a mixture of three or four easy-to-find "sweet" greens (beet greens, baby spinach, Swiss chard, miner's lettuce, pea shoots, mâche, orache, nettles, lamb's-quarters, and green amaranth) to which I add just one sprig of cilantro for fragrance.

Black-eyed peas are a popular legume in many Mediterranean regions, ranging from Catalonia (where they're cooked with moist stewed wild mushrooms or a spirited blend of salt cod and wild edible greens) to Cyprus (where they're stewed with greens and served with good olive oil and lemon) to Turkey (where they're enhanced with a unique burnished red pepper, then simmered with heaps of stewed greens).

Serve this delicious vegetable dish warm or cool for lunch along with some cheese, olives, and a glass of wine. Followed, in turn, in true Mediterranean spirit, by . . . you guessed it! . . . a nap.

1⅔ cups dried black-eyed peas

1 cup diced fennel bulb

2½ packed cups mixed tender leafy greens (see opposite page), washed, stemmed, and roughly cut up, about 5 ounces

¼ cup extra-virgin olive oil

1 cup chopped onion

3 scallions, finely chopped

1 sprig fresh cilantro, stemmed and roughly chopped

1 cup grated tomatoes

Pinch of fennel seeds, bruised in a mortar

Salt

Freshly ground black pepper

1. Soak the black-eyed peas according to package directions. Drain and cook in fresh water to cover until almost tender, about 30 minutes. Meanwhile, wash the fennel and the greens and let sit, dripping wet, on a plate.

2. In a 4-quart saucepan over medium heat, warm the olive oil. Add the onion, scallions, and the fennel and cook until soft, golden, and aromatic, 10 minutes. Add 1 cup water and continue to cook, stirring often, for 10 minutes. Add the greens to the saucepan along with the coriander, tomatoes, fennel seeds, and salt and pepper and cook for another 10 minutes.

3. Drain the black-eyed peas; discard the water. Add the black-eyed peas to the saucepan along with a few tablespoons water, if necessary, to keep everything moist. Simmer another 10 minutes and correct the seasoning. Serve warm or cool.

With thanks to Mirsini Lambraki for sharing this recipe.

you can't get a table, but you can try the food

author

Frank Pellegrino, owner of Rao's, a family-run Italian restaurant in East Harlem where it is famously impossible to get a reservation

why he wrote it

"For twenty-five years I have been trying to figure out what Rao's is all about. I give up. I can't. Many years ago the neighborhood people called it The Hole because you have to walk down four steps to the entrance. My Aunt Anna and Uncle Vincent called it The Saloon. I call it The Joint. It's all of the above. It's none of the above. It is itself, its own entity. It lives. It breathes. It communicates better than you and I can. It talks straight to your soul. . . . My sincerest hope is that this book, which emanates from this room called Rao's, brings a smile to your heart as well as to your palate."

why it made our list

We can't get a table at Rao's either. Ever since 1977, when Mimi Sheraton of *The New York Times* gave it a glowing review, reservations have been hard to come by. There are, after all, only eight tables available, with one seating per night, and the regulars who've been frequenting the establishment since before the review pretty much own those seats. This charming cookbook is about the closest most of us will ever come to experiencing Rao's, and so the author has included photos of the place and its famous customers, quotes from those who know it well, and recipes for the Italian specialties that keep them coming back week after week. The introduction traces the history of the restaurant from its founding in 1896, when Charles Rao bought a saloon at 114th Street and Pleasant Avenue. It's a fascinating read, and though we know it can't compare to being there, we're happy to have a taste.

chapters

Aunt Anna's Kitchen • Appetizers • Soups and Salads • Pasta • Risotto • Chicken • Meats • Seafood • Vegetables • Sweets

specifics

205 pages, 98 recipes,
32 color photographs,
44 black-and-white photographs,
$40. Published by Random House.

from the book

"Louis and Vincent kept the bar open during Prohibition. One of the neighborhood families, the Caianos, made their own wine in their cellar next door, and it was pumped into Rao's basement through a hose. Rao's sold the wine for a dollar a bottle."

RAO'S COOKBOOK
OVER 100 YEARS OF ITALIAN HOME COOKING

FRANK PELLEGRINO

Preface by Dick Schaap
INTRODUCTION BY NICHOLAS PILEGGI

SHRIMP OREGANATE

In this dish, you want a definite oregano flavor, but you do not want to overpower the delicate shrimp. Use a judicious hand when adding the oregano—fresh oregano works particularly well in this preparation.

SERVES 6

2 pounds large shrimp, peeled and deveined, butterflied, tails left on, patted dry

1 cup all-purpose flour

1 cup vegetable oil

2 cups dry white wine

1 cup chicken broth

Juice of 1 lemon

2 teaspoons minced garlic

2 teaspoons chopped, fresh oregano or 1 teaspoon dried oregano

Salt and pepper to taste

½ cup freshly grated Pecorino Romano cheese

Approximately 8 tablespoons unsalted butter

1 cup Bread Crumbs (see opposite page)

1. Preheat oven to 400° F.

2. Dredge shrimp in flour, patting them to make sure all sides are well coated.

3. Heat oil in a large sauté pan over high heat. When oil is very hot but not smoking, add shrimp and sauté for 3 minutes or until shrimp have just begun to brown. (Do not crowd pan; prepare shrimp in batches, if necessary.) Remove shrimp from pan and drain off all excess oil.

4. Return pan to medium-high heat. Add shrimp, wine, broth, lemon juice, garlic, oregano, and salt and pepper. Bring to a boil and cook for 1 minute.

5. Using a slotted spoon, remove shrimp from pan and place on a cookie sheet with sides. Pour sauce over the top of the shrimp.

6. Sprinkle cheese over each shrimp. Place ½ teaspoon butter on each shrimp, then generously coat the tops with Bread Crumbs.

7. Bake for 3 minutes.

8. Transfer shrimp to broiler for 1 minute or until tops are brown. Serve.

Note: At Rao's, for Shrimp Oreganate, we serve 7 shrimp per person. Two pounds of large shrimp should yield approximately 38 to 42 shrimp.

BREAD CRUMBS

Unless you make your own bread crumbs, you won't be following Rao's kitchen tradition. Use the finest-quality Italian bread you can find (we have been using Morrone from 116th Street in Manhattan for generations) and allow it to dry for at least two days. Then grate, using a handheld grater or a food processor fitted with the metal blade. Shake and push the bread crumbs through a medium strainer to get an even texture. And, remember, as Aunt Anna Rao used to say, "The better the bread, the better the crumbs."

Store, tightly covered and refrigerated, for no more than 1 week.

I guess one of my favorite memories about Rao's is the night Frankie stayed open late so I could celebrate my Broadway debut with family and friends. I've been lucky enough to dine there many times, and whether celebrating my girlfriend Lynn's birthday or just looking for a great meal, I don't think there's a better dining experience in New York. My personal favorites are the lemon chicken and the cheesecake . . . They're as good as it gets.

BRUNO KIRBY

Rao's Famous Lemon Chicken

Pollo al Limone

SERVES 6

---

2 2½- to 3-pound broiling chickens, halved   ¼ cup chopped Italian parsley

Lemon Sauce (recipe follows)

1. To attain maximum heat, preheat broiler for at least 15 minutes before using.

2. Broil chicken halves, turning once, for about 30 minutes or until skin is golden-brown and juices run clear when bird is pierced with a fork.

3. Remove chicken from broiler, leaving broiler on. Using a very sharp knife, cut each half into about 6 pieces (leg, thigh, wing, 3 small breast pieces).

4. Place chicken on a baking sheet with sides, of a size that can fit into the broiler. Pour Lemon Sauce over the chicken and toss to coat well. If necessary, divide sauce in half and do this in two batches.

5. Return to broiler and broil for 3 minutes. Turn each piece and broil for an additional minute.

6. Remove from broiler and portion each chicken onto each of 6 warm serving plates.

7. Pour sauce into a heavy saucepan. Stir in parsley and place over high heat for 1 minute. Pour an equal amount of sauce over each chicken and serve with lots of crusty bread to absorb the sauce.

LEMON SAUCE

---

2 cups fresh lemon juice   1½ teaspoons minced garlic

1 cup olive oil   ½ teaspoon dried oregano

1 tablespoon red wine vinegar   Salt and pepper to taste

1. Whisk together juice, oil, vinegar, garlic, oregano, and salt and pepper. Cover and refrigerate until ready to use. Whisk or shake vigorously before using.

robust, hearty cooking from the italian countryside

author

Cookbook writer Nancy Harmon Jenkins, a part-time resident of Tuscany

why she wrote it

"This book is . . . a look at what I think of and what has been presented to me as traditional Tuscan country food. In that sense, it's not eternal, not fixed in time, and in fact if I had been able to write this book in 1950 or 1900, it would have been quite different. But not entirely, because while some things change (violets become part of an insalata del bosco and Nutella fills the bombolone at Carnival), certain things persist, most of all the basic tastes of the Tuscans themselves, the underlying themes, of which there are so many variations, both seasonal and geographical."

why it made our list

Jenkins has had a farmhouse in Italy's Tuscan countryside for over 25 years and has learned much from her friends and neighbors there. The simple, robust recipes they've shared with her fill this down-to-earth collection, accompanied by tales of the life in the author's rural community. Reading this engaging book—and cooking from it—will transport you to another way of living and give you a thorough understanding of authentic Tuscan tastes and traditions.

chapters

Bread • Appetizers and Snacks • First Courses: Soups • First Courses: Pasta, Polenta, Farro, and Rice Dishes • Seafood • Chicken and Meat • Vegetables • Sweets and Desserts • The Wines of Tuscany • Tuscan Olive Oil • When You Go to Tuscany

previous books

Jenkins was one of last year's *Best of the Best* honorees for *Flavors of Puglia*. Her other books include *The Mediterranean Diet Cookbook*.

specifics

288 pages, 115 recipes,
8 color photographs,
12 black-and-white photographs,
$27.50. Published by Broadway Books.

from the book

"In the Tuscan farmhouses I know, the kitchen is not just the heart, it *is* the home, almost in its entirety, one large room that extends end to end across the front of the farmhouse. In this room all family activities take place, except for sleeping, giving birth, and dying, and sometimes even those have taken place in the kitchen."

FLAVORS OF Tuscany

Traditional Recipes from the Tuscan Countryside

Author of *Flavors of Puglia*

NANCY HARMON JENKINS

Tuscan Pot Roast
stracotto

8 TO 10 SERVINGS

With the exception of the glorious bistecca Chianina, Tuscans don't eat a lot of beef. Once the T-bones have been removed from a Chianina carcass, however, something has to be done with the rest of the meat, and *stracotto* is one thing to do with it. This kind of pot roast exists all over Italy, a real Sunday dish, elegant, flavorful, and practical for the cook, since the sauce for the pasta and the meat cook all at once and together. Americans may find it odd to serve two courses with the same fundamental flavors, but to Italians it's perfectly normal. What makes this particular treatment Tuscan is the presence of a robust Chianti wine in the sauce. Any flavorful red wine with a good acidic balance will do.

3 ½ pounds beef, such as top round, rolled and tied

3 or 4 cloves garlic, thinly sliced

2 medium carrots, scraped and thinly sliced

2 medium yellow onions, thinly sliced

1 thick stalk celery, thinly sliced

3 sprigs rosemary, leaves only, chopped

¼ cup extra virgin olive oil

1 ½ cups dry red wine

1 pound very ripe fresh tomatoes, peeled, seeded, and chopped, or 1 cup chopped canned tomatoes

1 tablespoon butter

1 tablespoon unbleached all-purpose flour

Salt and freshly ground black pepper to taste

Using a small sharp knife, make incisions all over the meat to a depth of ¼ to ½ inch and insert the garlic slices in them.

In a heavy saucepan over medium-low heat, gently sauté the carrots, onions, celery, and rosemary in the oil until the vegetables are beginning to soften but not brown. Add the garlic-studded beef, raise the heat to medium, and brown the beef on all sides, turning frequently. Add the wine and let it boil until reduced to about ½ cup. As soon as it's reduced, stir in the tomatoes. Cover and let simmer for about 1 hour.

Work the butter and flour together to make a paste, then stir thoroughly into the cooking juices. Cover tightly, reduce the heat to low, and let cook at a bare simmer for 2 hours longer, adding a little hot water, wine, or broth if the liquid in the pan reduces too much.

When the meat is done, lift it out of the cooking juices and set aside to rest for about 15 minutes, then slice off three thin slices of meat. Chop them with a knife as finely as possible.

Degrease the juices in the pan, setting aside about $\frac{1}{2}$ cup of the meat juices to garnish the meat. Season with salt and pepper. Add the chopped meat to the remaining juices and serve this as a sauce over pasta for a first course. Serve the meat as a second course with the reserved juices as a garnish. (This is often served with a contorno of puréed potatoes.)

Cantucci—Biscotti di Prato

ABOUT 36 BISCOTTI

These crisp thick cookies are meant to be dipped in a glass of vin santo or other sweet wine, or coffee, to soften them for eating. The town of Prato, north of Florence, claims them, but in fact they can be found all over Tuscany—and all over America these days. Biscotti, like biscuit, means twice-cooked; these are among the few biscuits that still reflect that original meaning.

A little butter for the cookie sheet
2 cups unbleached all-purpose flour and 2 cups pastry flour, or 4 cups Italian-style flour, plus a little more for the board and the cookie sheet
2 cups sugar
1 teaspoon baking soda
Pinch of salt
4 eggs
1 teaspoon pure vanilla extract
1 cup coarsely chopped toasted almonds
1 cup coarsely chopped toasted hazelnuts
1 egg white beaten with 1 teaspoon water

Preheat the oven to 375°F. Lightly grease and flour a cookie sheet.

In a mixing bowl, toss the flour, sugar, baking soda, and salt with a fork to mix well.

In a separate bowl, beat the eggs with the vanilla just enough to mix yolks and whites. Stir the eggs into the dry mixture, kneading with your hands in the bowl until you have a homogeneous mixture. Turn the dough out on a very lightly floured board. Sprinkle the nuts over the dough and continue kneading for a few minutes to distribute the nuts evenly throughout the dough. Set the dough aside to rest for 10 minutes or so.

Now divide the dough into 6 equal pieces and, using your hands, shape each piece into a long, thin log no more than 2 inches in diameter. As each log is finished, set it on the cookie sheet, keeping them a few inches apart; they expand while baking. Press the top of each log with your palm to flatten it slightly and give it an oval rather than a round section when sliced.

Paint each log with the egg white wash, then bake the logs for 20 to 30 minutes, or until they are dry and lightly colored. Remove from the oven and set aside, on the cookie sheet, until cool enough to handle. Lower the oven temperature to 300°F.

When the logs are cool enough to handle, slice them on the diagonal no more than ½ inch thick, using a long sharp knife. Lay the biscotti, flat side down, on the cookie sheet and return them to the oven for 15 to 20 minutes.

Transfer the biscotti to a rack to dry, cool, and harden for several hours. They can be kept in a cookie tin for 6 weeks or more.

an exploration into the heart of italian cooking

author

Lidia Matticchio Bastianich, co-owner of the New York City restaurants Felidia, Becco, and Frico Bar and host of the PBS series for which this book is a companion

why she wrote it

"Let me invite you on a journey with me from my childhood through my formative years and beyond to see how my love for food and my desire to share it have developed. In these pages, I talk about the growing of food, the harvesting and enjoyment of food, and the preparation, storing, drying, curing, and preserving of food. . . . I still vividly remember my early food experiences, which gave way to my lifelong love affair with Italian food. I would like to share these experiences with you."

why it made our list

There's certainly no shortage of Italian cookbooks these days, but what sets this one apart is its very personal approach to the cuisines of Bastianich's homeland. The story of her family's life in Italy and America is woven through the chapters, with fond memories of dishes prepared and eaten. "Our family has been through a lot together," she writes, "but when we are all gathered around Lidia's Italian table, I know everything will be fine forever." Of course, the fare on that table is pretty fine, too. Throughout the book, Bastianich emphasizes the importance of high-quality ingredients while clearly telling the reader what to look for when buying each one. The result is a collection that is both engaging and useful.

chapters

Appetizers • Soups • Fresh Pasta •
Dry Pasta • Rice • Gnocchi • Polenta •
Vegetables • Game and Chicken •
Meat • Fish and Shellfish • Sweets

previous books

Bastianich is also the author
of *La Cucina di Lidia*.

specifics

400 pages, 203 recipes,
19 color photographs, $26.
Published by William Morrow
and Company, Inc.

from the book

"I remember my grandmother Rosa telling me often how fortunate I was. While ladling out a sausage with my *pasta e fagioli*, she would explain that when she was my age, the flavor of meat in her *minestra* would have come from a prosciutto bone that was borrowed from the neighbors and then returned."

Lidia's Italian Table

More

Than 200

Recipes

from the

First Lady

of Italian

Cooking

LIDIA MATTICCHIO BASTIANICH

Seared Lamb Chops with Rosemary and Mint Sauce

Costatine d'Agnello alla Menta

For this dish, rib chops cut from a rack of lamb are best because of the length of the bones. Look for a bright red color a few shades lighter than beef and a big "eye" of meat—about 2½ inches wide.

MAKES 6 SERVINGS

For the chops

12 "frenched" rib lamb chops
   (about 3 pounds; see Note)
1 tablespoon fresh rosemary leaves
2 teaspoons extra virgin olive oil
1 teaspoon salt
1 teaspoon freshly ground black pepper

For the sauce

1 orange
1 pound meaty lamb bones
3 tablespoons extra virgin olive oil
1 tablespoon all-purpose flour
½ cup chopped onions
¼ cup sliced carrots
¼ cup sliced celery
1 tablespoon chopped fresh sage leaves
1 tablespoon chopped fresh rosemary leaves
1 tablespoon chopped fresh mint leaves
Salt and freshly ground black pepper
3 cups chicken stock or canned low-sodium
   chicken broth
1 cup water
½ cup dry white wine

Rub the chops with the rosemary, oil, salt, and pepper and let them stand at room temperature for up to 2 hours or refrigerate, covered, for up to 1 day.

Make the sauce. Preheat the oven to 425°F. Remove the zest—the orange part of the peel without the underlying white pith—from the orange with a vegetable peeler. Squeeze the juice from the orange. Reserve the zest and juice separately. Trim the lamb scraps of all fat and combine them with the lamb bones in a roasting pan. Pour 1 tablespoon of the olive oil over the trimmings and bones and toss to coat. Roast for 30 minutes. Sprinkle the flour over the bones and roast until the bones are well browned, about another 15 minutes.

Meanwhile, in a large nonreactive saucepan, heat the remaining 2 tablespoons oil over medium heat. Add the onions and cook, stirring occasionally, until softened, about 5 minutes. Add the carrots, celery, sage, rosemary, mint, and orange zest. Season lightly with salt and pepper and cook, stirring occasionally, until the vegetables are lightly browned, about 15 minutes. If the vegetables begin to stick, add a small amount of the stock and stir well.

Transfer the browned bones and meat scraps to the saucepan. Pour off and discard all the fat from the roasting pan. While the roasting pan is still hot, add the water, wine, orange juice, and the remaining chicken stock and scrape the bottom of the pan to release all the browned drippings. Pour the liquid into the saucepan and bring to a boil over high heat. Reduce the heat to a simmer and cook, skimming the foam and fat frequently from the surface, until the liquid is reduced to about 1½ cups, about 1¼ hours.

To serve

Braised Spring Legumes (page 122; optional)

Sprigs fresh mint

Discard the bones and strain the sauce through a fine sieve, pressing down hard on the solids to squeeze as much liquid as possible from them. Return the sauce to the saucepan and simmer over low heat until reduced to the consistency of gravy. Cover and keep warm in a warm place.

Heat a heavy griddle or large cast-iron pan over high heat. Add as many chops as will fit without touching. Cook the chops, turning them once, until well browned outside and rosy pink in the center, about 3 minutes. (For more well-done chops, add 1 to 2 minutes to the cooking time.) Repeat with the remaining chops, if necessary.

Spoon the sauce onto plates and arrange the chops over the sauce, with the bones crossing. Arrange the Braised Spring Legumes next to the lamb and decorate with mint sprigs.

Note: Ask the butcher to french the chops, or do it yourself: Cut the meat and fat away from each rib bone, starting at the point where the "eye" of meat meets the bone. Scrape the bone clean with the back side of a knife. There should be from 1½ to 3 inches of bone protruding. Save all trimmings from the chops to use in the sauce.

Braised Spring Legumes

🌿 Scaffata 🌿

This is a wonderful Roman spring dish that can be made when peas and favas in their shells are young and sweet. The name comes from the word *scaffare*—"to shell" in Roman dialect. It is especially good when served with roasted spring lamb or goat. The outermost, less tender leaves of a head of romaine, which you may not want to use in a salad, are perfect for this dish.

MAKES 6 SERVINGS

3 tablespoons extra virgin olive oil

1 cup chopped scallions (white and tender parts; about 6 scallions)

½ cup chopped onions

2½ pounds fresh peas in the pod, shelled

1¼ pounds fresh fava beans in the pod, shelled, blanched, and peeled

1 cup finely diced zucchini

½ teaspoon peperoncino (crushed red pepper)

Salt

2 cups thinly shredded romaine leaves

1 tablespoon finely shredded fresh mint leaves

In a large, heavy casserole with a tight-fitting lid, heat the olive oil over medium heat. Add the scallions and onions and cook, stirring, until wilted, about 4 minutes. Add the peas, fava beans, zucchini, and peperoncino and season lightly with salt. Stir well, reduce the heat to low, and cover the casserole tightly. Cook for 15 minutes, stirring occasionally.

Add the romaine and mint, cover the casserole, and cook, stirring occasionally, until the vegetables are very tender, about 25 minutes more. (The vegetables should give off enough moisture during cooking to prevent sticking or burning. If you find they are sticking, you can add a few tablespoons of water. Make sure the heat is very low and the pot is tightly covered before continuing to cook. It is fine, however, if the vegetables do brown a little.) Season to taste with salt and serve hot.

Seared Lamb Chops with Rosemary and Mint Sauce
and Braised Spring Legumes

resolutely authentic regional specialties

author

Giuliano Bugialli, famed cooking teacher and host of the PBS cooking series *Bugialli's Italy*

why he wrote it

"Some people do not agree with my passion for authenticity. They ask, if the recipe tastes all right, what difference does tradition make? My prejudice is that recipes that have been tasted over a long period have stood 'the test of time' and survived many changes of taste. And undoubtedly these traditional dishes tell you much about the values of a region. I have no interest in pedantic scholarship for its own sake, only in revealing as much as I can about a colorful, fun-loving people through the food they have long preserved."

why it made our list

Local specialties are the focus here, some of them found only in such small areas of Italy (a country where it sometimes seems every village has its own cuisine) that they have never been previously published. The recipes are organized by course, from antipasti to dessert, and—since Bugialli prizes authenticity—many are accompanied by the stories of their origins. "The only way to show how one sees and experiences one's native country," writes Bugialli, "is to travel through its regions, great and small cities, and share with people their gastronomic loves and experiences." It's like a grand tour of Italy, one dish at a time.

chapters

Antipasti (Appetizers) • Primi Piatti (First Courses) • Vegetables • Main Courses • Desserts

previous books

Among Bugialli's seven Italian-themed cookbooks are *The Fine Art of Italian Cooking* and *Giuliano Bugialli's Classic Techniques of Italian Cooking*.

specifics

320 pages, 190 recipes, 29 color photographs, $28. Published by William Morrow and Company, Inc.

from the book

"Recipes 'alla parmigiana' originally meant made in the homey style of a housewife from Parma. Because this usually meant that Parmigiano cheese was in the recipe, the meaning spread to dishes that were based on that cheese and even some other cheeses, sometimes in combination."

Bugialli's Italy

Traditional Recipes from the Regions of Italy

Giuliano Bugialli

INSALATA DI SEDANO E FINOCCHI
Celery and Fennel Salad
Makes 6 servings

The celery and fennel, shaved as thin as the shavings from a truffle cutter and topped with slivers of Parmigiano, are transformed by the merest two teaspoons of authentic balsamic vinegar into something really special. The authentic D.O.C. balsamic vinegar Aceto Tradizionale Balsamico from Modena is very concentrated and expensive, like truffles, but is used in very small quantities as a rare delicacy. When using this D.O.C. vinegar, you realize the true quality of this ingredient.

4 white inner stalks celery, all strings removed	2 teaspoons balsamic vinegar
2 medium-size fennel bulbs, cleaned and cut into quarters	1 large bunch arugula (*rucola* or *ruchetta*)
1 lemon	4 ounces Parmigiano cheese, cut into medium-size slivers
¼ cup extra virgin olive oil	1 ounce walnuts, coarsely chopped
Salt and freshly ground black pepper	Fresh basil and Italian parsley leaves
	Shelled walnuts in large pieces

Soak the celery and fennel in a bowl of cold water with the lemon, cut in half and squeezed, for half an hour. Drain the vegetables and use a truffle slicer or a mandoline to slice them very thin. Transfer the slices to a crockery or glass bowl and season with the oil, salt and pepper to taste, and the vinegar. Mix very well. Arrange the arugula leaves in a single layer on a serving platter, then arrange the vegetables in a layer over that. Over them lay the slivers of Parmigiano, then sprinkle with the chopped walnuts.

To serve, use a spatula so you can keep the layering as it is, without mixing the vegetables together with the cheese and nuts. Finally, sprinkle each portion with some basil and parsley leaves and a few walnut chunks.

TIMBALLI DI RICOTTA

Little Ricotta Budini

Makes 8 servings

In Italy this *budino* is made with sheep's milk ricotta, but it also works very well with cow's milk. The ricotta in Italy is very dry, so the ricotta used here must be drained very well before using. These *timballi* are really small soufflés, but Italians prefer them to be unmolded, so they do fall a little. They may also be eaten at room temperature, in which case they become the lightest of cheesecakes.

12 ounces whole-milk ricotta, drained

1½ ounces candied orange rind, cut into very small pieces

1½ tablespoons dark or light rum

½ cup plus ¼ cup superfine sugar

4 extra-large eggs, separated

Pinch of salt

1 tablespoon potato starch (*not* potato flour; see Note on page 128)

Grated rind of 1 small lemon with thick skin

Pinch of ground cinnamon

Granulated sugar as needed

TO SERVE:

About 2 tablespoons confectioners' sugar

Strips of zest of 1 medium-size orange with thick skin

Be sure the ricotta is very well drained and smooth. Soak the candied orange rind in the rum for 1 hour. Preheat the oven to 375 degrees and line the bottom of a large baking pan with paper towels or a cotton kitchen towel, to be used later as a water bath (*bagno Maria*).

Add the ½ cup sugar to the ricotta in a large bowl and mix very well. Add the egg yolks one at a time and mix as each is added. Then add the salt, potato starch, grated lemon rind, and cinnamon. Let rest, covered with plastic wrap, in the refrigerator, for at least 1 hour before using.

Butter eight custard cups or ramekins and coat them with granulated sugar. When ready, drain the candied orange rind and add it to the ricotta, discarding the unabsorbed rum. Beat the egg whites with the remaining ¼ cup sugar in a large copper bowl with a wire whisk until soft peaks form. Gently fold the whites into the ricotta mixture, then ladle into the prepared cups. The cups should be no more than two-thirds full. Place the cups in the baking pan and pour in enough lukewarm water to almost reach the level of the ricotta filling. Bake until the tops of the *timballi* are golden and very puffy, about 25 minutes.

Remove the cups from the water bath, run a paring knife all around the molds to be sure nothing is attached to the sides, then unmold onto individual dessert plates with the golden side on top. Using a very fine sieve, sprinkle the confectioners' sugar over, then a few orange zest strips. Serve hot.

VARIATIONS

- Use candied citron instead of orange rind.
- Use grated orange rind instead of lemon rind.
- Sprinkle unsweetened cocoa powder over the tops instead of confectioners' sugar.
- Do not unmold the *timballi*.

Note: Potato starch is available in some gourmet shops and the kosher section of many super-markets.

Timballi di Ricotta, if left in the molds, are small soufflés;
if unmolded, as Italians prefer, they become very light cheesecakes.

Udine (Friuli region): White celery in an Udine market in the Friuli region. Stalks of this celery are quite thick, with a lot of pulp. It is used mainly as a vegetable, not as an aromatic herb.

irreverence and recipes from a popular pair

authors

Clarissa Dickson Wright and Jennifer Paterson, British stars of the Food Network's *The Two Fat Ladies*

why they wrote it

As a second companion volume to their TV series.

why it made our list

Wright and Paterson have strong opinions about food and aren't afraid to express them. Fans of their no-holds-barred approach will love the attitude-packed introductions to the chapters and recipes, and series devotees will enjoy the behind-the-scenes photos that pop up throughout. As you might expect, most of the recipes are British in origin—but there are other influences here as well, just in case deviled kidneys aren't your cup of tea.

chapters

Light Dishes, Appetizers, and Savories • Main Courses • Puddings (Desserts) • Breakfasts • Teas • Cocktail Parties • Picnics

previous books

The first companion book to Wright and Paterson's TV show was *Cooking with the Two Fat Ladies*.

specifics

192 pages, 136 recipes, 26 color photographs, 22 black-and-white photographs, $25. Published by Clarkson N. Potter Publishers.

from the book

"Every food writer bangs on about the Mediterranean and Levantine civilisations' use of garlic, but turn to Skeat's *Etymological Dictionary* and there it is: garlic: Anglo-Saxon spearleek from gar, a spear. What, I wonder, did the Anglo-Saxons do with garlic that they took the trouble to name it? We are so brainwashed with information about the diet of bronzed southern peasants nowadays that we overlook our own heritage."

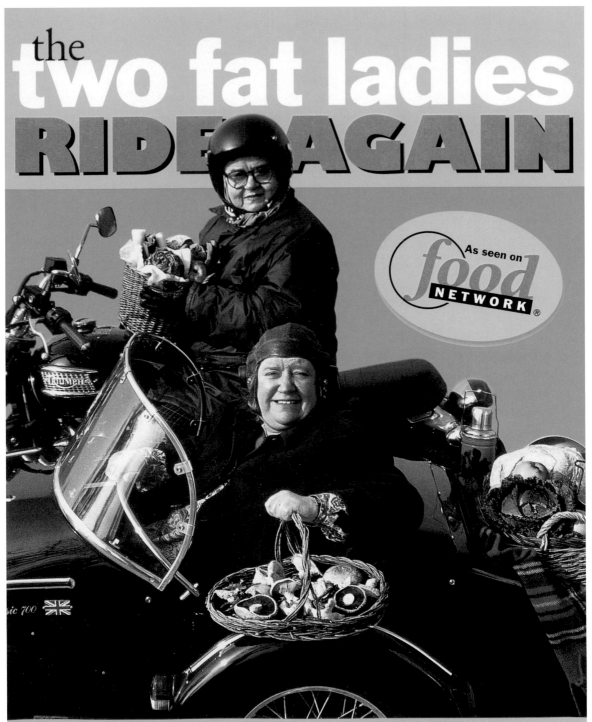

the
two fat ladies
RIDE AGAIN

As seen on *food* NETWORK®

Clarissa Dickson Wright AND Jennifer Paterson

BREAKFASTS

Driving a bike and sidecar is hard enough, without a cameraman in front of you

CLARISSA WRITES: Every nutritionist I have ever met agrees that breakfast is the most important meal of the day. Night is the longest period of time we go without food; in the morning we have the whole day in front of us and we need energy to tackle it. So what do we do? We stagger downstairs, grab a cup of something hot and probably instant and if we eat at all, it is probably cereal – with semi-skimmed milk even though the body cannot absorb the calcium in the milk without the fat, and osteoporosis is on the increase – or a swift piece of toast eaten on the run.

We have found out the hard way how difficult it is to find a good breakfast on the road. In one hotel, my poached eggs were served in a demi-lune salad dish, without toast but with a bunch of watercress and a free ant, to much ribald laughter from us! We have had eggs cooked in some tasteless, amorphous, artificial fat and tasting like blotting paper, and bacon which disgraced the poor pig who gave his all.

Currently we are staying at Boltongate Rectory, a Wolsey Lodge in Cumbria, and what a joy breakfast is. Nothing can surpass a well-laid breakfast table, and here the porridge is smooth and delicious and the eggs golden with proud yolks, while the bacon has just the right amount of salt. We are very jolly for it and sally forth to mob up the world in a much happier frame of mind. Breakfast beckons for us, as I hope it will for you.

Proper Scrambled Eggs

Apart from the omelet, eggs should be cooked slowly or they toughen. Think of those bullet-like fried eggs surrounded by black lace so beloved in the old transport cafes, or pub boiled eggs in vinegar with the consistency of rubber. This also calls to mind bought Scotch eggs, the scrambled eggs left in a chafing dish on the sideboard, a congealed yellow blancmange sitting in a pool of condensed water—all terrible and all to be avoided. Breakfast is really one of the most difficult things to prepare as all the ingredients require different times of cooking. This method of scrambling eggs not only produces a lovely creamy mass of eggs, but lets you get on with other things. I reckon about 3 eggs per person for a hearty helping, and I have yet to find that I have prepared too much.

Serves 4–6

12 eggs minus 3 of the whites
1 egg shell of water
salt and freshly ground pepper
½ cup (1 stick) unsalted butter
hot toast

Use a double boiler, porringer or simply a heatproof bowl set over simmering water. The eggs should be as fresh as possible, of course. Beat the eggs and water together very well and season with salt and lots of freshly ground pepper. Melt the butter in the top of the double boiler or bowl, pour in the eggs and give them a stir. Then you can get on with your other preparations for breakfast, just keeping an eye on the eggs and stirring every now and then to keep them creamy. When they have reached the consistency you require (this can take 15–20 minutes), pile them on to hot toast and serve with bacon, sausages or what you will.

JP

Chocolate Whisky Cake

Not much whisky here, but enough to give taste to a lovely cake.

½ cup golden raisins

4 tablespoons Scotch whisky

6 ounces bittersweet chocolate

½ cup (1 stick) butter or margarine

3 eggs, separated

¾ cup packed brown sugar

½ cup chopped walnuts

zest of 1 small orange, grated

½ cup self-rising flour

¼ teaspoon freshly grated nutmeg

FOR THE TOPPING:

4 tablespoons (½ stick) unsalted butter, at room temperature

1¼ cups confectioners' sugar, sifted

4 tablespoons Scotch whisky

Soak the golden raisins in the whisky for several hours, preferably overnight. Melt the chocolate and butter very gently in a heatproof bowl set over a pan of barely simmering water, then leave to cool. Beat the egg yolks with the sugar until pale and thick. Fold in the cooled chocolate mixture, golden raisins with any remaining whisky, the walnuts and grated orange zest. Add the flour and nutmeg and fold in gently. Whisk the egg whites until stiff and fold into the cake batter. Spoon into a greased 8-inch cake pan. Bake in the center of a preheated oven at 350°F for 1 hour, or until a skewer inserted in the center of the cake comes out clean. Leave in the pan for 15 minutes, then turn out on to a wire rack and leave to cool.

For the topping, cream the butter and sugar together until smooth. Add the whisky and beat until it has been absorbed. Spread over the top of the cake.

JP

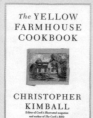

category **3**

general

This is our soup-to-nuts group, books that don't fit easily into any of the other categories because the recipes are from all over, for all sorts of ingredients, and for all courses. Judging by this year's entries, the difference between older all-purpose books and today's lies in the level of didacticism. With the exception of Newman, who just seems to be having a lot of fun, authors teach techniques, report kitchen-research results, provide diagrams, define terms, give lists of criteria for quality—essentially guide at every turn. Presumably, the need for copious detail exists because contemporary readers didn't absorb even basic cooking at their mother's knee; Mom was busy making a living. We can hope that the trend signals a renewed desire to cook well at home.

interest

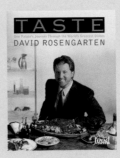
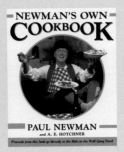

good-old, down-home, comfort-food favorites

author

Christopher Kimball, of Boston and the Green Mountains of Vermont, who is the founder, publisher, and editor-in-chief of *Cook's Illustrated* magazine

why he wrote it

"This is the unwritten code of the farmhouse: an expectation of hard work and a reliance on others to do their jobs tempered by modesty and an interest in the well-being of the community. In hard times, these were necessary traits for survival, but now that times have changed, I think that we could do worse than to take a moment to stop by the yellow farmhouse, take a seat at the table, backs warmed by the old green Kalamazoo, and share the food and the stories."

why it made our list

We're suckers for comfort food, and this book is packed with it. Flipping through it, reading the mouthwatering recipes and the nostalgic stories of small-town life, is like kicking off your shoes, burrowing into a comfy couch, and reveling in the feeling of home. The recipes have all been thoroughly tested, so cooking them will be as comforting as eating them. Well-thought-out charts and diagrams help, too. This is home cooking at its homiest.

chapters

The Country Kitchen • The Soup Pot • The Root Cellar • Rice and Beans • Covered Dish Suppers • Noodles and Macaroni • The Chicken Coop • The Meat Locker • The Summer Garden • Country Bakery • Farm Breakfast • The Cookie Jar • Cakes • The Dairy • The Apple Orchard • Summer Fruit • On the Farm for the Holidays • Preserving

previous books

Kimball is the author of *The Cook's Bible: The Best of American Home Cooking.*

specifics

416 pages, more than 250 recipes, $27.95. Published by Little, Brown and Company.

from the book

"Please taste the dish before serving to check for salt level as well as for the proper amounts of other seasonings. In my opinion, insufficient use of salt is perhaps the single greatest mistake by home cooks."

The YELLOW FARMHOUSE COOKBOOK

CHRISTOPHER KIMBALL

Editor of *Cook's Illustrated* magazine
and author of *The Cook's Bible*

Veal

Veal is a by-product of dairy farming. When bull calves are born, most of them are not needed by a dairy farmer. In the old days, many of these calves were simply slaughtered or given away. The story is told in our town about a farmer, during the Depression, who left two bull calves by the side of the road with a FREE sign next to them. He came back later to find three. However, after a while, a dairy-based formula was invented, the calves were fed for 6 weeks, and then they were brought to market.

Traditional veal has little flavor but a wonderful, soft texture. It is a flavor carrier much like the tenderloin muscle in beef. The sauce or seasoning is what gives it interest. Today, some veal is "naturally" raised, which means that it is not penned and is fed a more varied diet. This veal is darker and tastes much like mild beef. Putting aside the moral issues for the moment, the home cook needs to recognize these two varieties when shopping. I prefer the more traditional veal for its mild character and texture.

In our town in Vermont, we don't eat veal, although every August we do have an "ox roast" for which we prepare a young heifer (about 6 months old) that weighs about 180 pounds. This is no calf, and the meat tends to be tough, dark-colored, and fairly beefy. Each steamship round (the leg from knee to hip) is quite heavy, weighing in at about 25 pounds. This sort of meat bears no resemblance whatsoever to the light-colored, tender veal that is only 6 weeks old.

If purchasing chops, one can choose them from the loin, which are inordinately expensive ($10 to $12 per pound). A thick loin chop is what is most likely to be served in an expensive Italian restaurant. However, there is another common cut one might try: the shoulder blade chop, with two bones and a fair amount of

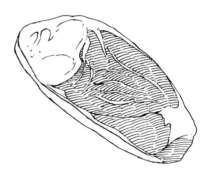

Veal round arm chops are a good alternative to the more expensive center-cut loin chops. A shoulder chop is roughly comparable in flavor and texture.

Veal shanks are the basis of the dish osso buco. The shank is the lower foreleg of the animal. Shanks should be cooked slowly at low oven temperatures, about 250 degrees.

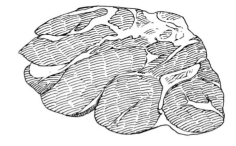

Veal shoulder chops are similar in taste, price, and texture to arm chops.

connective tissue. It can be quite large and is fairly tender and flavorful. This cut comes from the chuck, the forequarter of the animal. In terms of cooking chops, I tried all three methods tested on lamb and pork chops and found that sautéing the chops for 1 minute per side, covering, and then putting them into a 250 degree oven worked best. They were tender and juicy, and also had plenty of flavor from the stovetop searing.

Veal Shanks with Capers, Anchovies, and Sage

The perfume of fresh sage works well with this dish, along with the traditional lemon zest, which adds some zip. Be sure to cook the shanks long enough (up to 4 hours for very thick, large shanks). This dish can be made earlier in the day and then reheated on top of the stove over low heat (about 15 minutes). Be sure that none of the bitter pith — the white skin between the peel and the flesh — is attached to any of the lemon peel. I use a vegetable peeler instead of a knife, because it is easier to avoid taking any of the pith.

2½–3 pounds veal shank cut into pieces 1½ inches thick
Salt and freshly ground black pepper
2 tablespoons unsalted butter
2 tablespoons olive oil
¼ cup all-purpose flour
1 medium onion, chopped
4 anchovy fillets, chopped
2 carrots, finely chopped
4 cloves garlic, finely chopped
½ teaspoon dried thyme or 1 teaspoon fresh
½ teaspoon dried marjoram or 1 teaspoon fresh
½ cup dry white wine
⅔ cup chicken stock
1 cup chopped canned whole tomatoes (optional)
1 tablespoon grated lemon rind
2 tablespoons capers
2 teaspoons minced fresh sage or 1 teaspoon dried
¼ cup minced parsley

1. Heat oven to 250 degrees. Tie a string around the circumference of each piece of veal (or have the butcher do it for you) to keep meat from separating from bone. Season shanks with salt and pepper.

2. In a 12-inch-wide Dutch oven or sauté pan with a lid, melt the butter with olive oil over medium-high heat. When the foam subsides and the fat is very hot but not smoking, lightly flour the seasoned shanks and place them in the pot. Sauté for about 4 minutes per side, shaking pan occasionally to keep meat from sticking. The shanks should be golden brown on each side. Remove shanks and reserve. Put the onion, anchovies, and carrots in the pan, stir, and cook for 2 minutes. Add the next 6 ingredients (garlic through tomatoes) along with the veal shanks and bring mixture to a boil. Cover pan and place in oven.

3. Cook for approximately 2 hours (very large shanks can take up to 4 hours) or until the meat is very tender. The size of the shanks and the type of pot dramatically affect the cooking time. The internal temperature of the meat should be approximately 200 degrees.

4. Stir in lemon rind, capers, and sage. Bring to a simmer and cook uncovered for 4 minutes. Sprinkle each serving with minced parsley.

SERVES 4

Boston Cream Pie

The foundation for Boston Cream Pie was a cake referred to by James Beard as the One-Egg Cake and by Marion Cunningham in *The Fannie Farmer Cookbook* as the Boston Favorite Cake. It is made with cake flour, sugar, butter, milk, one or two eggs, vanilla, baking powder, and salt. Using this simple building-block recipe, many different variations were created, including, according to James Beard, Washington Pie, filled with jam and topped with powdered sugar; Boston Cream Pie, filled with a pastry cream and topped with powdered sugar; Martha Washington Pie, which is either the same as Washington Pie or split into three layers, one filled with jam and the other with pastry cream; and Parker House Chocolate Cream Pie, which is Boston Cream Pie topped with a thin layer of chocolate butter icing. The latter was invented either by a French chef, Sanzian, who was hired by Harvey Parker at his hotel's opening in October 1855 at the extraordinary annual salary of $5,000 (a good chef in Boston could be hired at that time for eight dollars per week) or by a German baker named Ward, who, shortly after the hotel opened, was also credited with inventing Parker House rolls. However, it is not clear whether, as Beard suggests, the term Boston Cream Pie already existed before the Parker House version. My guess is that Beard is right since Fannie Farmer also lists a recipe for "Boston Favorite Cake," suggesting that Boston Cream Pie is merely a variation. As for why it is called a pie, Jim Dodge, author of *Baking with Jim Dodge,* suggests that the cake was originally baked by early New England cooks in a pie pan. Why were pie plates used? My best guess is that pie plates, which predated cakes in the American kitchen, were common kitchen equipment, cake pans being less widely available. No matter the origins, the editors of *Cook's* found, in a blind tasting of 5

different cakes, that Foolproof Sponge Cake was ideal for Boston Cream Pie.

1   recipe Foolproof Sponge Cake (page 143)

PASTRY CREAM
2   cups milk
6   egg yolks
½   cup sugar
¼   teaspoon salt
¼   cup cornstarch, sifted
1   teaspoon vanilla extract
1   tablespoon rum
2   tablespoons unsalted butter, optional

RICH CHOCOLATE GLAZE
1   cup heavy cream
¼   cup light corn syrup
8   ounces semisweet chocolate, chopped into small pieces
½   teaspoon vanilla

1. Make Foolproof Sponge Cake.
2. *For the pastry cream:* meanwhile, heat milk in a small saucepan until hot but not simmering. Whisk yolks, sugar, and salt in a large saucepan until mixture is thick and lemon-colored, 3 to 4 minutes. Add cornstarch; whisk to combine. Slowly whisk in hot milk. Cook milk mixture over medium-low heat, whisking constantly and scraping pan bottom and sides as you stir, until mixture thickens to a thick pudding consistency and has lost all traces of raw starch flavor, about 10 minutes. Remove from heat; stir in vanilla, rum, and optional butter. Remove from heat, and transfer to another container placing a piece of plastic wrap directly on the surface of the filling to prevent a skin from forming; let cool to room temperature. (Can be refrigerated overnight.) To ensure that pastry cream does not thin out, do not whisk or vigorously stir it once it has set.

3. *For the glaze:* bring cream and corn syrup to a full simmer in a medium saucepan. Remove from heat; add chocolate, cover, and let stand for 8 minutes. (If chocolate has not completely melted, return saucepan to low heat; stir constantly until melted.) Add vanilla; stir very gently until mixture is smooth. Cool until tepid, so that a spoonful drizzled back into pan mounds slightly. (Glaze can be refrigerated to speed up cooling process, stirring every few minutes to ensure even cooling.)

4. While glaze is cooling, place one cake layer on a cardboard round on cooling rack set over a jelly roll pan. Carefully spoon pastry cream over cake and spread evenly up to cake edge. Place the second layer on top, making sure layers line up properly.

5. Pour glaze over middle of top layer and let flow down cake sides. Use a metal spatula if necessary to completely coat cake. Use a small needle to puncture air bubbles. Let sit about 1 hour or until glaze fully sets. Serve.

Foolproof Sponge Cake

The egg whites should be beaten to soft, glossy, billowy peaks. If beaten too stiff, it will be very difficult to fold in the whole-egg mixture.

½	cup cake flour
¼	cup all-purpose flour
1	teaspoon baking powder
¼	teaspoon salt
3	tablespoons milk
2	tablespoons unsalted butter
½	teaspoon vanilla extract
5	eggs, room temperature
¾	cup sugar

1. Adjust oven rack to lower middle position and heat oven to 350 degrees. Grease two 8- or 9-inch cake pans and cover pan bottom with a round of parchment paper. Whisk flours, baking powder, and salt in a medium bowl (or sift onto waxed paper). Heat milk and butter in a small saucepan over low heat until butter melts. Off heat, add vanilla; cover and keep warm.

2. Separate three of the eggs, placing whites in bowl of standing mixer fitted with the whisk attachment (or large mixing bowl if using hand mixer or whisk) and reserving the 3 yolks plus remaining two whole eggs in another mixing bowl. Beat the three whites on high speed (or whisk) until whites are foamy. Gradually adding 6 tablespoons of the sugar, continue to beat whites to soft, moist peaks. (Do not overbeat, as stiff, dry egg whites will be difficult to incorporate into the batter.) If using a standing mixer, transfer egg whites to a large bowl and add yolk/whole egg mixture to mixing bowl.

3. Beat yolk/whole egg mixture with remaining 6 tablespoons sugar. Beat on medium-high speed (setting 8 on a KitchenAid) until eggs are very thick and a pale lemon color, about 5 minutes (or 12 minutes by hand). Add beaten eggs to whites.

4. Sprinkle flour mixture over beaten eggs and whites; fold very gently 12 times with a large rubber spatula. Make a well in one side of batter and pour melted butter mixture into bowl. Continue folding until batter shows no trace of flour and whites and whole eggs are evenly mixed, about 8 additional strokes.

5. Immediately pour batter into prepared baking pans; bake until cake tops are light brown and feel firm and spring back when touched, about 16 minutes for 9-inch cake pans and 20 minutes for 8-inch cake pans.

6. Place one cake pan on a kitchen towel; run a knife around pan perimeter to loosen cake; cover pan with a large plate. Invert pan and remove it. Then invert cake onto cooling rack. Repeat with remaining cake. Remove parchment and continue with the recipe for Boston Cream Pie.

the kitchen reference for the new millennium

author

New York Times columnist Mark Bittman, who also writes on food and cooking for a multitude of magazines

why he wrote it

"Anyone can cook, and most everyone should. It's a sorry sign that many people consider cooking 'from scratch' an unusual and even rare talent. In fact, cooking is a simple and rewarding craft, one that anyone can learn and even succeed at from the get-go. . . . It remains for me to convince you that the process is an easy one. There are no 'secrets' to cooking—only guidance and experience."

why it made our list

Make room on your bookshelf: This massive collection, with more than 1,500 recipes and variations on 900-plus pages, is as much a reference book as a cookbook and is bound to be useful. The recipes tend toward the simple and basic, but Bittman offers plenty of variations for readers who want to play a little. Specific cooking times and temperatures, detailed diagrams, and a very large glossary of terms and techniques are especially useful, making this an excellent all-purpose kitchen companion.

chapters

Appetizers • Soups • Salads • Pasta • Grains • Breads • Pizza, Bruschetta, Sandwiches, Pitas, and Burritos • Fish • Poultry • Meat • Beans • Vegetables • Fruits • Desserts • Pies, Tarts, and Pastries • Cookies, Brownies, and Cakes • Eggs, Breakfast, and Brunch Dishes • Sauces, Salsas, and Spice Mixtures • Beverages

other books

Bittman is the author of *Fish: The Complete Guide to Buying and Cooking* and *Leafy Greens*. He's also the coauthor of another of this year's *Best of the Best* cookbooks, *Jean-Georges: Cooking at Home with a Four-Star Chef* (page 36).

specifics

944 pages, more than 1,500 recipes and variations, $25. Published by Macmillan General Reference USA.

from the book

"**Remember this about all knives: Dull ones are dangerous. They slip off the food you're cutting and right onto the closest surface, which may be your finger. Although you must be extremely careful with sharp knives—casual contact will lead to a real cut—at least they go where you want them to.**"

How to Cook
Everything

Simple Recipes for Great Food

Mark Bittman

The Basics of Split Chicken

Split or butterflied (or, to use an antiquated term, "spatchcocked") chicken is another form of whole chicken (or almost whole: the backbone is usually removed). Split chicken has its advantages: It can be grilled or sautéed, and it cooks more quickly than truly whole chicken. In fact, it cooks nearly as quickly as cut-up chicken, and retains more of its juice. Split chicken is not always readily available in the supermarket, but the procedure is easy to do at home; follow the illustrations below. (You can also ask the supermarket butcher to do it for you.)

Any recipe can be adapted for split chicken; follow the guidelines outlined here and season the chicken any of the ways you would for sautéed, grilled, roasted, or broiled whole chicken or parts.

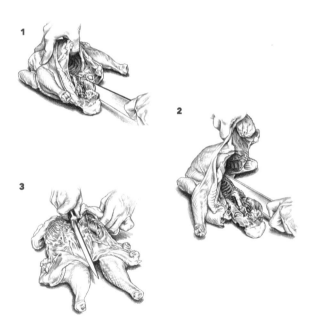

(Steps 1–2) To split a chicken: With the breast facing up, use a heavy knife to cut on either side of the backbone, cutting from front to rear. Once the backbone is removed, you will be able to lay the chicken out flat and flatten it on both sides. (Step 3) If you like, you can split the chicken into two halves.

Chicken Under a Brick
Pollo al Mattone
Makes 4 servings

Time: 45 minutes, plus optional marinating time

The great dish of Lucca, Italy, always made with the best olive oil available. I weight the chickens with a cast-iron pan and a couple of big rocks. The only problem is that handling the hot, heavy pan takes a steady, strong wrist, so use two hands. The effort is well worth it: This is the simplest and best method for producing a beautiful, crisp-skinned bird.

I specify rosemary here, which is delicious. But most herbs are equally wonderful: Try savory or dill (in similar quantity); parsley, basil, chervil, chives (use twice as much); or tarragon, marjoram, or thyme (use half as much).

1 whole (3- to 4-pound) chicken, trimmed of excess fat, then rinsed and patted dry with paper towels
1 tablespoon minced fresh rosemary leaves or 1 teaspoon dried rosemary, plus 2 sprigs fresh rosemary (optional)
2 teaspoons salt
1 tablespoon coarsely chopped garlic
2 tablespoons extra-virgin olive oil
1 lemon, quartered

❶ Follow the illustrations at left to remove the backbone and split the chicken. Mix together the rosemary leaves, salt, garlic, and 1 tablespoon of the olive oil and rub this all over the chicken. Tuck some of it under the skin as well. Allow to marinate, if time permits, for up to a day, refrigerated.

❷ When you are ready to cook, preheat the oven to 450°F. Preheat a large ovenproof skillet over medium-high heat for about 3 minutes. Press the rosemary sprigs if you are using them into the skin of the chicken. Put the remaining olive oil in the pan and wait a minute for it to heat up. Place the chicken in the pan, skin side down, along with any pieces of rosemary and garlic. Weight the chicken with another skillet or a flat pot cover and a couple of bricks or rocks. The basic idea is to flatten the chicken by applying a fair amount of weight evenly over its surface.

3 Cook over medium-high to high heat for 10 minutes; transfer, still weighted, to the oven. Roast for 15 minutes more. Take the chicken from the oven and remove the weight; turn the chicken over (it will now be skin side up) and roast 10 minutes more. To check for doneness, insert an instant-read thermometer into the thickest part of the thigh; it should read 160°F to 165°F. Serve hot or at room temperature (refrigerate if you will not be serving it within the hour), with lemon wedges.

The Basics of Bulgur

Bulgur (or bulghur), a traditional grain of the Middle East, is not just cracked wheat; it is wheat which is first steamed, then hulled, then dried, and then cracked. The result is a quick-cooking grain (in fact, you don't even cook some bulgur, you just soak it) that filled the historical need of conserving fuel and today provides convenience and great flavor.

The best-known use for bulgur is in tabbouleh, in which it plays a major role, along with parsley and/or mint. But bulgur makes wonderful pilaf-style dishes, especially when combined with vegetables or noodles.

Bulgur comes in four grinds, numbered one through four. Number One is so fine that it is almost always just soaked (see Basic Bulgur, right) rather than cooked. Number Two, considered medium, can be soaked or cooked. Number Three (coarse) must be cooked. Number Four is very coarse; you won't see it often. Most supermarkets stock Number Two, which you can consider all-purpose if you like; Number One and Number Three can be found in many natural foods stores, specialty food markets, and, of course, Middle Eastern stores.

Basic Bulgur
Makes 4 servings

Time: Less than 30 minutes

Bulgur, which has wonderful flavor, cooks up so nice and fluffy that it is actually a bit dry. Thus it really benefits from the addition of butter or some kind of sauce (pasta sauces, pesto, or the pan juices from meat are all delicious). This is also the way to make bulgur for inclusion in other dishes, such as tabbouleh.

> 1 cup medium-grind (Number Two) or fine-grind (Number One) bulgur
> 2½ cups boiling water

1 Place the bulgur in a bowl and pour the water over it. Stir once and let sit.

2 Fine bulgur will be tender in 15 to 20 minutes (sample some); medium in 20 to 25 minutes. If any water remains when the bulgur is done, squeeze the bulgur in a cloth or place it in a fine sieve and press down on it.

3 Serve immediately.

Lamb Patties with Bulgur
Kibbe
Makes 4 to 8 servings

Time: About 30 minutes, plus time to preheat the grill

Kibbe (or kibbeh, pronounced kibbey) is an important Middle Eastern (primarily Lebanese) dish that is made in a variety of forms, including raw and stuffed. This is a basic kibbe, a simple combination of ground lamb and cracked wheat (bulgur) that has wonderful flavor; serve it with a salad, or in a pita bread with raw vegetables, with Cucumber-Yogurt Dip with Mint (page 148).

1 cup fine-grind (Number One) or medium-grind (Number Two) bulgur (available in Middle Eastern or natural foods stores; see page 147)

2 cups boiling water

1 large or 2 medium onions

1 pound lean ground lamb

Salt and freshly ground black pepper to taste

1 tablespoon ground cumin

Pinch ground allspice

¼ teaspoon ground cinnamon

Minced fresh parsley, mint, or cilantro leaves for garnish

1 While you prepare the other ingredients, soak the bulgur in a bowl with boiling water for about 15 to 20 minutes for fine grind, 20 to 25 for medium grind. It will absorb most or all of the water; drain it if it does not. Start a charcoal or wood fire or preheat a gas grill or broiler; the fire should be quite hot, and the rack 3 to 4 inches from the heat source. (You can also sauté kibbe: Just before cooking, heat a large skillet over medium-high heat for 3 or 4 minutes, then add 2 tablespoons of butter or oil before adding the patties.)

2 Meanwhile, quarter the onion(s) and put them in a food processor; turn on the machine and puree. Add the lamb, salt, and spices, then pulse to blend. Add the drained bulgur and pulse a few more times. Try not to overprocess.

3 Remove the mixture and shape into 8 patties. Grill, broil, or sauté, turning occasionally. Kibbe are cooked to well done but not dry; total cooking time will be 10 to 12 minutes. Garnish and serve.

Baked Kibbe as an Appetizer: Preheat the oven to 375°F. Spread the kibbe mixture in an 8-inch square baking pan and score the top in a diamond pattern. Place a pine nut on each section and bake for about 20 minutes, or until cooked through and brown at the edges. Let cool for 5 minutes, then cut through the score marks. Garnish with parsley or cilantro and serve sections hot or at room temperature.

Cucumber-Yogurt Dip with Mint

Makes about 2 cups

Time: 10 minutes

A quickly made, low-fat sauce that is good for dipping vegetables or passing with grilled foods, especially lamb. Good when made with parsley or dill, too.

1 medium cucumber, peeled if desired

Salt and freshly ground black pepper to taste

1 cup plain yogurt

2 teaspoons minced onion, shallot, or scallion

1 tablespoon olive oil

3 tablespoons minced fresh mint leaves

1 Cut the cucumber in half lengthwise and scoop out the seeds. Chop it into ½-inch dice and combine it with all remaining ingredients.

2 Check seasoning and serve, or refrigerate until ready to use, but use within a few hours.

The Basics of Popovers, Biscuits, and Scones

These are last-minute rolls, made either for dinner or—in the case of scones—for an afternoon snack. They are light and easy. Biscuits, especially, can be made as part of a one-hour dinner without much effort, especially after a little practice. Like quick breads, they should all be handled as little as possible to keep them light and tender.

Yogurt or Buttermilk Biscuits

Makes 10 or more biscuits

Time: 20 to 30 minutes

These are the best, especially (I think) when made with yogurt. When made correctly—and you can do it the first time, I swear—they're sweet, slightly sour, crisp, and tender. Oh, and very, very fast. Don't substitute soured milk here; just move on to the Baking Powder Biscuit variation.

2 cups (about 9 ounces) all-purpose or cake flour,
    plus more as needed
1 scant teaspoon salt
3 teaspoons baking powder
1 teaspoon baking soda
2 to 5 tablespoons cold butter (more is better)
⅞ cup plain yogurt or buttermilk

1 Preheat the oven to 450°F.
2 Mix the dry ingredients together in a bowl or food processor. Cut the butter into bits and either pulse it in the food processor (the easiest) or pick up a bit of the dry ingredients, rub them with the butter between your fingers, and drop them again. All the butter should be thoroughly blended before proceeding.
3 Use a large spoon to stir in the yogurt or buttermilk, just until the mixture forms a ball. Turn the dough out onto a lightly floured surface and knead it ten times; no more. If it is very sticky, add a little flour, but very little; don't worry if it sticks a bit to your hands.
4 Press into a ¾-inch-thick rectangle and cut into 2-inch rounds with a biscuit cutter or glass. Place the rounds on an ungreased baking sheet. Gently reshape the leftover dough and cut again; this recipe will produce 10 to 14 biscuits.
5 Bake 7 to 9 minutes, or until the biscuits are a beautiful golden brown. Serve within 15 minutes for them to be at their best.

Baking Powder Biscuits: Use 4 teaspoons baking powder and sweet milk in place of yogurt or buttermilk. Proceed as above.

Cheese Biscuits: Stir in ½ cup grated Cheddar, Gruyère, Fontina, blue, or Parmesan cheese and ¼ teaspoon cayenne (optional) along with the yogurt or milk. Lightly grease the baking sheet and proceed as above. This will make 14 to 16 biscuits.

Drop ("Emergency") Biscuits: These cut 5 minutes off the prep time. Increase the yogurt or milk to 1 cup and drop tablespoons of the dough onto a greased baking sheet. Bake as above.

Sweet Potato Biscuits: A classic. Stir 1 cup cooked, drained, and pureed sweet potatoes or winter squash into the butter-flour mixture. Add only enough yogurt or buttermilk to form the dough into a ball, usually between ½ and ¾ cup (if your potatoes are very dry, you may need the whole ⅞ cup). Roll a little thinner—about ½ inch. Cut as above, into about 24 biscuits, and bake on a greased baking sheet at 450°F for 12 to 15 minutes.

homey american dishes
at the top of their form

author

Perfectionist Pam Anderson, executive editor of *Cook's Illustrated* magazine

why she wrote it

"Rather than continue to guess about the outcome of a recipe or wonder if the method I had always relied on was really the best, I decided to make a study of the dishes I prepared frequently. . . . I wanted a chicken pot pie that I'd actually have time to put on the table on weeknights, and macaroni and cheese that both my kids and I would eat. I wanted foolproof coleslaw and potato salads that would go with all sorts of dishes, and a cobbler recipe that I could vary with seasonal fruit and top in several different ways. For special occasions, I wanted dishes that would deliver the absolute best: Cornish hens that tasted as good as they looked, pork roast that was juicy and flavorful as well as lean, and rich and creamy cheesecake."

why it made our list

Anderson roasted more than 40 turkeys, cleaned and cooked more than 100 pounds of greens, baked more than 50 cobblers—and, through tireless trial and error, found the answers to questions that have been plaguing home cooks for years. She's determined the right pan for meatloaf, the right coating for fried chicken, the right temperature for prime rib, the right thickener for pie fillings. "From this book," promises Anderson, "you'll not only get infallible recipes, you'll learn why they work. Once you've had the secret cracked, you'll have a formula you can vary—as well as scores of general principles you can apply to all the dishes you'd love to turn into your own perfect recipes." Nice of Anderson to do all the work for us.

chapters

Taking Stock • Everyday Classics • Special Dinners • On the Side, but Not Forgotten • Bread Winners • Be-All and End-All Desserts

specifics

372 pages, more than 120 recipes, $27. Published by Houghton Mifflin Company.

from the book

"Remember the old Crisco commercials: 'It all comes back but 1 tablespoon'? I put this claim to the test with chicken and found it to be absolutely true: when the bird is fried in shortening, virtually all the fat remains in the pan and almost none is absorbed into the meat."

THE
Perfect Recipe

Getting It Right Every Time—

Making Our Favorite Dishes
The Absolute Best They Can Be

Pam Anderson
Executive Editor of *Cook's Illustrated*

Perfect Prime Rib

SERVES 6 TO 8

THERE ARE TWO DISTINCT CUTS on a rib roast. The first cut (ribs one to three) is closer to the loin end and is the more desirable of the two. It contains the large, single rib-eye muscle and is less fatty. The second cut (ribs four to seven) is closer to the chuck end and has a smaller rib-eye muscle and is more multi-muscled and fatty. Although some butchers charge extra for the first cut, others do not. Ask for the first cut. Even if you don't purchase your roast a week ahead of time, just a day or two of aging in the refrigerator will make it taste better. The longer the uncooked roast sits at room temperature, the higher its internal temperature and the shorter its roasting time. For this reason, I let the prime rib stand at room temperature several hours before roasting.

Although this size roast averages about 30 minutes per pound, larger roasts do not need proportionately longer cooking times.

> 1   3-rib standing rib roast (7 pounds), the first cut,
>   aged if possible (see page 154), set at room temperature
>   for up to 3 hours, and tied (see figure 1)
>   Salt
>   Ground black pepper

1. Adjust oven rack to low position and preheat oven to 200°F. Heat a large roasting pan over 2 burners set at medium-high heat. Place roast in hot pan and sear on all sides until nicely browned and about ½ cup of fat has rendered, 6 to 8 minutes.

2. Remove roast from pan. Set a wire rack in pan; set roast on rack. Generously season meat with salt and pepper.

3. Place roast in oven and roast until a meat thermometer registers 130°F for medium-rare, about 3½ hours. If roast is done sooner than you expect, simply turn oven as low as possible (preferably 150° to 170°F) and let stand until ready to serve.

4. Transfer roast to a cutting board, with rib bones perpendicular to board. Using a carving fork to hold roast in place, cut along rib bones to sever meat from bones as shown in figure 2. Set roast cut side down and carve meat across grain into ¾-to-1-inch-thick slices. Serve immediately.

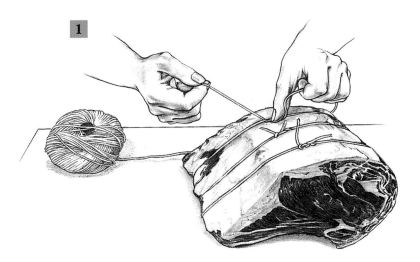

1. To keep the outer muscle from overcooking and separating from the roast, tie the roast at both ends and in the middle, with the twine running parallel to the bone. Remove the twine before carving.

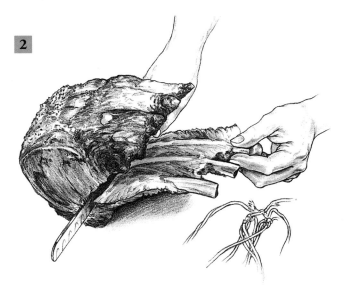

2. To facilitate carving, cut the rib bones away from the roast before serving.

DRY-AGED VERSUS WET-AGED BEEF

LIKE GOOD WINE, beef benefits from aging. This process allows the beef time to develop flavor and become more tender. All retail beef in this country is aged by one of two methods—dry-aging or wet-aging.

Dry-aged beef starts with a freshly slaughtered animal, which is hung in a cool, dry space, where it loses water and develops flavor. Because hanging quarters of beef take up refrigerator space and time and because the meat loses weight from dehydration and trimming to remove the dried exterior, it costs more, and for that reason many butchers no longer dry-age beef.

Most beef today is vacuum-packed in plastic at the processing plant and allowed to wet-age between the plant and the retailer. Wet-aged beef loses virtually no weight and comes butchered, packaged, aged and ready to sell.

To see if dry-aged beef is worth seeking out, I ordered a roast of each type from a restaurant supplier in Manhattan. Like a good, young red wine, the wet-aged beef tasted pleasant and fresh on its own. When compared to the dry-aged beef, though, its flavors were less concentrated, and the meat seemed washed out. The dry-aged beef engaged the mouth. It was stronger, richer and gamier-tasting, with a pleasant tang. The dry-aged and wet-aged beef were equally tender, but the dry-aged beef had an added buttery texture and tasted more mellow.

Dry-aged beef can be mail-ordered, or you may find a local butcher that's willing to age it for you. Because of the price, however, you may want to age it yourself, which simply involves making room in the refrigerator and remembering to purchase the roast a week or so early. To dry-age prime rib, pat the roast dry and place it on a wire rack set over a paper-towel-lined cake pan or plate. Set it in the refrigerator and let it age until ready to roast, up to seven days. *Before attempting to age meat, make sure your refrigerator registers lower than 40 degrees.* Before roasting, shave off the exterior meat that has completely dehydrated. (Between the trimming and dehydration, count on the roast losing a pound or so for a week's aging.)

The Ultimate Lemon Meringue Pie

MAKES ONE 9-INCH PIE, SERVING 8

AFTER MAKING THE MERINGUE, reheat the lemon filling before pouring it into the pie shell, so that the meringue does not weep. Beating the cornstarch mixture into the meringue not only prevents beading, but also keeps the meringue from shrinking.

Graham Cracker-Coated Pie Shell

1¼	cups all-purpose flour
1	tablespoon sugar
½	teaspoon salt
6	tablespoons (¾ stick) unsalted butter, chilled and cut into ¼-inch pieces
4	tablespoons vegetable shortening, chilled
½	cup graham cracker crumbs

Lemon Filling

1	cup sugar
¼	cup cornstarch
⅛	teaspoon salt
6	large egg yolks
1	tablespoon zest from 1 lemon
½	cup juice from 2-3 lemons
2	tablespoons unsalted butter

Meringue Topping

1	tablespoon cornstarch
¼	teaspoon cream of tartar
½	cup sugar
4	large egg whites
½	teaspoon vanilla extract

1. Pie Shell: Mix flour, sugar and salt in a food processor fitted with a steel blade. Scatter butter pieces over flour mixture, tossing to coat butter with a little flour. Cut butter into flour with five 1-second pulses. Add shortening; continue cutting in until mixture resembles coarse cornmeal with butter bits about the size of small peas, about 4 more 1-second pulses. Turn mixture into a medium bowl.

2. Sprinkle 3 tablespoons ice water over mixture. Using a rubber spatula, fold water into flour mixture. Press down on dough mixture with broad side of spatula until dough sticks together, adding up to 1 tablespoon more ice water if necessary. Shape dough into a ball with your hands, then flatten into a 4-inch-wide disk. Dust lightly with flour, wrap in plastic, and refrigerate at least 30 minutes before rolling.

3. Generously sprinkle an 18-inch work surface with 2 tablespoons graham cracker crumbs. Remove dough from wrapping; place disk in center of crumbs. Scatter a few more crumbs over disk top. Roll dough from center to edges into a 9-inch disk, rotating dough a quarter turn after each stroke and sprinkling additional crumbs underneath and on top as necessary to coat dough heavily. Flip dough and continue to roll, but not rotate, to a 13-inch disk, just under ⅛ inch thick.

4. Fold dough in quarters; place dough point in center of a 9-inch ovenproof pie pan. Unfold dough to cover pan completely, with excess dough draped over pan lip. Lift edge of dough with one hand and press dough into pan bottom with other hand; repeat process around circumference of pan to ensure that dough fits properly in pan and is not stretched in any way. Trim dough to ½ inch beyond lip all around. Tuck overhanging dough back under itself so folded edge is flush with lip of pan; press to seal. Flute dough by pressing thumb and index finger about ½ inch apart against outside edge, then use index finger or knuckle of other hand to poke a dent on inside edge through space created by other fingers. Repeat fluting around perimeter of pie shell.

5. Refrigerate dough until firm, about 30 minutes; prick shell at ½-inch intervals. Press a doubled 12-inch square of aluminum foil inside pie shell. Prick again to keep dough from ballooning during baking. Freeze pie shell while oven is preheating.

6. Adjust oven rack to lowest position and preheat oven to 375°F. Bake shell, checking occasionally to make sure it is not ballooning, pricking it if necessary, until shell is firmly set, about 15 minutes. Remove foil and continue to bake until shell is crisp and rich brown, about 10 minutes more.

7. Lemon Filling: Whisk sugar, cornstarch and salt together in a large, nonreactive saucepan. Add egg yolks, then immediately but gradually whisk in 1½ cups water. Bring mixture to a simmer over medium heat, whisking occasionally at beginning and more frequently as mixture begins to thicken, 8 to 10 minutes. Whisk in zest, then lemon juice and finally butter. Bring mixture to a good simmer, whisking constantly; simmer for 1 minute. Remove from heat, place plastic wrap directly on surface of filling to keep hot and to prevent a skin from forming.

8. Meringue Topping: Mix cornstarch and ⅓ cup water in a small saucepan. Bring to a simmer, whisking occasionally at beginning and more frequently as mixture thickens. When mixture starts to simmer and turn translucent, remove from heat.

9. Preheat oven to 325°F. Mix cream of tartar and sugar together. Beat egg whites with vanilla until frothy. Beat in sugar mixture, 1 tablespoon at a time, until sugar is incorporated and whites form soft peaks. Drop in warm cornstarch mixture, 1 tablespoon at a time, and continue to beat meringue to stiff peaks. Return saucepan of filling to very low heat during last minute or so of beating meringue to ensure that filling is hot.

10. Immediately pour filling into pie shell. Promptly distribute meringue evenly around edge, then center of pie, with a rubber spatula to keep it from sinking into filling and making sure it attaches to pie shell to prevent shrinking. Use back of a spoon to create peaks all over meringue. Bake until meringue is golden brown, about 20 minutes. Transfer to a wire rack and cool to room temperature. Serve.

trade secrets from four flourishing chefs

authors

French Culinary Institute faculty members Alain Sailhac, former chef at Le Cirque; Jacques Torres, chef-pâtissier at Le Cirque 2000; Jacques Pépin, cookbook author and TV personality; and André Soltner, former chef/proprietor of Lutèce

why they wrote it

To present "dishes that suit the lifestyles of people today: a lighter cuisine with smaller portions, reduced cooking times, more diversity and originality, all attractively presented on plates or platters. These recipes are a statement that defines a philosophy in tune with today's eclectic and demanding cook as well as with today's health concerns; they are a symbiosis between the desirable and the necessary."

why it made our list

If you diet as a way of life, why not do it with delicious French cuisine from celebrated chefs? The dishes are divided into menus that, writes Pépin, "follow the seasons and are favorable to your waistline and general health." Naturally, each recipe includes the number of calories, grams of fat, and milligrams of cholesterol for those counting any of the above. Even those who aren't will enjoy the contemporary approach to French food found here.

chapters

The French Diet—A Paradox with Benefits for Americans • French Cooking—Easy, Accessible, Delicious, and Healthy • Mastering the Basics • Spring Menus • Summer Menus • Autumn Menus • Winter Menus • Menus for Easy Entertaining

other books

Torres' *Dessert Circus* (page 256) and Pépin's *Jacques Pépin's Kitchen: Encore with Claudine* (page 166) are also among this year's *Best of the Best*.

specifics

336 pages, 186 recipes,
57 color photographs,
24 black-and-white photographs,
$30. Published by Rodale Press, Inc.

from the book

"**What comes to mind when you think of French food? Cheese, croissants, and foie gras, for sure. Pastries, soufflés, and duck à l'orange, no doubt. Butter, cream, and eggs, by all means. Good health? Get real. Well, we are getting real. And reality shows that, despite the apparent pitfalls of the French way of eating, these Europeans have much less heart disease than Americans.**"

THE FRENCH CULINARY INSTITUTE'S

SALUTE TO

HEALTHY
COOKING

from AMERICA'S FOREMOST FRENCH CHEFS

Food Photography by Maria Robledo

POTATO-MUSHROOM GALETTES
(Galettes de Pommes de Terre aux Champignons)

A potato galette is not only a tasty first course but also the base for an entrée of grilled or roasted meat or game. It can even be served for a light lunch with a tossed green salad on the side. To achieve the required thin, uniform potato slices, you will need a mandoline. You can prepare the galettes up to 1 hour in advance of serving and reheat them on a baking sheet for no more than 3 minutes in a very hot oven.

1	teaspoon canola oil
1	teaspoon unsalted butter
4	cups sliced mushrooms
2	small shallots, minced
3	sprigs fresh thyme
	Salt and freshly ground black pepper
3	large russet potatoes, peeled and sliced lengthwise into paper-thin slices
1	tablespoon olive oil

Warm the canola oil and butter in a large sauté pan over medium heat. Add the mushrooms and cook slowly, stirring frequently, for 5 minutes, or until the mushrooms release their juices. Continue cooking until all the moisture evaporates. Add the shallots and cook for 3 minutes. Strip the leaves from the thyme sprigs and add to the pan; discard the stems. Season with the salt and pepper. Remove from the heat.

Place the potatoes in a large bowl. Drizzle with the olive oil and toss until well-coated.

Place 2 medium nonstick sauté pans over medium-low heat. Place 1 potato slice in the center of each pan. Using one-quarter of the potatoes per pan, carefully form circles of slightly overlapping potato slices around the center slices, letting them fall slightly over the edge of the pan. Season with the salt and pepper. Cook for 4 minutes. If any gaps form between the slices, patch with slices cut to fit the gap.

Place one-quarter of the mushroom mixture in the center of each galette and evenly spread it out to cover the potatoes. As the potatoes become soft and flexible, begin folding them inward so that they slightly enclose the mushrooms and form a perfect disk-shaped galette. Cook for 25 minutes, turning occasionally so that the potatoes cook through and the galette is evenly browned, taking care not burn it. As you turn, season each side with salt and pepper.

POTATO-MUSHROOM GALETTES

Remove from the pans and place in a warm, dry spot. Repeat to make 2 more galettes using the remaining potatoes and mushroom mixture. Serve with the most evenly browned, symmetrical side of the galette facing up.

YIELD: 4 SERVINGS

PER SERVING

90 CALORIES
3 G. TOTAL FAT
0.6 G. SATURATED FAT
1 MG. CHOLESTEROL

FISH STEW, MARSEILLE-STYLE
(*Bouillabaisse du Cousin Marseillais*)

Not the typical rich bouillabaisse of Marseille but a healthier, still-delicious alternative. Saffron remains the constant, while you can use any fish you like as long as it is fresh. The flavors and aromas of this French stew should transport you to the blue waters, blue skies, and bright sun of the south of France. It is The French Culinary Institute chefs' favorite.

12	ounces sea bass fillets
12	ounces medium shrimp, peeled and deveined
½	cup anise liqueur
8	ounces fresh mussels
1	bulb fennel
2	tablespoons olive oil
1	medium onion, very thinly sliced
1	leek, with a little green attached, well-washed and very thinly sliced
5	cloves garlic, minced
6	cups Fish Stock (page 165)
4	very ripe plum tomatoes, peeled, cored, seeded, and chopped
2	small red potatoes, peeled and halved
2	sprigs fresh thyme
3	pinches of saffron threads
	Salt and freshly ground black pepper
¼	teaspoon cayenne pepper
1	tablespoon chopped fresh flat-leaf parsley
16	thin baguette slices, toasted

Cut the bass into chunks and place in a large bowl. Add the shrimp and liqueur. Cover and allow to marinate at room temperature for 30 minutes.

Squeeze each mussel in the palm of your hand and discard any whose shells open. Scrub the remaining mussels to remove grit; cut off the beards. Wash in 3 changes of cold water. Place the mussels in a medium saucepan and add cold water to cover by about 1″. Bring to a boil over medium-high heat. Cover and steam for 5 minutes, or until the mussels open. Discard any mussels that do not open. Remove from the heat and carefully lift the meat from the shells; discard the shells. Return the meat to the cooking liquid.

Remove any hard or discolored outer layers from the fennel bulb. Trim the root end and feathery tops. Cut in half lengthwise; cut crosswise into very thin slices.

Warm 1 tablespoon of the oil in a large nonstick saucepan over medium heat. Add the onions, leeks, and fennel. Cook slowly for 8 minutes. If necessary, lower the heat to keep the vegetables from browning. Stir in about half of the garlic. Cook for 3 minutes.

Add the stock, tomatoes, potatoes, thyme, and 2 pinches of the saffron. Season with the salt and black pepper. Cover and simmer for 10 minutes, or until the vegetables are cooked but still firm.

To make the *rouille*, use a slotted spoon to remove the cooked potatoes from the stew. Place in a blender or a food processor fitted with the metal blade. Add the cayenne, the remaining garlic, and 1 pinch of saffron. Process until smooth. With the motor running, add ½ cup of the vegetable cooking liquid and the remaining 1 tablespoon oil. Season with the salt and black pepper. Transfer to a small bowl and set aside.

Add the marinated fish and shrimp to the stew. Strain the liquid from the mussels and add to the stew. Cover and simmer over medium heat for 8 minutes, or until the fish and shrimp are opaque. Taste and adjust the seasoning.

Ladle the stew into 4 large shallow soup bowls, making certain that each bowl contains an equal assortment of fish, shellfish, and vegetables. Sprinkle each with an equal amount of mussels and parsley. Spread the *rouille* mixture on the toast. Arrange 4 baguette slices around the edge of each plate.

YIELD: 4 SERVINGS

PER SERVING

541 CALORIES
12 G. TOTAL FAT
2 G. SATURATED FAT
43 MG. CHOLESTEROL

FISH STEW, MARSEILLE-STYLE (PAGE 162)

FISH STOCK
(*Fumet de Poisson*)

Fish stock (also called fumet) is a clear, rich broth that's a very useful kitchen basic. We suggest that you triple this recipe and freeze the extra. Be certain that the fish skeletons are well-cleaned of gills and of any impurities around the head, or the stock will be cloudy. Snapper and sole make the finest fumets. Fattier fish, such as salmon, should be avoided.

2   pounds fish skeletons, well-cleaned with gills removed
1   leek, white part with a bit of green attached, well-washed and chopped
1   bay leaf
2   quarts water

If the skeletons are large, crack them into small pieces with a chef's knife. Place in a heavy stockpot. Add the leeks, bay leaf, and water. Bring to a boil over high heat. Reduce the heat to medium-low and simmer, uncovered, for 30 minutes.

Remove from the heat and strain through a fine sieve into a nonreactive container. Place the container in an ice-water bath and let cool.

Cover and refrigerate for at least 8 hours. Remove and discard any fat that has solidified on top.

Cover and store in the refrigerator for up to 2 days. Or pour into 1-cup containers, cover, label, date, and freeze for up to 6 months.

YIELD: 4 CUPS

PER CUP

36 CALORIES
0.4 G. TOTAL FAT
0.2 G. SATURATED FAT
16 MG. CHOLESTEROL

lessons in cooking from a master chef

author

PBS mainstay and FOOD & WINE contributor Jacques Pépin, who was inducted into the James Beard Foundation's Cookbook Hall of Fame in 1996

why he wrote it

As a companion to his PBS series, the second to costar daughter Claudine.

why it made our list

With sixteen cookbooks and three television series under his belt, Jacques Pépin has become one of the most well-known and most esteemed chefs in the country. Here, he presents a variety of international dishes grouped into menus. Each menu is prefaced by an informative discussion by Jacques, and Claudine's comments and reactions accompany many of the recipes. Jacques is the teacher and Claudine is his student; in guiding her, he is also guiding the inexperienced home cook through the menus. It's a delightful learning experience.

chapters

Great Sandwich Party • Special Celebration • Flavors of Italy • Heartwarming Winter Meal • The Inspired Chef • Everyday Cooking • Cuisine Bon Marché • A Kosher Menu for Friends • Modern American Cuisine • A *Bon Vivant* Feast • Old Favorites Revisited • Puttin' on the Ritz • Casual Corner Café • Comfort Food • Fall Colors Feast • Relaxing Summer Supper • The Making of a Cook • Cuisine Surprise • Contemporary French Cooking • A Food Lover's Delight • Cooking for Tonton Richard • A Menu for all Seasons • The Adventurous Cook • The Classic Cook • The Fish Connection • A Graduation Party

other books

Pépin's many cookbooks include the classics *La Technique* and *La Méthode*. He is a coauthor of another of this year's Best of the Best honorees, *The French Culinary Institute's Salute to Healthy Cooking* (page 158).

from the book

"The more you know, the less time it takes to put a good meal on the table. But if you never cook, you never master the routines that make it easy."

specifics

280 pages, 113 recipes, 55 color photographs, 40 black-and-white photographs, $27.95. Published by Bay Books and Tapes, Inc.

Jacques Pépin's Kitchen

ENCORE WITH CLAUDINE

COMPANION TO THE PUBLIC TELEVISION SERIES

Cream of Turnip and Sweet Potato Soup with Leek Julienne

TOTAL TIME

About 1 hour

YIELD

*4 servings
(about 6 cups)*

NUTRITION

*259 calories
8 g protein
13 g fat
8 g saturated fat
41 mg cholesterol
1325 mg sodium
28 g carbohydrate
2 g dietary fiber*

*One sweet potato
provides enough
beta-carotene
to supply the
recommended
daily amount of
vitamin A.*

While purple-topped turnips give this soup its distinctive taste, sweet potatoes are responsible for its beautiful orange color and creaminess. Earthy and elegant at the same time, it is the perfect beginning for almost any meal.

¾ POUND PURPLE-TOPPED TURNIPS, PEELED AND CUT INTO 1-INCH PIECES

1 SWEET POTATO (YELLOW OR ORANGE VARIETY), (ABOUT 8 OUNCES), PEELED AND CUT INTO 1-INCH PIECES

1 WHITE POTATO (6 OUNCES), PEELED AND CUT INTO 1-INCH PIECES

3½ CUPS LIGHT CHICKEN, BEEF, OR PORK STOCK, UNSALTED

1 TEASPOON SALT, PLUS ADDITIONAL TO TASTE, IF DESIRED

LEEK GARNISH

1 SMALL LEEK (ABOUT 4 OUNCES)

1 TABLESPOON UNSALTED BUTTER

½ CUP WATER

¼ TEASPOON FRESHLY GROUND BLACK PEPPER, PLUS ADDITIONAL TO TASTE, IF DESIRED

½ CUP LIGHT CREAM

1. Place the turnip, sweet potato, and white potato pieces in a pot with the stock and salt. Bring the mixture to a boil, then reduce the heat to low, cover, and cook gently for 45 minutes, or until the vegetables are very tender when pierced with a fork.

2. Meanwhile, prepare the leek garnish. Trim the leek to remove any damaged or fibrous outer leaves but retain most of the green top. Cut the leek crosswise into thirds, with each chunk about 4 inches long. Then, cut each segment in half lengthwise, and separate the layers. Stack the layers together so they are flat, and cut them into very thin lengthwise strips (a julienne). You should have about 1¾ cups. Wash and drain the leek in a colander.

3. Place the leek strips in a saucepan with the butter and water. Bring to a boil, reduce the heat to low, cover, and cook for 10 to 12 minutes, until the leek is tender. Set aside in any remaining cooking liquid.

4. When the vegetables in the soup are tender, process it in a food processor or with a handheld immersion blender until it is emulsified into a smooth-textured mixture. Add the pepper, cream, and the reserved leek julienne along with its liquid.

5. Bring the mixture back to a boil, adding additional salt and pepper to taste, if desired, and serve immediately.

Individual Chocolate Nut Pies

TOTAL TIME
About 1 hour

YIELD
4 servings

NUTRITION
556 calories
8 g protein
33 g fat
11 g saturated fat
71 mg cholesterol
289 mg sodium
64 g carbohydrate
4 g dietary fiber

The filling for this rich dessert is primarily a mixture of bittersweet chocolate, corn syrup, eggs, and mixed nuts. Baked in a classic graham cracker crust that has been molded into individual ramekins, it is easy to serve and quite delicious. The dessert can be made up to a day ahead and refrigerated, but should be rewarmed in a low-temperature oven to bring it back to room temperature for serving.

CRUST

5 GRAHAM CRACKERS (3½ OUNCES)

1½ TABLESPOONS UNSALTED BUTTER

1 TABLESPOON CANOLA OIL

2 TABLESPOONS SUGAR

FILLING

⅔ CUP MIXED NUTS (PECANS, ALMONDS, AND PIGNOLA NUTS, WITH THE PIGNOLA NUTS RESERVED IN A SEPARATE BOWL)

3½ OUNCES BITTERSWEET CHOCOLATE, BROKEN INTO PIECES

2 TEASPOONS UNSALTED BUTTER

1 TEASPOON CORNSTARCH

⅓ CUP LIGHT CORN SYRUP

1 LARGE EGG, LIGHTLY BEATEN WITH A FORK

1 TEASPOON PURE VANILLA EXTRACT

1. *For the Crust:* Place the graham crackers, 1½ tablespoons butter, canola oil, and sugar in the bowl of a food processor, and process for 1 minute, until the mixture is finely chopped, mealy, and starting to come together.

2. Divide the graham cracker mixture among four ramekins, each with a capacity of 1 cup, and press the mixture evenly into the bottom and around the sides of each cup to create a shell. Note: Although these desserts usually slide easily from their molds when cooled briefly after baking, lining your ramekins first with aluminum foil will eliminate any concerns about the crusts breaking when the desserts are unmolded.

3. Preheat the oven to 350 degrees.

4. *For the Filling:* Place the pecans and almonds in the bowl of a food processor, and process them for a few seconds to chop them coarsely. Stir in the pignola nuts, and divide the nuts among the graham cracker-lined ramekins.

5. Melt the chocolate and the 2 teaspoons butter in a microwave oven or in the top of double boiler set over hot water. Add the cornstarch, mix well, then add the corn syrup, and mix it in well. Add the egg and vanilla, and mix well. Divide the mixture among the four ramekins.

6. Arrange the ramekins on a tray, and bake the pies in the middle of the preheated 350-degree oven for about 25 minutes, until the filling is set but still somewhat soft in the middle. Cool the ramekins to lukewarm or room temperature on a rack.

7. At serving time, invert each of the ramekins onto a dessert plate, and, if using aluminum foil, gently peel it off the crusts. Carefully turn the ramekins right side up, and return them to the plates. Serve at room temperature.

a highly personal
collection of favorites

author

David Rosengarten, host of *Taste* on the Food Network

why he wrote it

"I want to show you how food crept into an American life—mine—and changed that life for the better. How one palate has wandered from the gastronomically unpromising streets of Brooklyn, New York, in the 1950's to the main international culinary avenues of the twenty-first century. Why is that important? I'm anxious to demonstrate what that path was like, in case you want to follow a similar path yourself."

why it made our list

Rosengarten knows what he likes and shares it here in a one-man show of recipes, opinions, and humor. He discusses the origins of each dish and why he is often disappointed with the versions he's tried—then reveals the much-better way he's found to make it. With his lists of criteria for quality, he teaches the reader what the dish should be and what to look for. Rosengarten believes that "taking the time to appreciate the pleasures of the table—if you're lucky enough to be able to do so—brings you about as close to a meaningful life as anything in this world can," and we can't argue with that.

chapters

My Favorite Light Appetizers • My Favorite In-Between Dishes • My Favorite Main Courses • My Favorite Desserts • Wine . . . and Other Good Things to Drink with Your Food

previous books

Rosengarten is the author of *The Dean & Deluca Cookbook* and coauthor of *Red Wine with Fish*.

specifics

345 pages, 97 recipes,
68 color photographs,
18 black-and-white photographs,
$45.00. Published by Random House, Inc.

from the book

"I'm sometimes asked what my last meal on earth would be. Without a nanosecond of hesitation, I always say that the light appetizer course has to be a gargantuan platter of raw, top-quality oysters—or else I refuse to go!"

TASTE

One Palate's Journey Through the World's Greatest Dishes

DAVID ROSENGARTEN

as seen on
food
NETWORK

THAI BEEF SALAD

MAKES 4 FIRST-COURSE SERVINGS

1/2 pound filet mignon, in one chunk that's 1 to 1 1/2 inches thick

4 cups firmly packed torn lettuce leaves *

1 cup firmly packed mint leaves, coarsely torn, plus whole leaves for garnish

1 cup cilantro leaves, chopped, plus whole leaves for garnish

1 cup sliced purple onion

1/2 cup firmly packed daikon (white radish) in julienne strips

1 cup finely diced fresh tomato

2 teaspoons finely minced fresh hot chili (preferably Thai bird peppers), or more to taste

4 teaspoons Thai fish sauce

6 tablespoons Basic Thai Salad Dressing (below)

1. Grill the beef to rare over a charcoal fire.

2. While the beef is grilling, combine the lettuces, mint, cilantro, onion, daikon, tomato, and chili in a large mixing bowl.

3. When the beef is rare, remove it from the grill, and let it rest for 5 minutes. Then slice it in ⅛-inch-thick slices, put them in a small mixing bowl, and toss with the fish sauce.

4. Add the beef to the bowl of lettuces, add the salad dressing, and toss.

5. Divide the salad among 4 serving plates, garnish each plate with mint and cilantro leaves, and serve immediately.

BASIC THAI SALAD DRESSING

MAKES 1¾ CUPS

1 cup freshly squeezed lime juice

1/2 cup fish sauce

4 tablespoons sugar

4 tablespoons thin-sliced tender center of lemongrass stalk

In a bowl, mix all the ingredients together until the sugar has dissolved. Use on Thai salads.

* For this salad, I like to use a combination of upscale lettuces—like frisée, radicchio, lolla rossa, mâche, et cetera. It's not exactly authentic, but it is delicious.

SOFT-SHELL CRABS

Peepers. Busters. Peelers. Southern terms of endearment for one of the great treats of American gastronomy . . . and one of the great oddities of the gastronomic world.

Why are soft-shell crabs odd? Because they're almost uniquely American. Theoretically, any crab-producing area anywhere in the world could specialize in soft-shell crabs—for soft-shells are, after all, just regular old hard-shell crabs that have shed their shells. They do this because their shells cannot grow, but their insides can—so the only way for a crab to get bigger is to shed its shell, grow its body, then accrue a larger shell.

But a whole industry has to be set up to capture these critters at just the right time and then care for them en route to the consumer. And the region from the Chesapeake Bay in Maryland down to the Gulf of Mexico in Louisiana—going back less than a hundred years—is the only crab-producing region in the world that has taken the trouble to set up a large-scale soft-shell crab industry. That's what's odd.

Indeed, most Europeans traveling to America for the first time find soft-shell crabs surprising (initially; then they find them delicious). Impervious to surprise may be travelers from the northeast coast of Italy, because the area around Venice is the only other coastal region I know of that's set up to produce soft-shell crabs (*moleche*)—but their industry is minuscule compared with ours.

So remember: soft-shell crabs are not freaks of nature. We have them in America because of a marketing decision. They are freaks of commerce.

Now, as to nature: the great blue crab of Maryland (which is actually found up and down the Eastern Seaboard and all the way over to Texas) spends most of its life—which would be about three years, if the crabbers left it alone—in a hard-shell condition. If it lived a full life, it would shed its shell as many as twenty-three times. Soft-shell crabbers, however, rarely allow that to happen. When crabs are large enough to go to market, the crabbers watch for telltale signs that the crabs are about to shed their shells; then they spring into action and catch them. The crabbers do have to spring, by the way, because if the crabs remain in the water for even a few hours after shedding, the new hard shells begin to form. Happily for the crabbers, hard shells will not form once the soft-shell crabs have been taken out of the water.

So what are the shedding clues? Ten to fourteen days before the blessed event, little white lines begin to appear on the shell. Crabbers pluck crabs with these lines from their natural waters and move them to holding floats. Two days before the shedding (or molting), the crab's hind legs turn from pink to red—and the vigil really begins. Skilled professionals in places like Crisfield, Maryland—the center of the industry—stay with the crabs round the clock so that the peelers may be plucked from the tank as soon as the shells come off. At the decisive hour, the body of the crab starts to expand, and, like a small, oddly shaped balloon, a bulbous dark mass begins to emerge slowly from the rear opening of the crab; after a lot of seemingly painful pushing and puffing and panting, the soft-shell crab emerges from its prison 25 to 40 percent larger than its former self.

For the first few hours after molting—when she's exposed and squeezable—the female crab, ironically, has her only opportunity to mate. Male crabs are furiously trying to grab her—but the bay crabber is trying to do the same, with an altogether different purpose in mind.

THE SOFT-SHELL CRAB PROBLEMS

On the gastronomic front, there are two groups of obstacles blocking your path to the blissful delectation of soft-shell crabs: buying difficulties and cooking difficulties.

Buying Difficulties. When soft-shell crabs are taken out of the water, they will live for only a few days. So they are shipped immediately, usually by air, to markets around the country. Unfortunately, the longer they're out of the water, the less sweet and intense they'll taste; that's why it's a good idea to make sure you're getting very fresh crabs, i.e., live crabs that are particularly lively looking, flailing around when provoked.

There is a season, of course, for live soft-shell crabs: they're a spring thing. But lately, live soft-shell crabs from warmer waters have been arriving in northern markets earlier in the year. I've seen Gulf of Mexico soft-shell crabs in New York as early as February. Now, I've got no prejudice against Gulf crabs—in fact, the best soft-shell crab I ever tasted was a Louisiana crab, at Uglesich's in New Orleans. But it has been my experience in the North that the best-tasting soft-shell crabs arrive from Maryland in June.

And one more tip: don't buy the larger crabs. Soft-shells usually range from 2 to 5 inches across, and many markets seem to think that Americans will pay more if the crabs are at the upper end of the continuum. I encourage my fish market, however, to get me the smaller ones; they seem more succulent, and I find them easier to cook well.

Now, if you love soft-shell crabs, you may be tempted to buy them frozen at other times of the year. In a word: don't. Not only are frozen soft-shell crabs more insipid in flavor, but they can be wet and watery—a problem that plagues even live soft-shell crabs and leads to all kinds of cooking difficulties.

Cooking Difficulties. So there you are, in a fine restaurant, with rising anticipation over the imminent arrival on your table of the season's first soft-shell crabs. The chef is sautéing them in butter, as many chefs do, and you can't wait. As soon as you cut into them, however, you realize that something is wrong: namely, they're squishy, watery, leaky, insipid. The plump meat you visualized just isn't there. It has probably happened to you so many times you've come to accept that this is the way soft-shell crabs are supposed to be.

And there's another problem as well. Though I fully appreciate the softness of soft-shell crabs—after all, the point of the thing is that you can eat the whole crab—sometimes I find them too soft, find myself yearning for a little crunch, a little textural resistance. And this is why I believe one of the secrets of cooking soft-shell crabs to be *the restoration of the shell.* Yes, some supreme power took the shell off—but supreme chefs restore a little firmness to the crab that makes it perfect.

One of the best ways to do this is by deep-frying the crab. Japanese chefs in America get this dead right. They quarter the crabs (creating even more surface area to crunch up), toss them in some flour, dip them in beaten egg, then roll them in a particularly crunchy type of bread crumb called *panko.* After the crabs fry for a few minutes at 365 to 375 degrees, they're crisp and altogether wonderful on the outside.

They may, however, still be watery on the inside. Why? Because they are supposed to be like this. In order to crawl out of its shell, a crab has to convert some of its flesh into water. Of course, soft-shell crabs are watery. But now—read on—they don't have to be.

A few years ago I was on a mission to solve the watery-within problem, and I tested scores of methods. The one I finally came up with is something of a miracle: while you're sautéing the crabs in a pan, you lay a heavy weight—like a brick—over the crabs. The weight forces the crabs to spit out all their excess liquid while helping to develop a crunchy sear on the sides of the crabs that're next to the pan. The result tastes intensely of crab, but the meat within has practically the texture of lobster.

WEIGHTED AND PANFRIED SOFT-SHELL CRABS

This is it. The ultimate soft-shell crab cooking method, the one that removes all the watery liquid from inside the crab. Try it!

MAKES 4 SERVINGS

1 cup flour

1 tablespoon salt

1 teaspoon fresh ground black pepper

1/2 teaspoon cayenne

12 small soft-shell crabs, cleaned

Unsalted butter for pan frying

1. In a bowl, mix together the flour, salt, black pepper, and cayenne.

2. Dredge the crabs in the flour, shaking off the excess.

3. Choose several heavy frying pans that will hold the crabs in one layer without crowding. Place the pans over moderately high heat, and add enough butter to create a thin layer (about ¼ inch) in each pan. After the foam subsides, add the floured crabs and weight them (with bricks, other heavy pans, or anything you can improvise). Cook for 2 to 3 minutes, or until the crabs are golden brown on the underside. Turn the crabs over, and weight them again. Cook for 2 to 3 more minutes, or until the other side is golden brown. Transfer them to paper towels to drain briefly, and serve, 3 to a portion.

star-studded recipes
from a real celebrity chef

authors

Movie star and salad-dressing mogul Paul Newman and his Newman's Own partner, author and playwright A. E. Hotchner

why they wrote it

"It's our belief that eating well is the best revenge, and the recipes collected herein have been chosen with that in mind. These are our favorite recipes and those of our families and friends. Our guidelines were that the dishes be simple, imaginative, and digestible. Don't expect to find exotic game birds floating in a cream and brandy sauce or lobster stuffed with caviar and foie gras. These are the kind of wholesome, tasty dishes that would bring joy to the heart of Butch Cassidy and Ernest Hemingway if the two of them happened to have dinner together."

why it made our list

It's a pretty irresistible package: recipes from celebrities, proceeds to a children's charity, and Paul Newman on the cover. There are plenty more photos of the blue-eyed one inside and also of his famous friends, all performing at the Hole in the Wall Gang Camp for children with cancer and other serious illnesses, which this book will benefit. Most of the recipes manage to feature Newman's Own products on their ingredient lists—the money from all that salad dressing and spaghetti sauce goes to charity, too—but substitutions are offered. "If you have the questionable taste of preferring some others," advises Newman, "suit yourself."

chapters

Starters • Soups, Stews, and Chilies • Main Courses • Pastas, Pizza, and Rice • Vegetables and Side Dishes • Breads and Snacks • Desserts

specifics

223 pages, 131 recipes, 23 color photographs, $25. Published by Simon & Schuster.

from the book

"My adult life has been spent in the family of women: my wife, Joanne; five daughters; my housekeeper, Caroline; and a succession of wire-haired terriers, all males who were immediately castrated upon arrival. No wonder I took to wearing an apron by way of disguise, lest I become a capon. What started out as a protective measure became, over time, a stunning discovery of culinary treasures."

NEWMAN'S OWN COOKBOOK

PAUL NEWMAN

and A. E. HOTCHNER

Proceeds from this book go directly to the Hole in the Wall Gang Fund

Holly Hunter's Zucchini Pancakes with Smoked Salmon and Yogurt-Dill Sauce

These are elegant and beautiful and make a great first course or entree for brunch. You can also quarter the finished pancakes and serve them as an appetizer. Don't stint on the quality of smoked salmon. This is a case where more is more.

■ **SERVES 6**

YOGURT-DILL SAUCE

1 cup plain low-fat yogurt
¼ cup finely chopped fresh dill
salt and freshly ground black pepper
    to taste
juice of 1 lemon

PANCAKES

2 medium zucchini, ends trimmed
2 large Idaho potatoes, scrubbed but
    not peeled
1 small red onion, thinly sliced and cut
    into julienne strips
2 tablespoons olive oil

salt and freshly ground black pepper to
    taste
2 tablespoons vegetable oil for cooking
1½ teaspoons unsalted butter, melted,
    for cooking

ACCOMPANIMENTS

2 cups mixed baby greens
12 ounces sliced Norwegian smoked
    salmon or gravlax (2 slices per
    serving)
½ cup chopped chives for garnish
very thin lemon slices for garnish
freshly ground black pepper to taste

To make the sauce: In a ceramic or plastic bowl, combine all the ingredients, cover, and chill. (If you are making the sauce in advance, add the lemon juice just before serving, or the yogurt will separate.)

To make the pancakes: Grate the zucchini and potatoes on the large-hole side of a hand-held box grater or in a food processor fitted with the shredding disk. Put the grated vegetables in a bowl and add the onion, olive oil, salt, and pepper.

Preheat the oven to 300°F. In a 7½-inch nonstick omelet pan, heat 1 teaspoon of the vegetable oil together with ¼ teaspoon of the melted butter over medium-high heat until hot. Pour ¾ cup of the grated vegetables and spread the mixture to the edges of the pan, pressing down firmly with a rubber spatula, to form a pancake about ¼ inch thick. Cook about 3 minutes, until the edges begin to brown. Gently lift the pancake with the spatula, to check the underside. If it is deep golden brown in color, turn (or flip) the pancake and cook 3 to 4 minutes more, until golden. Remove the pancake to a paper-towel-lined plate to drain, then transfer to a baking sheet. Place in the oven to keep warm.

Make pancakes with the remaining ingredients in the same manner, being sure to add 1 teaspoon of oil and a bit of butter to the pan before making a new pancake.

To serve, put a generous ¼ cup of greens on each of 6 salad plates. Spread each pancake with about 2 tablespoons (or more to taste) of yogurt-dill sauce, then put a pancake on each plate on the greens. Arrange 2 slices of salmon on top of each pancake. Garnish each serving with some chives, several lemon slices, and a generous grinding of pepper. Serve the remaining sauce in a bowl on the side.

Matthew Broderick's Grilled T-bone Steak with Sweet Onion Marmalade and Campfire Mustard Sauce

Steak doesn't get any better than this, and when paired with roasted new potatoes, it's too good to be true. If this seems like a lot of work, remember that both the marmalade and the campfire mustard sauce can be made up to four days in advance. Keep covered in the refrigerator. Then it's just a question of making the potatoes and grilling the steaks. It's well worth the effort.

■ **SERVES 6**

6 T-bone steaks (12 to 14 ounces each)
salt and freshly ground black pepper to
taste

ONION MARMALADE

2 tablespoons unsalted butter
4 Vidalia onions, thinly sliced
6 shallots, thinly sliced
10 cloves garlic, thinly sliced
½ cup port wine
¼ cup balsamic vinegar

CAMPFIRE MUSTARD SAUCE

½ cup Dijon mustard
½ cup Pommery (French whole-grain)
mustard
¼ cup honey mustard
¼ cup balsamic vinegar
1 teaspoon freshly ground black
pepper

Bring the steaks to room temperature, then season with salt and pepper.

Meanwhile, make the onion marmalade: Melt the butter in a large cast-iron skillet. Add the onions, shallots, and garlic, and cook over high heat, stirring, for 10 minutes, until the onions are soft. Add the port and vinegar, and cook about 5 to 10 minutes, until the liquid is almost evaporated. Remove the pan from the heat but keep the marmalade warm.

To make the mustard sauce: Combine all the ingredients in a bowl.

Preheat a grill or broiler until hot. Grill the steaks for 4 to 4½ minutes per side for rare, 6 to 7 minutes per side for medium-rare.

Serve each steak topped with some warm marmalade. Serve the mustard sauce separately in a bowl.

"Pops" Newman's Coffee-Toffee Macadamia Crunch

For Bob Gadsby, a love for popcorn as a child developed into an art form as a bachelor. Even though his wife is now queen of the kitchen, popcorn is one area where he reigns supreme. His 1996 prize-winning recipe combines popcorn with rich, buttery macadamia nuts and just a hint of coffee. Bob donated his award to the Boundary County Library and the Volunteer Fire Department. ■ MAKES ABOUT 13 CUPS

One 3½-ounce bag Newman's Own All-Natural Flavor Oldstyle Picture Show Microwave Popcorn (about 10 cups) or your favorite
2 cups coarsely chopped macadamia nuts
1½ sticks (12 tablespoons) unsalted butter or margarine

1 cup sugar
½ cup packed light brown sugar
¼ cup coffee-flavored liqueur or strong coffee
¼ cup light corn syrup
2 teaspoons vanilla extract

Butter a large roasting pan.

Pop the popcorn according to the package directions. Pour into the prepared pan and add the macadamia nuts. Toss to mix.

In a 2-quart saucepan, combine the butter, sugar, brown sugar, liqueur, and corn syrup, and bring to a boil over medium heat, stirring constantly. Continue cooking and stirring until the mixture reaches 290°F on a candy thermometer. Remove the pan from the heat and stir in the vanilla extract. Pour over the popcorn mixture and stir until evenly coated.

Cool until firm and break into pieces.

Store in an airtight container.

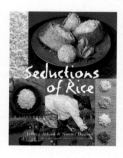

category **4**

special

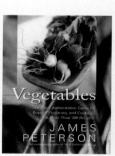

subjects

Grilling was the hot topic of the year. We tested eight books on this subject alone and found two that deserve to be honored here. Both cover technique thoroughly and include loads of recipes. In fact, the hallmark of the special-subject cookbooks, which in the past have often included mainly small volumes on narrow topics, is their expansion to the proportions of complete reference books. For all of these books, the authors have clearly done their homework.

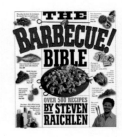

plain-old, reliable rice made fascinating

authors

Photographers, writers, and world travelers Jeffrey Alford and Naomi Duguid

why they wrote it

"The world of rice is so huge, it would be presumptuous to think that we could include every rice here, or discuss every important rice tradition. Instead we've tried to give an introduction to the world of rice. We hope this book will help you navigate that world with ease, finding your own ways, bringing dishes to your table with confidence and pleasure, day in and day out."

why it made our list

Any book that makes a simple staple like rice seem exciting gets our full attention. With stunning photographs and enticing recipes, this is an excellent kitchen cookbook that's also pretty enough for your coffee table. The authors, who traveled extensively to take the pictures and collect the recipes, guide the reader on an extended tour through countries like Mexico, Vietnam, and Japan, offering traditional preparations for rice all along the way. It's an amazingly delicious journey.

chapters

Beginning with Rice • The World of Rice • White Rice, Black Rice, Congee • Jasmine, Sticky Rice, Thai Red • Gohan, Sushi, Mochi • Basmati, Gobindavog, South Indian Red • Chelo, Polo, Pulao • Pilaf, Paella, Risotto • Yassa, Mafe, Diebou Dien • Hoppin' John, Rice and Peas

previous books

Alford and Duguid are also the authors of *Flatbreads and Flavors: A Baker's Atlas.*

specifics

467 pages, 186 recipes,
46 color photographs,
223 black-and-white photographs,
$35. Published by Artisan.

from the book

"Our favorite way to eat rice is out of a bowl, the way it is commonly eaten in China. We also like eating rice from a small dinner plate using a dessert spoon to pick it up, Thai style. And when we are in South India, we eat it from a banana leaf with our hands, and then we think that is the best way."

Seductions of Rice

of Rice

A COOKBOOK

Jeffrey Alford & Naomi Duguid

Authors of *Flatbreads and Flavors: A Baker's Atlas*

Editor's Choice Award

most fascinating to read

Golden Chicken Kebabs

Makes 12 to 15 kebabs; serves 6 to 8 with rice

PERSIAN *CHELO* RICE IS OFTEN EATEN WITH GRILLED LAMB OR CHICKEN KEBABS. These savory chicken kebabs are marinated in a blend of yogurt, garlic, saffron, and dried mint before being grilled over charcoal or broiled. Easy and delicious.

Serve the kebabs with a plate of fresh herbs (basil, tarragon, flat-leaf parsley) and Special Everyday Persian Rice (page 190) or any cooked long-grain rice. You might want to offer Oasis Salad (page 192) as an accompaniment.

2 pounds boneless skinless chicken thighs
or breasts or a combination

Marinade

1 cup plain yogurt (whole-milk or 2%)

1 tablespoon minced garlic

⅛ teaspoon saffron threads, dry-roasted
(see page 191), crushed to a powder,
and dissolved in 2 tablespoons warm
water

1 tablespoon crushed dried mint
(optional)

½ teaspoon salt

½ teaspoon freshly ground black pepper

Cut the chicken into small pieces, ½-inch cubes or smaller, discarding any fat or tough connective tissue.

Combine the yogurt with the remaining marinade ingredients in a small bowl and mix well. Place the chicken pieces in a shallow bowl, pour the marinade over, and stir to ensure that all of the chicken is well coated. Let stand, refrigerated, for at least 3 hours or as long as 24 hours.

Preheat a charcoal or gas grill or a broiler.

Thread the chicken pieces onto metal skewers. Place only a few pieces of chicken on each skewer, and don't cram the pieces together tightly. (If they are packed together, rather than just lightly touching, they will not cook evenly.)

Grill or broil 5 to 6 inches from the heat, turning the skewers after 3 minutes for about 10 minutes, until the chicken is cooked through. Serve hot or at room temperature.

above
Special Everyday Persian Rice (page 190)
with Golden Chicken Kebabs (page 188),
Oasis Salad (page 192), and fresh herbs

left
Small rice shop in Sapa,
northern Vietnam

Special Everyday Persian Rice
chelo

Serves 6

As the more elaborate form of everyday Persian rice, *CHELO* is a wonderful treat, usually served with kebabs or with a moist stew-like *khoresh*. The rice is soaked, then briefly cooked in plenty of boiling water. To create a delicious crust and perfectly textured rice, the rice is then returned to the pot and gently steamed for thirty minutes. But first the bottom of the pot is covered with oil or butter with a binder such as egg or yogurt (or both) and a thin layer of rice or some flatbread or thinly sliced potatoes. This bottom layer cooks to a golden crispy crust known as the *tahdig* and is served beside or on top of the finished dish.

Though the instructions may seem elaborate, you'll understand the sequence and be delighted by the perfection of the results after you've made this rice once. Serve it with Golden Chicken Kebabs (page 188), with a yogurt sauce and sliced ripe tomatoes or cucumbers.

2½ cups basmati rice (see Note)

¼ cup salt

Water

¼ cup vegetable oil or 4 tablespoons butter

2 tablespoons plain yogurt (whole-milk or 2%)

1 large egg

1 teaspoon saffron threads, dry-roasted (see opposite page), crumbled to a powder, and dissolved in 3 tablespoons warm water (optional)

Wash the rice thoroughly, then place in a large pot with 3 tablespoons of the salt and enough cold water to cover by 2 inches. Let soak for 2 to 3 hours.

Drain well in a fine sieve. In the same pot, bring 4 quarts of water to a vigorous boil. Add the remaining 1 tablespoon salt, then gradually sprinkle in the rice. Stir gently to prevent sticking, and bring back to the boil. After the rice has been boiling for 2 minutes, test for doneness. The rice is ready when the outside is tender but there remains a slight uncooked resistance at the core of the grain. If the core of the grain is brittle, it's not done enough. Continue to check the rice until done, usually about 4 minutes, then drain in the sieve and rinse with tepid to cool water (to prevent it from cooking any more).

Place the pot back over high heat and add the oil or butter and 1 tablespoon water. In a small bowl, whisk together the yogurt and egg. Stir in about ½ cup of the rice, then place in the sizzling oil and spread over the bottom of the pot. Gradually add the remaining rice, sprinkling it in to form a mound. Use the handle of a wooden spoon to make three or four holes through the mound to the bottom, then cover the pot with a lid wrapped in a tea towel. (The towel helps seal the lid and absorbs moisture from the rising steam.) Heat over medium-high heat until steam builds up, 1 to 2 minutes, then lower the heat to medium-low and cook for about 30 minutes. When it is done, the rice will be tender and fluffy with a flavorful crust, the *tahdig,* on the bottom.

The *tahdig* comes off more easily if, before removing the lid, you place the pot in an inch of cold water (in the sink) for a minute. Then remove the lid and, if you're using saffron, gently spoon about 1 cup rice into the saffron water mixture; stir to blend. Mound the remaining rice on a platter. Sprinkle on the saffron rice, if you have it. Place chunks of the crust on top or on a separate plate; it's a big treat.

Note: You can substitute brown basmati for white. Boiling until tender will take 12 to 15 minutes, depending on the rice; begin testing the rice at 11 minutes after it comes back to the boil.

saffron   Saffron threads are the pistils of a crocus (*Crocus sativa*), gathered by hand in the spring. Spain produces most saffron; Kashmir is also known for its saffron. Saffron is used for its color and delicate flavor. Because it is rare and expensive, as well as giving food a beautiful color, it is associated with festive dishes. Available in specialty stores and by mail order, saffron should be bought as threads, rather than powdered, and stored in a cool, dry place. Before using, heat the saffron threads gently in a dry skillet to dry them out thoroughly, then reduce them to a powder in a mortar. Dissolve the powder in a little water before adding it to dishes.

Uighur men cooking kebabs in western Xinjiang

Oasis Salad

COMING INTO AN OASIS FROM THE DESERT CAN BE HALLUCINATORY. ONE moment you're in a vast, open, shadeless space, the sun beating down, the next you've entered the leafy calm of the poplars and cottonwoods that mark the edge of the oasis. Water gurgles in open irrigation ditches, birds sing, and green vegetables thrive in well-tended gardens. Everything smells moist and fresh, and there's a softness to the air. It's tempting to cross back out into the desert just to reexperience the transition, but if you're like us, you're usually too eager for fresh vegetables and a cool drink to take the time.

It's no wonder then that oasis dwellers are famous for their sweet melons, plump red tomatoes, and crisp fresh cucumbers and radishes. These fruits of the desert heat and oasis waters feel like a triumph of human will and effort over nature. And no wonder that most meals along the Silk Road, except in winter, feature at least one salad, very simply dressed. (Wintertime is the season for pickles, a wonderful way to have the crisp bite of radishes and carrots in the cold season.)

When you serve this salad, imagine that you are seated under a canopy of grape vines, sipping hot tea from bowls and eating pilaf and kebabs.

1 cup coarsely chopped red or white (daikon or icicle) radish

1 cup coarsely chopped peeled English cucumber

2 cups ripe tomato chunks

1 teaspoon salt, or to taste

¼ to ½ cup loosely packed fresh coriander leaves, coarsely chopped

Combine all the ingredients in a bowl and toss gently to blend. Serve at room temperature.

Oaxacan Rice Pudding

arroz con leche oaxacana

ALL FLAVORS SEEM MORE INTENSE AND COMPLEX IN OAXACA, FROM THE chocolate *atole* to the *mole* sauces. This rice pudding, so like Spanish rice pudding, packs a pleasant extra bit of flavor from the ginger that simmers with the rice.

6 cups whole milk

½ cup medium or long-grain rice, broken (see Note)

2 inches cinnamon stick

½-inch ginger

2 small strips lime zest

¼ teaspoon salt

½ cup sugar

3 large egg yolks

¼ cup raisins

Place the milk, rice, cinnamon stick, ginger, lime zest, salt, and sugar in a large heavy non-reactive pot. Bring almost to a boil, then lower the heat and simmer, stirring occasionally, for 1 hour. Remove the cinnamon stick, ginger, and zest.

Preheat the oven to 350°F. In a medium bowl, beat the egg yolks. Stir in about ½ cup of the rice, then mix back into the rice in the pot. Add the raisins, reserving a few for garnish. Transfer to a large shallow ovenproof dish and bake for 10 to 20 minutes, until the eggs have set. Let stand at room temperature for 10 minutes before serving. Serve warm or at room temperature, in individual bowls, garnished with the reserved raisins.

Note: To break rice, pound briefly in a large mortar, or place on a countertop, cover with a tea towel, and roll briskly with a heavy rolling pin, pressing firmly as you do so.

A small shrine in Oaxaca's main market

making the most of your favorite flavorings

editor

Judith Hill, editor in chief of FOOD & WINE Books

why we wrote it

"To make the most of herbs and spices, you must get to know them fairly intimately. And giving you an opportunity to do just that is the main point of this book. We have concentrated on dishes that are as quick and easy as all the other recipes in the *Quick from Scratch* series and in addition emphasize the nature of a spotlighted herb or spice. We hope you'll find that using this volume not only helps you to make good food fast but also to learn exactly what individual herbs and spices taste like."

why it made our list

We're particularly proud of our latest *Quick from Scratch* entry and think it has a rightful place on any list of the year's best, both for the deliciousness of the dishes and for the usefulness of the information. As we developed these recipes, we carefully considered the flavors of every herb and spice, which led us to understand each of their effects more completely than we had before. If you've ever used herbs and spices as a matter of habit rather than with clear knowledge of how they interact with other ingredients, then you need season blindly no more. With this book, you can enjoy learning and eating at the same time.

sections

Herbs • Spices

previous books

Other entries in the *Quick from Scratch* series include *Pasta*, *Chicken*, *Fish and Shellfish*, *Italian*, *One-Dish Meals*, *Vegetable Main Dishes*, and *Soups and Salads*.

specifics

192 pages, 75 recipes, 75 color photographs, $25.95. Published by FOOD & WINE Books.

from the book

"**There's an easy way to determine the freshness of dried herbs and spices: Smell them. If the aroma is faint or nonexistent, the flavor will be, too. It's not a crime to throw out old herbs and spices. Most are not what they should be after a year on your shelf.**"

BASIL *It may be best known as the herb that puts the green in pesto, but with its enchanting fragrance and hints of mint, licorice, and clove, basil can bring excitement to all manner of dishes. A member of the mint family, basil comes in many varieties. Sweet is the most common; others include lemon, cinnamon, the purple-hued opal, and holy basil, which is commonly used in Thai cooking. Whatever kind you choose, it should be fresh; in the process of drying, the flavor seems to evaporate from the leaves along with the moisture. Because heat also destroys the flavor, add basil generously at the end of cooking.* 🌿 **USES** *Basil is at its peak in the summer and is well paired with summer vegetables like eggplant, peppers, and zucchini. It's never better, though, than with tomatoes. Top sliced tomatoes with basil and a splash of vinegar for a simple salad, or use chopped rather than sliced tomatoes in the same combination for a tasty no-cook pasta sauce. Fold chopped basil into unsweetened whipped cream, and swirl the cream into tomato soup. Try also: stuffing chicken breasts with basil and goat cheese; mixing chopped basil with butter to top a grilled steak or chop; using basil in place of lettuce on sandwiches.*

THAI CHICKEN WITH BASIL

An abundance of whole basil leaves joins chicken and fiery red chiles for a quick, delicious, and decidedly spicy stir-fry. Holy basil is the most authentic choice, but any variety will do.

🍷 **WINE RECOMMENDATION**
Look for a rich but dry white wine, such as a pinot gris from the Alsace region in France.

SERVES 4

1⅓ pounds boneless, skinless chicken breasts (about 4), cut into 1-by-2-inch pieces

2 tablespoons Asian fish sauce (nam pla or nuoc mam)*

1½ tablespoons soy sauce

1 tablespoon water

1½ teaspoons sugar

2 tablespoons cooking oil

1 large onion, cut into thin slices

3 fresh red chiles, seeds and ribs removed, cut into thin slices, or ¼ teaspoon dried red-pepper flakes

3 cloves garlic, minced

1½ cups lightly packed basil leaves

*Available at Asian markets and many supermarkets

1. In a medium bowl, combine the chicken with the fish sauce, soy sauce, water, and sugar. In a large nonstick frying pan or a wok, heat the oil over moderately high heat. Add the onion and cook, stirring, for 2 minutes. Stir in the chiles and garlic; cook, stirring, 30 seconds longer.

2. Remove the chicken from the marinade with a slotted spoon and add it to the hot pan. Cook until almost done, stirring, about 3 minutes. Add the marinade and cook 30 seconds longer. Remove from the heat and stir in 1 cup of the basil. Serve topped with the remaining ½ cup basil.

MARJORAM Sweet marjoram is quite a different herb entirely from wild marjoram, otherwise known as oregano. The two are similar enough so that they can sometimes be substituted for each other, but don't consider them as one and the same. You can distinguish marjoram by its paler flavor, aroma, and color. And whereas oregano is usually dried, marjoram is okay dried but best fresh. Marjoram's flavor has also been compared to that of thyme, and it can replace that herb as well. Though it's milder than oregano, fresh marjoram is not subtle; you'll want to use it sparingly. To avoid loss of flavor, add fresh marjoram to dishes toward the end of cooking. Dried, on the other hand, should go in early. 🌿 **USES** Sautéed mushrooms taste delicious with marjoram. So does lamb, whether as grilled brochettes or in a Greek meat sauce. Try also: tossing chopped marjoram with olive oil, cooked broccoli, and sausage for a terrific pasta sauce; adding it to chicken braised with carrots; stirring a little into fettuccine Alfredo; simmering it in a pot of beans; sautéing veal scaloppine and then deglazing the pan with a little cream and a touch of marjoram to make a quick sauce.

SAUTÉED CARROTS WITH LEMON AND MARJORAM

Lemon juice and garlic balance sweet sautéed carrots flavored with fresh marjoram. A simple yet exceptional side dish, it goes equally well alongside meat, fish, or poultry.

SERVES 4

- 3   tablespoons olive oil
- 1   large clove garlic, minced
- 2   pounds carrots (about 16), cut diagonally into ½-inch slices
- 1   teaspoon sugar
- ½   teaspoon salt
- ¼   teaspoon fresh-ground black pepper
- 1   tablespoon chopped fresh marjoram, or 1 teaspoon dried marjoram
- 4   teaspoons lemon juice

1. In a medium nonstick frying pan, heat 1½ tablespoons of the oil over moderately low heat. Add the garlic, carrots, sugar, ¼ teaspoon of the salt, the pepper, and the dried marjoram, if using. Cook, covered, stirring occasionally, for 5 minutes.

2. Uncover the pan. Raise the heat to moderate and cook, stirring frequently, until the carrots are very tender and beginning to brown, about 8 minutes longer.

3. Remove the pan from the heat. Stir in the remaining 1½ tablespoons oil and ¼ teaspoon salt, the lemon juice, and the fresh marjoram, if using.

SAGE *Once limited to stuffing for the holiday bird, sage has come into its own. Credit can go largely to the renaissance in America of Italian regional cooking, which makes good and frequent use of sage. The herb's flavor is undeniably strong, almost musty, yet can enhance even the most delicate of dishes. Stronger still is dried sage; use it sparingly. Though the herb comes in many, many decorative varieties, the two commonly used for cooking are narrow-leaved and broad-leaved sage.* 🌿 **USES** *Sage is a key ingredient in sausages and, in fact, is delicious with any rich meat or poultry, such as pork or goose. At the other extreme, sage has a great affinity for delicate trout. It's a classic with cannellini beans and delicious with both tomatoes and cheese. Try also: sautéing sage leaves in brown butter to top ravioli, fish, veal cutlets, or even cauliflower; combining chopped sage with prosciutto and fontina cheese as a stuffing for chicken breasts or pork chops; tossing chunks of winter squash with sage and olive oil and then roasting; putting sage leaves under the skin of a chicken before roasting; steeping the leaves in warm water for an interesting herbal tisane.*

GRILLED FONTINA, MUSHROOM, AND SAGE SANDWICHES

The grilled cheese sandwich grows up in our sophisticated version that starts with nutty, smooth-melting fontina cheese and adds a layer of sage-accented sautéed mushrooms.

WINE RECOMMENDATION
A crisp, dry, Italian white—such as Soave, Frascati, or pinot grigio—will refresh your mouth after every bite of this flavorful sandwich.

SERVES 4

3 tablespoons butter, 2 melted
1/2 pound mushrooms, cut into thin slices
1/4 teaspoon salt
1/8 teaspoon fresh-ground black pepper
4 teaspoons chopped fresh sage, or
  1 1/4 teaspoons dried sage
8 slices from a large round loaf of country-style bread, or other bread
1/2 pound fontina, grated (about 2 cups)

1. In a large nonstick frying pan, heat 1 tablespoon of the butter over moderate heat. Add the mushrooms, salt, pepper, and dried sage, if using, and cook, stirring frequently, until golden brown, about 5 minutes. Stir in the fresh sage, if using. Put the mushrooms in a bowl and wipe out the pan.

2. Using a pastry brush, coat one side of 4 slices of the bread with half of the melted butter. Put them, buttered-side down, on a work surface. Top the bread with the cheese and then the mushrooms. Cover with the remaining 4 slices of bread; brush the tops with the remaining melted butter.

3. Heat the frying pan over moderately low heat. Add the sandwiches and cook, turning once, until golden, 5 to 10 minutes per side.

ALLSPICE *True to its name, allspice tastes like a mixture of cloves, cinnamon, and nutmeg, with a dash of black pepper. It grows in the form of berries that resemble peppercorns and are dried in the same way. In fact, adding a handful of allspice berries to your pepper mill along with the peppercorns makes an interesting variation on ground pepper. Though some recipes do require whole berries (for pickling and marinating) or crushed berries (with meats, poultry, and fish), ground allspice is the common form and the one called for most often.* ❋ **USES** *Allspice is a flavoring from the New World that is now used around the globe. It enhances vegetable and rice dishes and is a perfect all-purpose spice in desserts such as cakes, pies, puddings, and custards. Try also: using allspice in pâtés and sausage and with ham; tossing crushed allspice berries into shrimp or beef stir-fries; mixing the crushed berries with the black pepper for steak au poivre; adding ground allspice to sautéed carrots; making it part of a spice rub for pork; putting allspice in chutneys and relishes; letting it spice up applesauce, cheesecake, fruit quick breads, and butter cookies.*

BAKED CUSTARD WITH ALLSPICE

Classic and homey baked custard benefits from a dusting of allspice instead of the usual nutmeg. Custards don't get much quicker to prepare than this one.

SERVES 4

- 2 cups milk
- 2 large eggs
- 2 large egg yolks
- ⅓ cup sugar
  Pinch salt
- 1 teaspoon vanilla extract
- ¼ teaspoon ground allspice

1. Heat the oven to 325°. Bring water to a simmer for the water bath. In a medium saucepan, bring the milk almost to a simmer, stirring occasionally.

2. In a medium bowl, whisk together the eggs, egg yolks, sugar, and salt until just combined. Pour the hot milk over the egg mixture, whisking. Stir in the vanilla. Strain the custard into a large measuring cup or pitcher and skim any foam from the surface.

3. Divide the custard among four 6-ounce custard cups or ramekins. Sprinkle the tops with the allspice and put them into a small roasting pan. Pour enough of the simmering water into the roasting pan to reach about halfway up the side of the custard cups. Carefully transfer the roasting pan to the middle of the oven and bake until a knife stuck in the center of the custard comes out clean, 45 minutes to 1 hour. Remove the cups from the water bath and let cool. Refrigerate until cold, at least 1 hour.

everything you've wanted to know about vegetables

author

Chef, cookbook author, and food authority James Peterson

why he wrote it

"When I set out to write *Vegetables*, I went to the local chain bookstore to look at other vegetable books. . . . In my perusal of the competition I found few recipes for the simplest dishes—things like glazed carrots, mashed potatoes, sautéed spinach, and steamed asparagus—dishes to cook on a Wednesday evening. So I decided to write a book that would include not just new or unfamiliar dishes but also the tried-and-true dishes that many of us grew up with."

why it made our list

Packed with recipes, instructional photos, and useful information on buying, storing, and preparing, this is a complete and convenient, must-have guide to vegetables. It provides basic information on just about every vegetable that exists, along with plenty of ways to prepare each of them, ranging from comfortingly familiar to fairly unique. Bonuses include a comprehensive chart on vegetable yields and a terrific seasonal availability guide. There's something here for everyone who ever cooks vegetables.

chapters

Techniques for Cooking Vegetables • Vegetable Salads • Fried Vegetables • Vegetable Gratins and Casseroles • Grilled Vegetables • Pasta, Gnocchi, and Risotto • Pickles and Brine • Pureed Vegetables • Roasted Vegetables • Four Flavorful Favorites • Braising • Soups • Vegetable Stews • Tasty Starters for Parties and Meals • Sauces, Salsas, Pastes, Rubs, and Flavorful Blends

previous books

Peterson has written three other comprehensive cookbooks—*Sauces*, *Splendid Soups*, and *Fish and Shellfish*.

specifics

448 pages, more than 300 recipes, 189 color photographs, $35. Published by William Morrow and Company, Inc.

from the book

"I was not a big fan of radishes until I picked up the French habit of sandwiching the radish in a tiny chunk of crusty bread and smearing the whole thing with butter as a before-dinner hors d'oeuvre. The process is so addictive that you'll have no trouble eating a bunch of radishes and a rather shocking amount of butter."

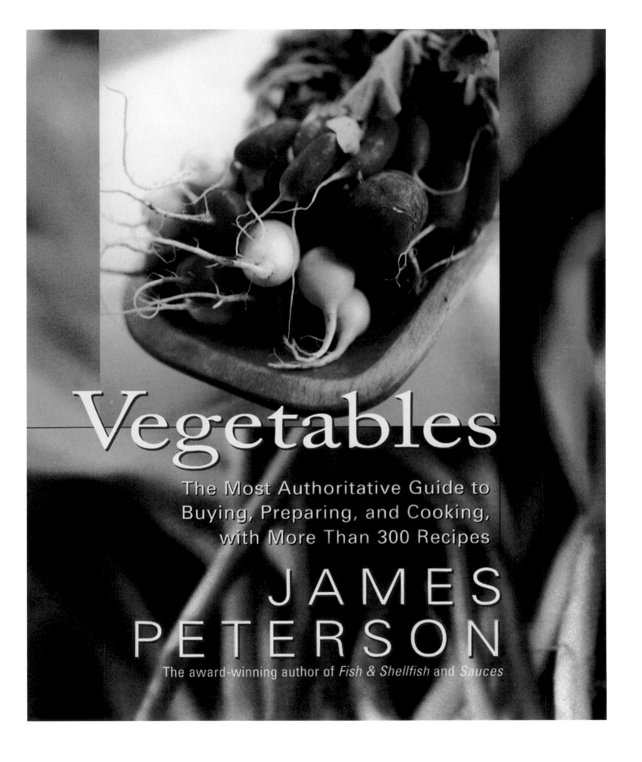

Vegetables

The Most Authoritative Guide to
Buying, Preparing, and Cooking,
with More Than 300 Recipes

JAMES PETERSON

The award-winning author of *Fish & Shellfish* and *Sauces*

Sautéed Radicchio, Orange, Bacon, and Pecan Salad

This salad makes a lovely start to a winter dinner. The sweet oranges and the smoky bacon are a perfect accent to the gentle bitterness of the radicchio, and the pecans give the whole thing a contrasting texture. I use double-smoked slab bacon, which is lean, has a good flavor, and is easy to cut into cubes, but thickly sliced packaged bacon will also work—just be sure to buy a brand that says "naturally smoked" and not "smoke flavored." "Smoke flavored" brands taste like soap.

All the cooking for this salad can be done earlier the same day; only the final assembly has to be done at the last minute. This salad should be served at room temperature or slightly cool, not chilled.

Makes 4 first-course servings

> 1 cup shelled pecans
>
> 2 to 3 bunches radicchio (¾ pound total)
>
> 4 thick slices bacon, cut into ¼-inch cubes
>
> 3 tablespoons extra-virgin olive oil
>
> ¼ cup sherry vinegar or balsamic vinegar, or more to taste
>
> salt and freshly ground black pepper
>
> 4 navel oranges, cut into skinless wedges (see box, right)

Toast the pecans for 15 minutes in a 350°F oven, or until they brown very slightly and start to smell toasty.

Pull any wilted leaves off the radicchio bunches and cut the bunches in half through their cores. Slice each half as thin as you can—⅛-inch shreds are ideal—with a chef's knife or vegetable slicer.

Heat the bacon cubes in a heavy-bottomed skillet over medium heat until they render fat and barely start to turn crispy, about 8 minutes. Drain off the fat (you can save bacon fat for other recipes) and pour the olive oil into the pan. Turn the heat up to high and stir in the shredded radicchio. Stir the radicchio for about 5 minutes or until it has shrunk to about half and is completely wilted. Add the vinegar, stir for 1 minute more (you'll see the color of the radicchio brighten), and transfer to a mixing bowl. Toss the radicchio with the pecans and the bacon cubes and season to taste with salt and pepper and a little more vinegar if needed. Let cool.

Place the salad in mounds on individual plates. Arrange the orange segments in a circular pattern over the salad. Serve immediately.

Cutting an Orange into Skinless Wedges or Slices

Slice the top and bottom of the orange just deep enough to expose the flesh. Set the orange flat on a cutting board and with a very sharp knife, trim off the peel, following the contours of the orange so a minimum of flesh is left on the peel. Cut off any of the white membrane that still clings to the orange. If you're serving the orange in slices, just cut it into round slices about ¼ inch thick.

If you're serving the orange in wedges, hold the orange in your left hand (if you're right-handed) over a bowl and cut between each orange segment, along both sides of the thin membrane that separates each segment, with a very sharp stainless steel paring knife. Cut only to the center of the orange. Continue in this way, cutting on both sides of each membrane until all the orange segments fall into the bowl. Give the pulp left in your hand a good squeeze to get out all the juice.

Dried Mushrooms

One of the great things about dried mushrooms is that you can keep them on hand for emergencies and last-minute inspirations. I keep a bag of dried porcini, tightly wrapped, in my refrigerator for flavoring simple pasta dishes and for giving an elegant and subtle savor to vegetables.

The best dried mushrooms for flavoring vegetables are porcini, morel, and shiitake. To use porcini and morel, rinse them with cold water and soak them for about 30 minutes in barely enough warm water to cover. Dried shiitakes need to be soaked for 5 hours in cold water or for 30 minutes in boiling water. Squeeze the water out of the mushrooms (save it) and chop the soaked mushrooms or slice them thinly.

Italian-style Corn with Dried Porcini and Prosciutto

I *can combine dried porcini mushrooms and prosciutto with just about anything and be happy with the results. This dish came about one evening when I had set out to make polenta with mushrooms but decided to use fresh corn instead.*

Makes 4 side-dish servings

> ½ cup (about ¾ ounce) dried porcini mushroom slices
> one ⅛-inch-thick slice prosciutto, including the fat around the edges (about 2 ounces)
> 1 tablespoon butter (optional)
> 1 small onion, minced
> 1 teaspoon finely chopped fresh marjoram or thyme, or half as much dried
> 2 cups corn kernels (from about 5 ears plump corn-on-the cob)
> ¼ cup water
> salt and freshly ground black pepper

Quickly rinse the porcini mushrooms and soak in warm water until soft, about 30 minutes. During soaking, turn the dried mushrooms around in their liquid every few minutes to get them to soften. Squeeze the water out of the mushrooms—save the water—and chop the mushrooms to the size of small peas.

Cut the fat off the edge of the prosciutto. Finely chop the prosciutto and the fat, keeping the two separate. If the prosciutto doesn't have any fat, use the butter instead.

Put the chopped prosciutto fat or butter in a heavy-bottomed 4-quart pot over medium-low heat. If you're using prosciutto fat, allow about 10 minutes for the fat to render and release into the pan. Stir the chopped prosciutto, onion, and marjoram into the rendered fat or butter and cook gently over medium heat for about 5 minutes.

Stir the chopped porcini into the prosciutto mixture. Carefully pour in any of the porcini soaking liquid, leaving any grit behind in the bowl. Cook gently over medium heat for 5 minutes, until everything begins to caramelize and stick to the sides of the pan. Stir in the corn and ¼ cup water. Cover the pan and simmer gently for 10 minutes. Check after 6 or 7 minutes. If the water has run dry add a tablespoon or two more. Season to taste with salt and pepper and serve immediately.

Leeks

Leeks are the royal members of the onion family. They have a subtle earthy flavor that's hard to get enough of and are especially delicious when cooked with cream or in soups, or when served cold in a mustardy vinaigrette.

Leeks are expensive and it's always a little discouraging to use only a small part of the whole leek, the white. In restaurants the leek greens are tied up into bundles with herbs and used as bouquet garnis in big pots of stock, but at home, unless you have a pot of broth simmering on the stove, it can be hard to find a use for them. They are occasionally used in pureed vegetable soups.

In most parts of the country, leeks are available year-round, but they're at their peak season in the fall. Inspect leeks carefully before you buy to make sure that the greens are bright and fresh with no signs of yellowing or wilting, and make sure they stick straight out instead of hanging limply. Check the white part of the leek—the outer membrane should be pure white with no brown or slimy spots.

Leeks need to be carefully washed because sand and mud have a nasty way of hiding in between the leaves and membranes of the white. To wash leeks, cut off the greens leaving a couple of inches of pale green attached to the white. Use a sharp knife to whittle off the tough outer green membranes from the pale green end of the leek. This reveals that what was green on the outside is really white or very pale green on the inside. To rid leeks of grit, cut the leeks in half lengthwise or, if the leeks must be left whole, only down to an inch above the root end. Hold the leeks under cold running water with the green end facing down (if it's facing up the water will drive grit farther down into the leek) and fold back the membranes, one by one, rubbing between thumb and forefinger to rinse out grit. Trim off the hairy root end exactly where it joins the base of the leek. Don't cut above the bottom or the leek will fall apart (see color photos, opposite page).

Leek Gratin

This is the easiest and best way I know to cook leeks, but if you're on a diet, forget it—the leeks are baked in heavy cream. I admit to a certain glee when showing this dish to my students, their mouths open in horror as I pour over the cream, but once they take a bite they all give up their scruples. This dish is delicious served with roast beef, lamb, or chicken.

Makes 4 side-dish servings

> 6 to 8 medium leeks, all except 2 inches of green removed
> 1 cup heavy cream
> salt and freshly ground black pepper

Preheat the oven to 375°F.

Whittle off the dark green outer layers of the leeks without cutting off the pale green or white layers at the center (see color photo, opposite page). Cut the leeks in half lengthwise and rinse out any sand or grit.

Arrange the leeks, flat side down, in a medium (about 8-cup) oval gratin dish or baking dish just large enough to hold them in a single layer. There's no need to butter the dish since the cream prevents the leeks from sticking. If they don't quite fit, turn some of them on their sides. Pour over the cream and sprinkle with salt and pepper.

Bake the leeks until the cream has thickened and been almost entirely absorbed by the leeks, about 35 minutes. A couple of times during the baking, use a spoon to baste the leeks with the cream and press the leeks down into the cream to prevent those parts not submerged from browning and getting tough. Serve immediately or turn the oven down to 200°F and hold for up to 30 minutes.

a. Cut the greens off the whites, leaving about an inch of green attached to the white.

Cleaning Leeks

b. Cut off the root, exactly where it joins the white.

c. Trim off the outermost green leaves left attached to the white.

d. Cut the whites in half lengthwise. (If you want to leave the whites whole, leave about ½ inch of the root end.)

e. Hold the leek whites under cold running water with the cut side up. Rub each layer between thumb and forefinger to detach any grit.

Leek Gratin

putting meat back
on the dinner table

authors

Bruce Aidells, owner and founder of the Aidells Sausage Company, and food writer Denis Kelly

why they wrote it

"Because of pressures to lower the fat in the American diet, producers have been breeding and raising animals to be leaner. . . . The new meat demands a new approach, and that's our mission in this book: to show you how to prepare today's cuts so that they're tender, juicy, and full of flavor."

why it made our list

Meat has fallen out of fashion in recent years—reviled not only for being too fat but somehow just not politically correct—and we're happy to see it making a comeback. Aidells and Kelly are unapologetically enthusiastic about beef, pork, lamb, and veal, and offer here a wealth of information on every cut there is, how to choose the best of each, and how to prepare it so it's as good as it can possibly be. And lest you think you know everything, the authors offer mythbusting tips with titles like "Basting: A Wasted Effort," and "The Other White Meat Should End Up Slightly Pink!" Informative, comprehensive, fun to read, and packed with good recipes, this cookbook reclaims meat's rightful place at the table.

chapters

Meat Basics • Cooking Today's Meat • Beef: America's Most Popular Meat • Pork: The Most Versatile Meat • Lamb: Ethnic Favorite and Epicure's Delight • Veal: A Tender Delicacy

previous books

Aidells and Kelly are the authors of *Real Beer and Good Eats*, *Hot Links and Country Flavors*, and *Flying Sausages*.

specifics

604 pages, 304 recipes, 16 color photographs, $35. Published by Houghton Mifflin Company.

from the book

"When you cook roasts, stews, and even steaks, there is usually meat left over. But don't think 'leftovers.' Think of this as an opportunity to make an even tastier dish the second time around."

The Complete Meat Cookbook

A Juicy and

Authoritative

Guide to

Selecting,

Seasoning,

and Cooking

Today's Beef,

Pork, Lamb,

and Veal

Bruce Aidells and Denis Kelly

Not-Like-Mom's Meat Loaf

1 ounce dried porcini or
    other mushrooms,
    soaked in boiling water
    for at least 30 minutes
1 cup soft fresh bread
    crumbs
½ cup heavy cream
2 tablespoons olive oil
1 cup finely chopped
    onions
2 garlic cloves, minced
½ pound fresh shiitake,
    porcini, or other wild
    mushrooms, stems
    removed if using
    shiitakes; thinly sliced
2 large eggs, lightly
    beaten
1 tablespoon
    Worcestershire sauce
¼ cup chopped fresh
    parsley
1 teaspoon dried thyme
1 tablespoon kosher salt
1 teaspoon freshly ground
    black pepper
1 pound ground beef
    round (85% lean)
1 pound ground pork
1 pound ground veal
    or turkey
3 slices pancetta, bacon,
    or lean salt pork,
    about ⅛ inch thick

Serves 8, with leftovers
■ GOOD FOR A CROWD ■ GREAT LEFTOVERS

NO DOUBT ABOUT IT, Mom made a great meat loaf, but wild mushrooms give this delicious version flavors she never dreamed of. We like to make plenty, because the leftovers are wonderful in sandwiches. Try cold slices on split baguettes with garlic mayonnaise, sliced red onions, and cornichons. It is excellent served hot with a fresh tomato or marinara sauce. Beaujolais is the perfect wine here, whether you serve the meat loaf hot or cold.

Remove the dried mushrooms from the soaking liquid. If using shiitakes, remove and discard the stems. Chop the mushrooms and set aside. (Save the soaking liquid for use in soups, stews, or pasta sauces.)

In a small bowl, soak the bread crumbs in the cream while you prepare the rest of the ingredients.

Preheat the oven to 350°F. In a large skillet, heat 1 tablespoon of the olive oil over medium heat. Add the onions and sauté until softened, about 5 minutes. Add the garlic and sauté for 2 minutes longer, stirring frequently. Remove the onions and garlic to a large bowl and set aside. Add the remaining 1 tablespoon olive oil to the pan and increase the heat to high. Put in the soaked dried mushrooms along with the fresh mushrooms and sauté, stirring constantly, until the mushrooms release their liquid and it evaporates, about 5 minutes. Add the mushrooms to the onions in the bowl.

Stir in the eggs, Worcestershire sauce, parsley, thyme, salt, and pepper. Mix well, then add the ground meats and soaked bread crumbs with any liquid. Knead gently, using your hands, until everything is well blended. Rinse a large loaf pan (10 by 5 by 4 inches) with cold water and pack the meat into it. Invert the loaf onto a foil-lined baking sheet (with 1-inch sides) or a shallow baking dish or gratin pan and remove the loaf pan. (Or you can form a loaf on the baking sheet or in the pan.)

Place the slices of pancetta, bacon, or salt pork on top of the meat and bake for 1 to 1½ hours, or until the internal temperature is 155°F. Remove the meat loaf from the oven and let it rest, loosely covered with foil, for 10 to 20 minutes before slicing.

Nogales Steak Tacos

Nogales Steak Tacos

Serves 6 to 8
■ COOKING ON A BUDGET (CHUCK STEAKS) ■
■ FIT FOR COMPANY ■ GOOD FOR A CROWD ■

THE STEAKS WE ATE IN NOGALES were most likely chuck steaks cut from the area closest to the prime rib. Look for chuck steaks with a good portion of rib bone and very little of the blade bone—or you can use bone-in rib steaks. The marinade in this recipe will tenderize the somewhat tougher chuck steaks adequately, but it adds flavor to the more tender rib steaks, too. This is also a superb marinade for fajitas made from skirt or flank steak. Chiles and other Mexican ingredients are available in Latino groceries or by mail-order. Begin the recipe the day before you plan to serve it.

———

■ **Flavor Step** ■ Mix all the ingredients in a bowl and whisk together, or put the ingredients into a food processor and pulse briefly. Lay 1 steak in a nonreactive dish. Puncture the meat all over on both sides with a fork or skewer. Pour over half the marinade. Put the other steak on top and repeat the process. Reverse the steaks to make sure that both are well coated with the marinade. Cover with plastic wrap and refrigerate overnight, turning the steaks occasionally to ensure full penetration of the marinade.

About an hour before grilling, remove the steaks from the refrigerator. Soak 6 mesquite wood chunks or 2 cups of mesquite, oak, or hickory chips in water. Fire up a covered charcoal grill with about 60 briquettes or the equivalent of mesquite charcoal. When the coals are completely covered in gray ash and you can hold your hand over them only for a count of two, scatter the mesquite chunks or chips over the coals.

■ **Flavor Step** ■
NOGALES STEAK
MARINADE

6 garlic cloves, mashed with 1 teaspoon kosher salt in a mortar or on a cutting board

¾ cup fresh sour orange juice (from Seville oranges) OR ¼ cup fresh orange juice plus ½ cup fresh lime juice

2 tablespoons tequila (optional)

2 tablespoons ground chiles (ancho or New Mexico)

1 cup chopped fresh cilantro

1 tablespoon chopped fresh oregano or 1½ teaspoons dried

2 teaspoons salt

1 tablespoon coarsely ground black pepper

¼ cup olive or vegetable oil

2 ¾-to-1-inch-thick chuck steaks, cut closest to the prime rib, OR two 1-to-1¼-inch-thick rib steaks (each about 1½ pounds) Salt and freshly ground black pepper

24 corn tortillas, preferably handmade (or the freshest machine-made you can find)

1 pound mild white cheese, such as *queso asadero,* California Monterey Jack, or Wisconsin Muenster or brick, cut into ¼-by-1-by-3-to-4-inch strips

6 fire-roasted pasilla chiles or 10 Anaheim chiles (see below), sliced, OR equivalent canned green chiles, preferably Ortega brand, sliced

GARNISHES

1 cup Lime-Pickled Red Onions (opposite page)
  Guacamole
  Salsas of your choice, such as green chile salsa and salsa cruda

Remove the steaks from the marinade and pat dry with paper towels. Season lightly with salt and pepper. Put the steaks on the grill and cover the kettle immediately. Adjust the vents so that no flare-ups occur. Cook until steaks are done to your liking, 6 to 8 minutes per side for medium-rare to medium (consult the Doneness Chart, page 218). Set the steaks aside on a platter and cover loosely with foil to keep warm while you prepare the tortilla/cheese setups.

Preheat the oven to 300°F. Briefly heat each tortilla over the direct heat of the grill to soften it (or heat each tortilla in a heavy skillet over high heat to soften). Heat the tortillas only enough to make them pliable, so they don't crack when folded over the cheese. Place 2 pieces of cheese on each tortilla and fold in half. Wrap 6 or so folded tortillas in foil, and keep warm in the oven. Repeat the process for all 24 tortillas. It takes about 10 minutes to heat the folded tortillas in the oven and barely melt the cheese—don't keep them in the oven too long or the cheese will ooze out. Pay attention to timing: if you put the tortilla packets in the oven when the steaks are done and let the steaks rest for 10 minutes, that should work out fine. You can leave the tortillas in their foil packets for serving or, if you'd like to be more authentic, wrap them in large cloth napkins or dish towels.

FIRE-ROASTING CHILES OR BELL PEPPERS

CHAR AND BLISTER THE PEPPERS, turning occasionally, over an open flame or under a hot broiler. Put them into a plastic or paper bag for 10 to 15 minutes or so to sweat and loosen the skins. Scrape off the skins and remove the stems and seeds. You can wash the peeled peppers under cold running water if you want, but this can reduce the flavor slightly. Ortega brand canned fire-roasted green chiles are an acceptable substitute for fresh mild chiles.

Be careful when handling hot chiles. Use rubber gloves or wash your hands thoroughly after touching them.

To serve, cut the steaks against the grain into strips 3 to 4 inches long and about ¼ inch thick. Put the bones on a separate platter. Set out the fire-roasted chiles, pickled onions, tortilla/cheese setups, guacamole, and salsas, and encourage your guests to go for it. Pass around the steak bones for true carnivores to gnaw on and toss over their shoulders to the dogs. Beer (preferably Mexican) goes great here, but a spicy Zinfandel would also be delicious.

LIME-PICKLED RED ONIONS
Makes 1 cup

TRY THESE ZESTY ONION SLICES in tacos, burritos, and quesadillas. They're great on sandwiches of all sorts too, from roast beef to grilled Cheddar cheese. You can also use them to liven up grilled fish or chicken breasts.

- 1 large red onion, thinly sliced
- ¼ cup fresh lime juice
- 1 tablespoon olive oil
- ½ teaspoon salt
- 2 tablespoons chopped fresh cilantro
- 1 teaspoon chopped fresh oregano or ½ teaspoon dried

Mix all the ingredients together and let the onion marinate for at least 3 hours at room temperature. The onion will keep for up to 4 days, covered, in the refrigerator.

THE DONENESS CHART

USDA-recommended temperatures reflect the government's concern for safety. It's up to you whether it's more important to enjoy a rare steak or be totally sure the meat is risk free.

VERY RARE

	REMOVE FROM HEAT	IDEAL TEMPERATURE (AFTER RESTING)	USDA RECOMMENDS
Beef steaks/lamb chops	115° to 120°F	115° to 120°F	none
Beef/lamb roasts	110° to 115°F	115° to 125°F	none

Very rare (what the French call *bleu*) should be reserved for beef or lamb. The center of the meat will be soft and the color of raw meat (cherry red for beef, purple red for lamb). The rest of the meat will be bright pink and quite juicy. We find that when large roasts such as prime rib are removed from the oven at 110° to 115°F, they often reach a final temperature of 125°F or more after 20 to 30 minutes of rest and may be considered rare rather than very rare. The internal temperatures of very large roasts (8 pounds or more) that rest for 45 minutes may increase by 15°F.

RARE

	REMOVE FROM HEAT	IDEAL TEMPERATURE (AFTER RESTING)	USDA RECOMMENDS
Beef steaks/lamb chops	120°+ to 130°F	125°+ to 130°F	140°F
Beef/lamb roasts	115°+ to 120°F	125° to 130°F	140°F

Beef and lamb are the only meats cooked to the rare stage (*saignant* in French). The meat will be fairly soft and bright pink to red in the center, not blood-red as in very rare. Some blood-red areas may remain near the bones and in the very center of large roasts. The meat is very juicy.

MEDIUM-RARE

	REMOVE FROM HEAT	IDEAL TEMPERATURE (AFTER RESTING)	USDA RECOMMENDS
Beef steaks/lamb chops/veal chops	130°+ to 135°F	130° to 140°F	150°F
Beef/lamb/veal roasts	125°+ to 130°F	130° to 140°F	150°F

Beef, lamb, and veal can be reliably cooked to this popular degree of doneness. The meat is quite pink in the center with no blood-red areas and has begun to turn grayish around the edges. It is firmer than rare but still quite juicy. Often lamb described as "rare" in restaurants is served at this temperature.

MEDIUM

	REMOVE FROM HEAT	IDEAL TEMPERATURE (AFTER RESTING)	USDA RECOMMENDS
Beef steaks/lamb/veal chops	135°+ to 150°F	140°+ to 150°F	160°F
Beef/lamb/veal roasts	130°+ to 140°F	140° to 150°F	160°F

Meat defined as medium has a wider temperature range (15 degrees) than rare or medium-rare. This doneness is fine for fattier cuts of beef, lamb, or veal, such as cross-rib roast, prime rib, leg of lamb, or rack of veal. The meat will be pink in the center and gray at the periphery, the texture quite firm, the grain compact. Pale veal may need to be cooked to 145° to 155°F to develop its best flavor. Pork is safe to eat at 145° to 150°F, but most cuts need higher temperatures for the best flavor. Pork chops may be eaten in this range, since they risk drying out beyond 155°F.

MEDIUM-WELL

	REMOVE FROM HEAT	IDEAL TEMPERATURE (AFTER RESTING)	USDA RECOMMENDS
Beef steaks/lamb/veal/pork chops less than 1¼ inches	150°+ to 165°F	155° to 165°F	170°F
Beef/lamb/veal/pork roasts/ pork chops 1¼-1½ inches or more	145°+ to 155°F	150° to 165°F	170°F

Beef or lamb should be cooked by moist or very slow heat to this range; otherwise, the meat will be dry. Fatty cuts such as lamb shoulder or beef chuck will still be juicy, however. The meat will usually be uniformly gray, with a pinkish tint near the bones. Pork and milk-fed veal are best cooked to this temperature; the juices may be faintly pink. The meat should still have some juiciness. Pork loin, especially boneless pork loin, should reach a final temperature of 150° to 160°F; remove it from the oven at 145° to 150°F. Thick pork chops (1¼ inches) may be cooked to 145°F and allowed to rest for 5 or 10 minutes for a final temperature of 150°F.

WELL DONE

	REMOVE FROM HEAT	IDEAL TEMPERATURE (AFTER RESTING)	USDA RECOMMENDS
Pork/veal roasts	165°+	170° to 185°F	170°

Meat is overcooked at this stage unless it is fatty and naturally juicy, as are cuts like spareribs or Boston butt. Pork loin or chops will be hard and dry.

hearty and satisfying servings of soup

author

Cookbook writer and *New York Times* contributor Barbara Kafka

why she wrote it

"When I am trying to think what I want to eat, the answer is often soup. It may be as a snack, as an accompaniment for a sandwich, as an opener of a meal, as the main course of a meal, or as an entire meal or party. . . . Sadly, I cannot invite all of you to my house, but I think there is a full array of recipes here for happiness."

why it made our list

A good, hearty soup brings us to the table every time, and this book is full of them. Many are substantial enough to serve as a main course, and the recipes are unfailingly quick and easy. Kafka takes soup seriously, but she's not above taking shortcuts: "I have shocked more than a few purists by starting with commercial broth," she writes. "I consider that sharing the soup is more important than perfection; but I also think that I cheat intelligently. . . . When I don't have the long simmering time for the chicken broth, I disguise and enjoy." Whether you choose to cheat or use Kafka's recipes for homemade stock, the enjoyment part's no trouble at all.

chapters

Family Soups • Vegetable Soups • Bird Soups • The Meat of the Matter • Swimmers in Soup • "Oats, Peas, Beans, and Barley Grow . . . " • The Soul of Soup • From Stock to Soup

previous books

Kafka's books include *Roasting: A Simple Art, Microwave Gourmet,* and *Party Food.*

specifics

480 pages, 298 recipes,
16 color photographs,
16 black-and-white photographs,
$35. Published by Artisan.

from the book

"**Soup is the solvent of memory. For many of us it is love. When I am tired and want comfort, when I want to share happiness, or when I want flavor, my first desire is soup.**"

soup

A WAY OF LIFE

barbara kafka

corn chowder

THIS MAKES A beautiful bowl—red, green, yellow, and white—of late summer's best.

1 pound (450 g) mashing potatoes, peeled and cut into ½-inch (1-cm) dice

1 medium onion, cut into ¼-inch (.5-cm) dice

1 large green bell pepper, cored, seeded, deribbed, and cut into ¼-inch (.5-cm) dice

1 large red bell pepper, cored, seeded, deribbed, and cut into ¼-inch (.5-cm) dice

Kernels from 4 ears corn

4 medium scallions, trimmed and thinly sliced across

2 medium ribs celery, peeled and cut into ¼-inch (.5-cm) dice

1½ cups (375 ml) milk

½ cup (125 ml) heavy cream

2 teaspoons kosher salt

Freshly ground black pepper, to taste

Hot red pepper sauce, to taste

IN A MEDIUM SAUCEPAN, bring the potatoes, onion, peppers, and 1 cup (250 ml) water to a boil. Cover, lower the heat, and simmer for 10 minutes.

Stir in the corn, scallions, celery, milk, and cream. Return to just under a boil. Lower the heat and simmer for 10 minutes, stirring frequently to avoid scorching. Season with the salt, pepper, and hot red pepper sauce.

MAKES ABOUT 8 CUPS (2 L); 8 FIRST-COURSE SERVINGS

winter duck soup

THIS IS A MEAL in a bowl. If there are guests who will not be happy cutting up their duck in the bowl, remove the pieces when the soup is cooked, skin them and cut the meat from the bone, and return to the soup.

One 5-pound (2.25-kg) duck, cut into 14 pieces (see opposite page; back, neck, and wing tips reserved for stock)

1 medium yellow onion, cut into ¼-inch (.5-cm) dice

3 medium cloves garlic, smashed, peeled, and very finely chopped

8 cups (2 l) duck stock, Basic Chicken Stock (page 226), or commercial chicken broth

1 bay leaf

1 large carrot, peeled and cut into ½-inch (l-cm) dice

½ small celery root, trimmed, peeled, and cut into ½-inch (1-cm) cubes

1 small turnip, peeled and cut into ½-inch (1-cm) cubes

¾ pound (360 g) mashing potatoes, peeled and cut into ½-inch (1-cm) dice

1 medium parsnip, peeled and cut into ½-inch (1-cm) dice

1 medium bunch parsley, leaves only, coarsely chopped

1½ tablespoons kosher salt, or less if using commercial broth

Freshly ground black pepper, to taste

IN A LARGE FRYING PAN, starting with the skin-side down, cook the duck pieces over high heat until they are golden in color and have lost their raw look, 7 to 10 minutes per side. Remove from the pan and place in a colander to drain.

Spoon 2 tablespoons of the fat from the pan into a large tall stockpot (reserve the remaining fat for another use). Stir in the onion. Cook for 3 minutes over medium heat. Stir in the garlic and cook for 2 minutes.

Add the stock and bay leaf and bring to a boil. Add the duck, carrot, celery root, and turnip. Return to a boil. Lower the heat and simmer for 15 minutes, skimming off excess fat as needed. The soup can be made ahead up to this point and refrigerated for up to 2 days.

If refrigerated, reheat. Add the potatoes, parsnip, parsley, and salt to the soup. Return to a boil, lower to a simmer, and cook for 15 minutes, or until the duck and vegetables are tender. Season to taste with pepper.

MAKES 12 CUPS (3 L); 6 TO 8 MAIN-COURSE SERVINGS

TO CUT UP A BIRD

Remove the giblet package from the body of the bird. Reserve the neck and gizzards for stock. Save the liver for another use. Work with strong sharp kitchen shears and a large heavy knife. The latter is especially important when cutting the bird into fourteen pieces.

To cut a bird into eight serving pieces: Cut through the skin connecting each leg/thigh to the body of the bird. Separate each leg/thigh from the carcass by pulling it away and down so that the joint becomes loose. Where the thigh meets the carcass, the joint should pop out. Cut through the place where the bone has popped out of the joint. This easily separates the thigh from the carcass.

Lay each leg/thigh piece on the counter skin side down. There will be a diagonal line of visible fat running between the leg and the thigh. Cut along this line to separate the leg from the thigh.

Using the same skin-cutting, bending-back, and popping-out method, separate each wing from the carcass, cutting the wing away through the joint. Cut the wing tips off and reserve for stock.

Tilt the carcass up so that it is propped on the neck opening. Cut down between the back and the breast, leaving the portion of the rib bones not covered by meat attached to the back portion. Cut down along either side of the breastbone to separate the breast into two pieces.

There will be eight serving pieces, plus the back, neck, and wing tips.

To cut a large bird such as a goose or duck into fourteen serving pieces: Cut the bird into eight pieces, as above.

Cut each breast crosswise in half. Do the same with each thigh. Cut through the joint between the remaining wing pieces to make two pieces. Leave the legs whole, or, if desired, cut off the knobby ends.

There will be fourteen serving pieces, plus the back, neck, and wing tips. For more manageable pieces, if the back is being used, it can be cut across into two pieces.

basic chicken stock

ONE OF THE SAD REALITIES of contemporary life is the almost total unavailability of fowls, aged birds of substantial size that are tough but full of flavor and lots of enriching gelatin in the bones. Today's birds are slaughtered young, before they start producing thin-shelled eggs with double yolks. Those of us who are women can sympathize—osteoporosis and lessened fertility.

The live-poultry markets of the past are disappearing. However, Asian markets will often sell chicken feet that can be added to the other bones to enrich the stock. There is very little point in using (wasting) chicken meat to make stock unless the chicken is wanted for the soup or another purpose such as salad. Many supermarkets sell backs and necks, or chicken wings can be used. I keep a plastic bag in the freezer and throw in odds and ends of unused chicken parts—necks and wing tips—until I have enough to make stock. Hearts and gizzards can be used; livers cannot.

As I roast chicken frequently, I break up the carcass after everyone has eaten and add it, along with any gizzards, hearts, and bones from the plates to my bag or to my pot. Stock made with bones from a roast will have a somewhat darker, deeper flavor; I don't bother to roast fresh parts or bones when I get them. I simply cover them with water and proceed as in this recipe.

For Roasted Chicken Stock, use the bones left over from roasting a chicken, cover with water, and simmer until the bones fall apart. The bones from one 5-pound (2.25-kg) chicken will make about 6 cups (1.5 l) stock. Even though the stocks made in the oven and in the slow-cooker cook for more than twice as long as stock made on the stove, the gelling quality and flavor are the same. This is due to the gentle cooking methods, which extract flavor and gelatin at a slower rate.

If it is at all possible, the stock should be refrigerated overnight. The fat will rise to the surface and harden, making it easier to remove. The sediment will settle to the bottom of the stock. To separate the sediment from the bottom of liquid stock, spoon the clear stock from the top, leaving the sediment behind. If the stock has gelled, turn it out of its bowl and scrape off the sediment-laden layer. I tend to eat it.

Any of these stocks needs only seasoning and the vegetable(s) of choice, a starch such as rice or noodles, or an herb—dill is always good with chicken—to be a soup. Dumplings such as matzo balls and filled pastas, wontons included, are other possible add-ins. If using a slow-cooker, use only half the quantities listed.

5 pounds (2.25 kg) chicken backs and necks
12 cups (3 l) water

TO MAKE THE STOCK on top of the stove, in a tall narrow stockpot, bring the bones and water to a boil. Skim the fat. Lower the heat and simmer gently, so bubbles are barely breaking the surface of the liquid, for at least 4 hours and up to 12; add water as needed to keep the bones covered. Skim as necessary to remove as much fat as possible. If the pot is covered with an otoshi-buta (a Japanese wooden lid that fits inside the pot, leaving an inch [2 cm] of space all around) or a lid slightly ajar, there will be less evaporation.

To make the stock in the oven, place a rack on the lowest level of the oven and heat the oven to 250°F (121°C; gas mark #½; #½ British regulo).

In a tall narrow stockpot, bring the bones and water to a boil. Skim the fat. Place in the oven for 4 hours; add water if needed. Remove and skim the fat. Return to the oven for at least 5 hours and up to 8.

To make the stock in a slow-cooker, start with 2½ pounds (1.1 kg) bones and 6 cups (1.5 l) water for a 4-quart (4-l) cooker. Place the bones in the slow-cooker and pour the water over. Cover and turn the heat on low. Cook for 11 to 12 hours.

In all methods, the bones will be falling apart when the stock is done.

Strain the stock through a fine-mesh sieve. Skim fat. Cool to room temperature. Refrigerate for 3 hours.

Remove the fat from the top of the stock and the sediment from the bottom (see opposite page). Use immediately, or refrigerate for up to 3 days or freeze.

MAKES 10 CUPS (2.5 L) ON TOP OF THE STOVE, 8 CUPS (2 L) IN THE OVEN,
6 CUPS (1.5 L) IN A SLOW-COOKER

a celebration of
sizzle and smoke

author

Grill-master Steven Raichlen, the acclaimed food writer, cooking teacher, and syndicated columnist

why he wrote it

"An idea began to take hold of my imagination: to explore how the world's oldest and most universal cooking method varies from country to country, region to region, and culture to culture. To travel the world's barbecue trail—if such a trail existed—and learn how pit masters and grill jockeys solve that age-old problem: how to cook food over live fire without burning it."

why it made our list

It's not your usual steak-and-burger book (though if it's burgers you want, you'll find a fascinating international selection). We were impressed by the array of global grilling traditions Raichlen has assembled here and by the clarity of the information he offers on the basics: the different effects of gas and charcoal grills, how to light and cook on each of them, the advantages of rotisserie cooking. Raichlen asserts that "the bottom line is that I want you to make these recipes." With dishes as interesting and tasty as these, we're happy to oblige.

chapters

A Crash Course on Grilling and Barbecuing • Thirst Quenchers • Warm-ups • Blazing Salads • Grilled Bread • What's Your Beef • High on Hog • A Little Lamb • Ground Meat, Burgers, and Sausages • Bird Meets Grill • Water Meets Fire: Fish on the Grill • Hot Shells: Lobsters, Shrimp, Scallops, and Clams • Vegetables: Greens Meet Grill • Vegetarian Grill • Rice, Beans, and Beyond • Sidekicks: Pickles, Relishes, Salsas, and Slaws • Sauces • Rub It In • Fire and Ice: Desserts

previous books

Among Raichlen's 16 books are *Miami Spice* and the *High-Flavor, Low-Fat Cooking* series.

specifics

576 pages, more than 500 recipes, 19 black-and-white photographs, $18.95. Published by Workman Publishing Company, Inc..

from the book

"Barbecue lends itself to obsession. If you're afflicted with an obsessive personality like me and you start to delve into the world of barbecue, you may soon find all your spare time literally going up in smoke."

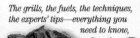

GRILLED GARLIC BREAD FINGERS

U.S.A.

METHOD:
Direct grilling

Barbecue, by its very nature, requires a lot of standing around the grill waiting for foods to cook. But idle time shouldn't be hungry time. These slender bread strips—nice and garlicky—make a perfect munchie while you're waiting for more substantial fare to cook. Cutting the bread into fingers maximizes the surface area, ensuring even crusting and browning on all sides. The lemon zest adds a dimension you won't find in most garlic breads. And because you maximize the surface area, this recipe works well even on supermarket French bread. In the interest of health, I like to brush the bread with olive oil, but you could certainly use the melted butter.

1 loaf French bread (about 20 to
    24 inches long; see Note)
½ cup extra-virgin olive oil or melted
    unsalted butter
4 cloves garlic, minced
1 teaspoon grated lemon zest
¼ cup minced fresh Italian (flat-leaf) parsley
Salt and freshly ground black pepper, to taste

1. Preheat the grill to medium-high.

2. Cut the loaf crosswise into 4 equal pieces. Then cut each piece lengthwise into 4 equal pieces to make 16 "fingers," each 5 to 6 inches long.

3. Heat the oil in a small saucepan over medium-low heat. Add the garlic, lemon zest, and parsley and simmer until the garlic just begins to brown, 3 to 5 minutes. Remove the garlic oil from the heat and season with salt and pepper.

4. When ready to cook, generously brush the bread fingers all over with the garlic oil. Starting crust side down, arrange the fingers on the hot grate and grill, turning with tongs, until nicely browned, 2 to 4 minutes per side. Don't take your eyes off the grill for a second; grilled bread burns very easily. Transfer to a bread basket and serve immediately.

Makes 16 pieces; serves 6 to 8

Note: My favorite bread for this recipe are the soft, puffy "French" or "Italian" loaves sold in the supermarket bread aisle. You can also use a long, crusty bakery-style baguette, but the result will be *very* crusty.

BEER CAN CHICKEN

U.S.A.

METHOD:
Indirect grilling

SPECIAL
EQUIPMENT:
1½ cups
mesquite chips,
soaked in cold
water to cover
for 1 hour and
drained

This odd recipe makes some of the most moist, succulent, flavorful barbecued chicken I've ever tasted. The secret: an open can of beer is inserted into the cavity of the bird, which is cooked upright on the grill. Besides being incredibly tender, the bird makes a great conversation piece. The recipe was inspired by the Bryce Boar Blazers, a barbecue team from Texas I met at the Memphis in May World Championship Barbecue Cooking Contest. The proper beverage? Beer, of course.

1 large whole chicken (4 to 5 pounds)
3 tablespoons Memphis Rub (opposite page)
    or your favorite dry barbecue rub
1 can (12 ounces) beer

1. Remove and discard the fat just inside the body cavities of the chicken. Remove the package of giblets, and set aside for another use. Rinse the chicken, inside and out, under cold running water, then drain and blot dry, inside and out, with paper towels. Sprinkle 1 tablespoon of the rub inside the body and neck cavities, then rub another 1 tablespoon all over the skin of the bird. If you wish, rub another ½ tablespoon of the mixture between the flesh and skin. Cover and refrigerate the chicken while you preheat the grill.

2. Set up the grill for indirect grilling (see page 233), placing a drip pan in the center. *If using a charcoal grill,* preheat it to medium.

If using a gas grill, place all the wood chips in the smoker box and preheat the grill to high; then, when smoke appears, lower the heat to medium.

3. Pop the tab on the beer can. Using a "church key"–style can opener, make 6 or 7 holes in the top of the can. Pour out the top inch of beer, then spoon the remaining dry rub through the holes into the beer. Holding the chicken upright, with the opening of the body cavity down, insert the beer can into the cavity.

4. When ready to cook, if using charcoal, toss half the wood chips on the coals. Oil the grill grate. Stand the chicken up in the center of the hot grate, over the drip pan. Spread out the legs to form a sort of tripod, to support the bird.

5. Cover the grill and cook the chicken until fall-off-the-bone tender, 2 hours. If using charcoal, add 10 to 12 fresh coals per side and the remaining wood chips after 1 hour.

6. Using tongs, lift the bird to a cutting board or platter, holding a large metal spatula underneath the beer can for support. (Have the board or platter right next to the bird to make the move shorter. Be careful not to spill hot beer on yourself.) Let stand for 5 minutes before carving the meat off the upright carcass. (Toss the beer can out along with the carcass.)

Serves 4 to 6

MEMPHIS RUB

I'm not sure where the American version of a spice rub was born, but if I had to guess a birthplace, I'd name Memphis. Memphans make extensive use of rubs—often to the exclusion of mop sauces or barbecue sauces. This rub is especially delicious on smoke-cooked ribs and pork shoulders.

¼ cup paprika
1 tablespoon firmly packed dark
    brown sugar
1 tablespoon granulated sugar
2 teaspoons salt
2 teaspoons Accent (MSG; optional)
1 teaspoon celery salt
1 teaspoon freshly ground black pepper
1 to 3 teaspoons cayenne pepper, or to taste
1 teaspoon dry mustard
1 teaspoon garlic powder
1 teaspoon onion powder

Combine all the ingredients in a jar, twist the lid on airtight, and shake to mix. Store away from heat and light for up to 6 months.

Makes about ½ cup; enough for 4 to 6 racks of ribs

"ONION WATER" LAMB CHOPS
O Be Peyaz

AFGHANISTAN

METHOD:
Direct grilling

ADVANCE
PREPARATION:
2 hours for
marinating
the meat

The Afghan name of this dish—*o be peyaz*—means, literally, "onion water." The lamb chops are marinated in an intensely flavored mixture of onion juice, saffron, turmeric, and chiles. Most Afghan meats are marinated for several days prior to cooking, but these chops can be grilled after a couple of hours. The recipe was inspired by the Khyber Pass restaurant in New York City. The onion juice has a tenderizing and aromatizing effect on the lamb, and it's used throughout the Islamic world. Serve the chops with pita bread and basmati rice.

8 loin lamb chops (each 4 to 5 ounces
    and 1½ inch thick)
¼ teaspoon saffron threads
1 tablespoon warm water
1½ pounds onions, peeled and
    quartered
1 to 3 serranos or other hot chiles,
    minced
1 teaspoon ground turmeric
2 teaspoons salt
1 teaspoon freshly ground black
    pepper

1. Trim most of the excess fat off the lamb chops.

2. Place the saffron in a small bowl and grind it to a fine powder with a pestle or the end of a wooden spoon. Add the warm water, stir, and let stand for 5 minutes.

3. Place the onions in a food processor and process, in batches if necessary, until the onions are puréed and quite watery. Transfer the contents of the workbowl to a fine-meshed strainer and set over a large, deep nonreactive bowl and drain, pressing the solids with the back of a rubber spatula or wooden spoon to extract the juice; you should have about 2 cups. Discard the contents of the strainer.

4. Add the chile, turmeric, salt, pepper, and the dissolved saffron to the onion juice. Whisk until the salt is dissolved. Add the lamb chops and turn to coat thoroughly. Cover and let marinate, in the refrigerator, for 2 hours, turning several times.

5. Preheat the grill to high.

6. When ready to cook, remove the chops from the marinade and blot dry with paper towels. Oil the grill grate, then arrange the chops on the hot grate and grill, turning with tongs, until cooked to taste, about 6 minutes per side for medium.

7. Transfer the chops to serving plates or a platter and serve immediately.
Serves 4

PUTTING IT ALL TOGETHER

As you use the recipes in this book, you'll be instructed to preheat the grill, set it up for direct or indirect cooking, and make various adjustments in the temperature. Here are brief explanations of these instructions.

Preheat the grill to high

If you are using a charcoal grill, light the coals. Rake the hot coals over the bottom of the grill. Open the top and bottom vents wide. Use the 3-second test to determine when the coals are the proper temperature for cooking: Hold your hand about 6 inches above the coals. If you can keep it there for 3 seconds (count "one one-thousand, two one-thousand, three one-thousand") and only 3 seconds, the fire is the right temperature. If you have a thermometer, the surface temperature of the grilling area should be about 500°F. Allow about 30 minutes to bring the coals to the right temperature for cooking.

If you are using a gas grill, set all the burner dials on high. Preheat the grill until the internal temperature is at least 500°F. This will take 10 to 15 minutes.

Preheat the grill to medium-high

For a charcoal grill, light the coals, but rake them out into a thinner layer or let them burn for another 5 to 10 minutes longer than you did for high. You should be able to hold your hand over the fire for 5 seconds.

For a gas grill, preheat to high, then turn the burner dials down to medium-high. The firebox temperature should be about 400°F.

Preheat the grill to medium

For a charcoal grill, light the coals, but rake them out into a yet thinner layer or let them burn for another 5 to 10 minutes longer than you did for medium-high. You should be able to hold your hand over the fire for 7 seconds.

For a gas grill, preheat to high, then turn the burner dials down to medium. The firebox temperature should be about 350°F.

Preheat the grill to medium-low

For a charcoal grill, light the coals, but rake them out into a yet thinner layer or let them burn for 5 to 10 minutes longer than you did for medium. You should be able to hold your hand over the fire for 10 seconds.

For a gas grill, preheat to high, then turn the burner dials down to medium-low. The firebox temperature should be about 325°F.

Preheat the grill to low

For a charcoal grill, light the coals. Rake them out into a very thin layer or let them burn for 15 to 20 minutes longer. You should be able to hold your hand over the coals for 12 seconds.

For a gas grill, preheat to high, then turn the burner dials down to low. The firebox temperature should be about 300°F.

Set the grill up for direct cooking

For a charcoal grill, light the coals. Rake them out directly under the section of the grate where you plan to do the cooking.

For a gas grill, it's best to preheat the whole grill, then turn off the burners you don't need. Gas grills respond almost instantaneously; control the heat by adjusting the gas flow.

Set the grill up for indirect cooking

For a charcoal grill, light the coals. When they are blazing red, use tongs to transfer them to opposite sides of the grill, arranging them in two piles. Let the coals burn until they are covered with a thin layer of gray ash. Set the drip pan in the center of the grill, between the mounds of coals. Place the food on the grate over the drip pan, and cover the grill. You'll need to add about 10 to 12 fresh briquets to each side after an hour of cooking.

For a two-zone gas grill, preheat to high, reduce the heat on one side to medium-high or medium and turn the other side off. Place the food and drip pan (if using—many gas grills have built-in drip pans) on the *off* side. Adjust the gas flow so that the temperature inside the firebox stays around 350°F.

For a three-zone gas grill, set the front and rear (or left and right) burners on medium, leaving the center burner off. Place the food and drip pan in the center. Again, adjust the gas flow so that the temperature inside the firebox stays around 350°F.

casual and carefree as a summer afternoon

authors

Husband-and-wife travel and food writers Cheryl Alters Jamison and Bill Jamison, authorities on American regional cooking

why they wrote it

"Our goal is to capture the rapture of the open sky and the open flame, to celebrate the elemental glories of grilling and the deliciously unpretentious foods that form the roots of the craft. The recipes take a fresh, hearty look at the foods Americans love to cook outdoors, reveling in full grill flavor and the creative fun of working directly with fire."

why it made our list

This book, a tip of the toque to every spatula-wielding outdoor cook, honors all-American grilling. The Jamisons start with a thorough description of different techniques and types of equipment and then proceed to an enormous body of outdoor recipes—hamburgers and hot dogs (of course), lots of kebabs, appetizers, even flame-cooked desserts. Scattered throughout the book are entertaining servings of barbecue trivia, techniques, and traditions. It's all easy, breezy fun, the way cooking outside should be.

chapters

An American Grill Pantry • Happy-Hour Skewers and Spreads • Fired-Up Pizzas and Tortillas • Hot Burgers and Haute Dogs • Serious Steaks • Party-Perfect Pork, Lamb, Veal, and Venison • Fowl Play • Sizzling Fish and Shellfish • Getting Fresh in the Garden • Flame-Kissed Salads, Pastas, and Other Delights • S'mores and More • All-American Accompaniments

previous books

Among the Jamisons' other cookbooks are two volumes on grilling, *Smoke and Spice* and *Sublime Smoke*.

specifics

512 pages, 277 recipes, $27.95. Published by The Harvard Common Press.

from the book

"Covered cooking is almost foolproof, one of the reasons that many grill manufacturers and other authorities recommend the method. You put on food, close the cover, and let the grill do the rest. . . . It's a perfect system if you don't enjoy cooking. Open grilling requires careful control of the fire, which makes it both more challenging and rewarding."

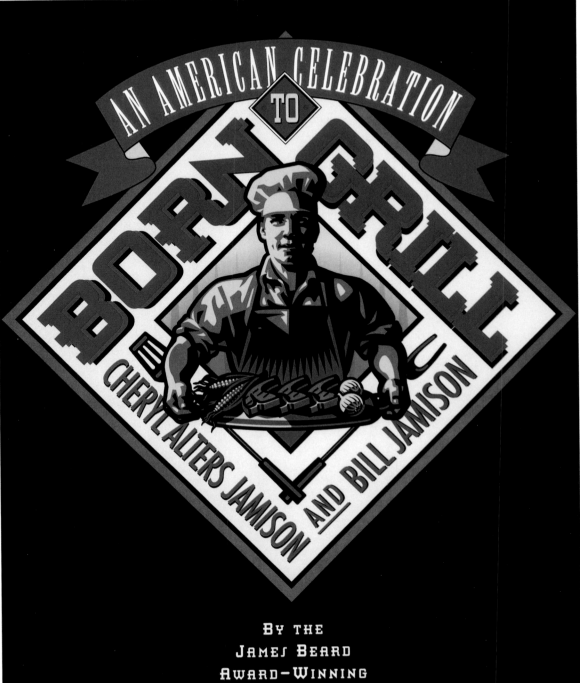

AN AMERICAN CELEBRATION

TO

BORN GRILL

CHERYL ALTERS JAMISON AND BILL JAMISON

BY THE
JAMES BEARD
AWARD-WINNING
AUTHORS

PAELLA MIXED GRILL

This is our favorite special-occasion grill dish, a circus of cooking and a carnival of good eats. For maximum showmanship, do as much of the cooking outside as the size and capability of your grill will allow. We give instructions for cooking the rice on a side burner or kitchen stove, but we prefer to do it on top of the grate if it's easy to vary temperatures on the grill. In either case, grill the seafood, chicken, and sausage at the same time or immediately afterward. However you manage the multiple but simple steps, you'll have the hot-doggers in the crowd salivating with gluttony and envy alike.

SERVES 8 OR MORE
. . . .

PAELLA CHICKEN
2 teaspoons olive oil
1 plump garlic clove, minced
1 teaspoon paprika
1 teaspoon minced fresh thyme or ½ teaspoon dried thyme
¼ teaspoon kosher salt or other coarse salt
Two 6-ounce boneless, skinless individual chicken
    breasts, pounded to ½- to ¾-inch thickness

PAELLA SHRIMP
¾ pound medium shrimp, peeled and, if you wish, deveined
1 teaspoon Mexican hot sauce, such as Cholula, El
    Tapatío, or Búfalo
½ teaspoon olive oil
¼ teaspoon kosher salt or other coarse salt

PAELLA SQUID
½ pound small squid bodies, preferably about 3 inches
    in length, with tentacles separated, cleaned, or
    ½ pound squid steaks
Juice of ½ lemon
1 teaspoon olive oil
¼ teaspoon kosher salt or other coarse salt

. . . . . .

Three 5-ounce to 6-ounce fresh uncooked Italian
    sausages
8 to 12 hard-shell clams, such as cherrystones or
    littlenecks, or mussels, cleaned of grit

¼ cup extra-virgin olive oil
1 medium red onion, diced
1 medium green bell pepper, diced
1 medium red bell pepper, diced
1½ tablespoons minced garlic
3 cups short-grain rice, such as arborio (Italian rice
    for risotto)
1½ teaspoons crumbled saffron threads
6 cups chicken stock, preferably homemade
Kosher salt or other coarse salt
½ cup halved briny green olives
½ cup halved briny black olives
½ cup baby peas, fresh or frozen, or slivered cooked
    artichoke hearts
½ cup minced fresh parsley

- - - - - - - - - - - - - - - - - - -

At least 1 hour and up to 8 hours before you plan to begin cooking, marinate the chicken. In a small bowl, combine the oil, garlic, paprika, thyme, and salt. Rub the paste over the chicken breasts, place them in a plastic bag, and refrigerate. About 1 hour before you plan to begin cooking, combine the shrimp in a small bowl with the hot sauce, oil, and salt, and in another bowl, combine the squid with the lemon juice, oil, and salt. Refrigerate the shrimp and squid.

Fire up the grill for a two-level fire capable of cooking at the same time on both high heat and medium heat. If you want to cook the rice over the grill fire, you'll need a capability for medium-low heat as well.

Remove the chicken, shrimp, and squid from the refrigerator and let them, the sausage, and the clams sit covered at room temperature for 20 to 30 minutes while you prepare the rice.

In a 12- to 14-inch heavy skillet or paella pan, warm the oil over medium heat. Add the onion, peppers, and garlic and sauté several minutes until softened. Stir in the rice and continue cooking until translucent but not brown, about 4 to 5 minutes. Mix the saffron into the stock and pour the stock over the rice. Add salt to taste. Cook the rice over medium-low heat uncovered, without stirring, until the liquid is absorbed, 15 to 20 minutes. Late in the cooking, insert a spoon or spatula to the bottom of the rice in

several spots, without stirring, to make sure the rice is cooking evenly. Shift the position of the pan over the heat if it is getting more done on the bottom in one area than elsewhere. When done, the perfect paella rice is moist throughout but has just a little crust on the bottom and side portions.

Remove the pan from the heat and scatter the olives, peas or artichokes, and parsley over the rice. Cover it immediately with foil and keep warm in a very low oven or on a corner of the grill.

Transfer the shrimp, squid, sausage, and clams to the grill, placing them over high heat, and add the chicken over medium heat. Grill the shrimp and squid for 3 to 4 minutes, turning once. The squid tentacles will be done about a minute sooner than the bodies. When done, the shrimp should be just opaque with lightly charred edges and the squid should feel firm yet tender. Remove them from the heat and cover with foil. Cook the clams until they pop open wide, about 8 to 10 minutes, and cover them too. Discard any clams that don't

open within a couple of minutes of the others.

Grill the sausages on high for 3 to 4 minutes, rolling them to sear evenly, and then move them to medium heat and continue cooking for an additional 15 minutes or until cooked through. Cook the chicken over medium heat for 10 to 12 minutes, turning once, until opaque throughout but still juicy.

Slice the squid and sausages into rings and the chicken into bite-size pieces. Stir all the grilled ingredients into the rice and serve immediately.

TECHNIQUE TIP: Though our paella is an Americanized amalgam of ingredients, it's true to its Spanish roots in cooking the rice over an open fire in an open pan. To maintain that spirit, and provide full attention to the multiple ingredients on the grill, we don't recommend cooking the paella (either the rice or the grilled toppings) covered. If you enjoy the dish and want to do it often, consider investing in a proper paella pan; The Spanish Table in Seattle (206-682-2827) carries an astonishing range of sizes and varieties.

GRILLED BANANA SPLIT WITH CHOCOLATE-TOFFEE MELT

Save this fruit fantasy for a special party, perhaps a birthday, the Fourth of July, or just the next available Saturday. Warming the bananas on the grill mellows their taste and softens their texture, making them as meltingly luscious as the ice cream and the toffee candy sauce.

· · · · · · · · · · · · · · · · · · ·

1 cup sugar
⅛ cup half-and-half
6 tablespoons butter
6 medium bananas
Three 1.4-ounce Heath Bars or 4 to 5 ounces chocolate-
    covered toffee, chopped into chunks
6 large scoops each of two kinds of ice cream, such as
    vanilla, butter pecan, praline, chocolate, or banana
Whipped cream

Toasted almonds, for garnish

· · · · · · · · · · · · · · · · · · ·

Fire up the grill, bringing the temperature to medium.

Combine the sugar and half-and-half in a heavy medium saucepan. Bring the mixture to a full rolling boil, stirring occasionally. Stir in the butter and remove from the heat.

Just before grilling, slice the bananas, still in their skins, lengthwise.

Transfer the bananas cut-side down to a well-oiled grate. Grill the bananas uncovered over medium heat for 3 to 4 minutes. Turn the bananas skin-side down, brush their cut surfaces with a few teaspoons of the sugar–half-and-half mixture, and grill them for 2 to 3 additional minutes, until soft and lightly colored. If grilling covered, cook for the same amount of time, turning once midway and basting then.

Remove the bananas from their skins. If you own long banana split dishes, leave the banana halves whole and place two of them in each dish. If not, cut the bananas into bite-size chunks and divide them among individual serving dishes.

Return the sugar–half-and-half mixture to medium-low heat and stir in the toffee chunks. Cook briefly until the chocolate and toffee have partially melted (leaving some chunkiness) and stir well. Top each dish of banana with one scoop of each ice cream and some of the chocolate-toffee melt. Add whipped cream, top with almonds, and serve immediately.

TECHNIQUE TIP: Banana split dishes seem to be making a retro comeback everywhere from flea markets to chic cookware stores. Williams-Sonoma (800-541-2233) sells them by mail order.

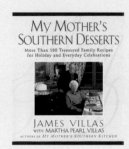

category **5**

desserts

After a dearth last year, a wealth of dessert books surfaced this time around. And half of our chosen batch are from professional pastry chefs who work in famous restaurants or important shops—clear evidence that the celebrity-chef phenomenon has expanded to include those on the sweet side of the kitchen. For further proof, you have only to take a look at the television-chef lineup. Paragon of pastry Pierre Hermé, for instance, has his own show in France, while Jacques Torres displays his wizardry on a series here in America. Luscious desserts abound in this group of books, which made our choice of best recipes more difficult than in any other category. We just had to keep tasting and tasting and tasting. It's a tough job, but someone's got to do it.

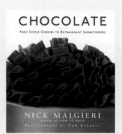

elegant, enchanting desserts, the pride of the south

author

James Villas, the food and wine editor at *Town & Country* magazine, writing with his original cooking teacher—his mother, Martha Pearl Villas

why he wrote it

Preserving this "aspect of our Southern culinary heritage" is crucial. "Which, of course, is the reason I decided to write this book under the steady guidance, ardent supervision, and suspicious eye of Mother every step of the way."

why it made our list

Talk about irresistible desserts: When we tested and tasted these goodies in our FOOD & WINE kitchen, a line formed to polish off every last crumb! Looking through this impressive collection of beloved family recipes, it's difficult to find one that's not appealing. There's something delightful about them and about the anecdotes of growing up with a Southern mama that Villas scatters liberally throughout. In true Southern tradition, there's a dessert here for any possible occasion—birth, death, and everything in between. But a sweet tooth is the only excuse you'll need to try them all.

chapters

Christmas and New Year's • Valentine's Day, St. Patrick's Day, and Kentucky Derby • Mother's Day and Easter • Memorial Day and Father's Day • July Fourth and Labor Day • Halloween, Election Day, and Thanksgiving • Birthdays and Christenings • Weddings and Graduations • Bereavements and Shut-Ins • Picnics and Cookouts • Bridge Luncheons, Book Clubs, and Charity Socials • Cocktail Parties and Formal Dinners • Morning Coffees, Afternoon Teas, and Weekend Brunches • Ice Cream Socials • Friendship Gifts • Dessert Basics: Cakes, Pastry Shells, Frostings, and Sauces

previous books

Mother and son also collaborated on *My Mother's Southern Kitchen*; James Villas's solo endeavors include *Stews, Bogs, and Burgoos*, a *Best of the Best* honoree last year.

specifics

287 pages, 182 recipes, 16 color photographs, $25. Published by William Morrow and Company, Inc.

from the book

"**If there is a tendency in some parts these days to reduce desserts at formal home dinners to flourless cakes, herb sorbets, and anemic berry 'soups,' rest assured that no such trend will ever find its way to the table of Martha Pearl Villas.**"

MY MOTHER'S
SOUTHERN DESSERTS

More Than 180 Treasured Family Recipes
for Holiday and Everyday Celebrations

JAMES VILLAS
WITH MARTHA PEARL VILLAS

AUTHORS OF *MY MOTHER'S SOUTHERN KITCHEN*

most delectable sweet recipe

Snowflake Coconut Cake with Seven-Minute Frosting

SNOWFLAKE COCONUT CAKE WITH SEVEN-MINUTE FROSTING

Like her mother and grandmother, Mother still saves any extra milk drained from fresh coconuts just so she can make this wondrous, moist cake that graces the table after babies of relatives and friends have been christened—served ceremoniously, of course, with small glasses of chilled sweet white wine. Just the mention of ordinary coconut cakes made with canned flaked coconut and frosted with a heavy, overly sweet, innocuous white icing makes Mother cringe. "They're dry as a bone, tasteless, just awful," she says with a scowl, "so if you're not willing to deal with fresh coconut and produce a nice, light frosting in a double boiler, you'd be better off making another cake." And that's that!

1 medium-size coconut
2¼ cups granulated sugar
3 cups cake flour
2 teaspoons baking powder
1 cup (2 sticks) butter, softened
1 cup milk
1 teaspoon pure vanilla extract
6 large egg whites
Seven-Minute Frosting (page 246)

Pierce the eyes of the coconut with an ice pick or small screwdriver, strain the milk into a container, add enough water to measure 1 cup, and pour into a small saucepan. Add ¼ cup of the sugar, bring to a boil over moderate heat, stirring, and set aside to cool. Crack the coconut with a hammer and remove the meat from the shell. Trim off the brown skin with a sharp paring knife and discard, grate the coconut onto a plate, and set aside.

Preheat the oven to 350°F. Grease and flour three 8-inch round cake pans, tapping out any excess flour, and set aside.

In a medium-size mixing bowl, combine the flour and baking powder and mix well. In a large mixing bowl, cream the butter and the remaining 2 cups sugar together with an electric mixer till light and fluffy. Beat the dry mixture alternately with the milk and vanilla into the creamed mixture till well blended, ending with the dry mixture.

Wash and dry the mixer beaters, then, in another large mixing bowl, beat the egg whites till stiff but not dry peaks form. With a rubber spatula, gently fold them into the creamed mixture. Scrape the batter evenly into the prepared pans and bake till a cake tester or straw inserted in the center comes out clean, about 30 minutes. Cool the cakes in the pans for about 10 minutes, then turn them out onto a wire rack to cool completely.

Place a cake layer on a cake plate, drizzle about one quarter of the coconut milk mixture over the top, spread about ¾ cup of the frosting over the top, and sprinkle about one quarter of the grated coconut over the frosting. Repeat with the second layer, then top with the third and spread the remaining frosting over the top and around the sides of the cake and press the remaining grated coconut into the top and sides. Drizzle the remaining coconut milk over the top, cover the cake with plastic wrap, and chill for at least 24 hours before serving.

YIELD One 3-layer 8-inch cake; 10 to 12 servings

 *Martha's Sweet Note*

If batter scraped into a baking pan seems uneven and I want a perfectly even cake layer, I gently "spank" the bottom for even distribution and to minimize any bubbles that have formed.

SEVEN-MINUTE FROSTING

This feathery-white vanilla frosting was conceived to complement Mother's inimitable Snowflake Coconut Cake (page 245). The frosting is really very elemental, so experiment with it on any number of your favorite cakes.

5 large egg whites
2½ cups granulated sugar
½ cup water
½ teaspoon pure vanilla extract

In the top of a double boiler, combine the egg whites, sugar, and water and beat slowly with an electric mixer till well blended. Over boiling water, beat the mixture briskly till stiff peaks form, about 7 minutes. Remove the pan from the heat and beat in the vanilla. Continue beating till the frosting is thick and smooth, then use immediately.

YIELD About 3 cups frosting; enough for the top and sides of a 3-layer 9- or 10-inch cake

SOUR CREAM COFFEE CAKE

*T*his, in Mother's opinion, is the queen of all coffee cakes and the one that usually joins company with the Champagne punch, egg, sausage, and grits casserole, country ham biscuits, fried green tomatoes, fresh fruit compote, and strawberry preserves at one of her more elaborate Sunday brunches. It's not the easiest coffee cake to make, but if you love fresh coffee cake, you'll remember this one for a long time. Best of all, it freezes beautifully and can be reheated in a matter of ten to fifteen minutes.

3 cups all-purpose flour
1½ teaspoons baking powder
1½ teaspoons baking soda
¼ teaspoon salt
1½ cups (3 sticks) butter, softened
1½ cups granulated sugar
2½ teaspoons pure vanilla extract, plus 2 tablespoons pure vanilla extract combined with 2 tablespoons water
3 large eggs
1½ cups sour cream
¾ cup chopped walnuts
¾ cup firmly packed dark brown sugar
1½ teaspoons ground cinnamon
Confectioners' sugar for dusting

*P*reheat the oven to 350°F. Generously grease a 10-inch Bundt or tube pan and set aside.

*I*n a medium-size mixing bowl, combine the flour, baking powder, baking soda, and salt, mix till well blended, and set aside. In a large mixing bowl, cream the butter and granulated sugar together with an electric mixer till light and fluffy, then add the 2½ teaspoons vanilla and the eggs, beating well after each addition. Gradually beat in the sour cream, then add the flour mixture and beat till the mixture is well blended. In a small bowl, combine the walnuts, brown sugar, and cinnamon and mix well.

*S*poon one third of the batter into the prepared pan and sprinkle half of the nut mixture over the surface, taking care not to sprinkle all the way to the edges of the pan (which could cause the cake to break when turned out). Repeat with the second third of the batter and the remaining nut mixture, and top with the remaining batter. Spoon the vanilla-water mixture evenly over the top and bake the cake in the center of the oven for 30 minutes. Reduce the heat to 325°F and continue baking till the cake feels quite firm and a cake tester or straw inserted in the center comes out clean, about 45 minutes. Cool the coffee cake on a wire rack for 10 minutes before loosening the edges with a knife and turning it out onto a serving plate. Let cool completely and dust with confectioners' sugar just before serving in wedges.

YIELD One 10-inch Bundt or tube cake; 10 to 12 servings

CHOCOLATE PECAN PIE

When it was noticed that my nephew, Charles Royal, wouldn't touch Mother's sacred Southern pecan pie when he was a child, she modified the recipe by deleting the corn syrup and adding chocolate, only to realize that she'd created a pie with an altogether different flavor and texture. To this day, Mother still makes this pie for Charles's birthday, and I must grudgingly admit that once you've tasted this creamy chocolate version, the regular classic leaves a little something to be desired. "I've learned that lots of children won't eat plain nut desserts," Mother explains, "but add a little chocolate—to cakes, pies, cookies—and they gobble them up."

⅔ cup evaporated milk
2 tablespoons butter
One 6-ounce bag (1 cup) semisweet chocolate chips
2 large eggs, beaten
1 cup granulated sugar
2 tablespoons all-purpose flour
¼ teaspoon salt
1 teaspoon pure vanilla extract
1 cup chopped pecans
1 unbaked 9-inch Basic Pie Shell (opposite page)

Preheat the oven to 375°F.

In a small saucepan, combine the evaporated milk, butter, and chocolate, stir constantly over low heat till the chocolate melts completely, and remove the pan from the heat.

In a large mixing bowl, combine the eggs, sugar, flour, salt, vanilla, and pecans and stir till well blended. Add the chocolate mixture and stir well, then scrape into the pie shell. Bake the pie just till the filling is soft in the center when the pie is gently shaken, 40 to 45 minutes. Cool the pie completely on a wire rack.

YIELD One 9-inch pie; 6 to 8 servings

BASIC PIE OR TART SHELL

1½ cups all-purpose flour
½ teaspoon salt
½ cup Crisco shortening
4 to 5 tablespoons ice water

*I*n a large mixing bowl, combine the flour and salt, then cut in the shortening with a pastry cutter or two knives till the mixture resembles coarse meal. Stirring with a wooden spoon, gradually add the water till a ball of dough is formed. Wrap the dough in plastic wrap and chill till ready to use.

*T*o bake the pie or tart shell, preheat the oven to 425°F, grease a 9- or 10-inch pie plate or tart pan, and set aside.

*P*lace the chilled dough on a lightly floured surface and roll it out from the center (not to and fro) with a lightly floured rolling pin to a ⅛-inch thickness. Carefully fold the pastry in half, lay the fold across the center of the prepared plate or pan, unfold it, and press it loosely into the bottom and sides of the plate or pan. Prick the bottom and sides with a fork, trim and crimp the edges, place on a heavy baking sheet, and bake till the shell browns evenly, 12 to 15 minutes. Allow the shell to cool completely on a wire rack.

(Note: For pies calling for either a double or lattice crust, use 2 cups all-purpose flour, 1 teaspoon salt, ⅔ cup Crisco shortening, and 5 to 7 tablespoons ice water.)

YIELD One 9- or 10-inch pie or tart shell

SPICY PIE SHELL *Decrease the salt to ¼ teaspoon and add ½ teaspoon each ground cinnamon and nutmeg. Mother uses this shell to add flair to fillings that tend to be a bit bland. Try it for pumpkin pies, sweet potato pies, apple pies, or any pear tart.*

a book to make
chocolate lovers swoon

author

Dessert authority Nick Malgieri, director of the baking department at Peter Kump's Cooking School in New York City

why he wrote it

To share a lifelong passion for collecting chocolate recipes. "My quest for additions to my collection has taken me from southern France to British Columbia—it's never too long a trip if there is chocolate at the end of it. . . . I have taught innumerable classes in making chocolates and chocolate desserts, and although my previous books have all had a goodly amount of chocolate desserts in them, this is my first all-chocolate book. I hope you enjoy using it as much as I have enjoyed writing it."

why it made our list

Chocolate lovers—and we count ourselves among them—will swoon over the delectable recipes and luscious photos that fill this book. There's something here to cater to every kind of craving: chocolate cookies, chocolate cakes, chocolate puddings and pies, sauces and soufflés, ice cream, confections, even chocolate beverages. As with his earlier books, Malgieri's recipes are clearly written; whether the result is a quick chocolate fix or an elaborate showpiece, the instructions are complete and easy to follow. How sweet it is!

chapters

Chocolate Basics • Cakes • Cookies • Creams, Mousses, Custards, and Soufflés • Ices and Frozen Desserts • Pies, Tarts, and Other Pastries • Chocolate Confections • Sauces and Beverages • Decorating Desserts with Chocolate • Showpieces and Decorating Projects

previous books

Malgieri also served up great desserts in *How to Bake*, *Nick Malgieri's Perfect Pastry*, and *Great Italian Desserts*.

specifics

478 pages, 255 recipes and "projects," 95 color photographs, $40.
Published by HarperCollins Publishers, Inc.

from the book

"The first truffles were made from the scraps left over from cutting dipped chocolates into uniform shapes. At the end of the day, all the scraps would be combined, placed in a mixer, and beaten. The result was piped out into small irregular balls, chilled, roughly coated with tempered chocolate, and rolled in cocoa, so they looked like Périgord truffles covered with earth."

CHOCOLATE

FROM SIMPLE COOKIES TO EXTRAVAGANT SHOWSTOPPERS

NICK MALGIERI
Author of HOW TO BAKE
PHOTOGRAPHS BY TOM ECKERLE

SUPERNATURAL BROWNIES

■ ■ ■

Makes about twenty-four
2-inch-square brownies

16 tablespoons (2 sticks) unsalted
   butter

8 ounces bittersweet or semisweet
   chocolate, cut into ¼-inch pieces

4 large eggs

½ teaspoon salt

1 cup granulated sugar

1 cup firmly packed dark brown
   sugar

2 teaspoons vanilla extract

1 cup all-purpose flour

One 13 × 9 × 2-inch pan, buttered
   and lined with buttered
   parchment or foil

Though the name sounds an exaggeration, you'll agree that these brownies are absolutely out of this world.

1. Set a rack at the middle level of the oven and preheat to 350 degrees.

2. Bring a saucepan of water to a boil and turn off heat. Combine butter and chocolate in a heatproof bowl and set over pan of water. Stir occasionally until melted.

3. Whisk eggs together in a large bowl, then whisk in salt, sugars, and vanilla. Stir in chocolate and butter mixture, then fold in flour.

4. Pour batter into prepared pan and spread evenly. Bake for about 45 minutes, until top has formed a shiny crust and batter is moderately firm. Cool in pan on a rack. Wrap pan in plastic wrap and keep at room temperature or refrigerated until next day.

5. To cut brownies, unmold onto a cutting board, remove paper, and replace with another cutting board. Turn cake right side up and trim away edges. Cut brownies into 2-inch squares.

SERVING: Serve the brownies on their own or with ice cream and hot fudge sauce.

STORAGE: The best way to store brownies is to wrap them individually and keep them at room temperature in a tin or plastic container with a tight-fitting cover. Or freeze them.

NOTE: If you have a 12 × 18-inch commercial half-sheet pan, you may double this recipe easily.

VARIATION

Add 2 cups (½ pound) walnut or pecan pieces to the batter.

SWISS CHOCOLATE SANDWICH COOKIES

• • •

Makes about 18 sandwich cookies

CHOCOLATE COOKIE DOUGH

12 tablespoons (1½ sticks) unsalted butter, softened

4 ounces semisweet chocolate, melted and cooled

1¾ cups all-purpose flour

GANACHE FILLING

⅓ cup heavy whipping cream

1 tablespoon unsalted butter

1 tablespoon light corn syrup

2 ounces bittersweet chocolate, cut into ¼-inch pieces

2 ounces milk chocolate, cut into ¼-inch pieces

FINISHING

Confectioners' sugar

2 cookie sheets or jelly-roll pans lined with parchment or foil

This recipe is adapted from that great work *Swiss Baking and Confectionery* by Walter Bachmann, a Swiss pastry chef who lived in London after the Second World War.

1. To make the dough, beat the butter by hand in a medium bowl just until it is evenly softened. Quickly beat in the melted chocolate, then the flour. Continue to mix until dough is smooth.

2. Scrape the dough out onto a piece of plastic wrap and press it into a rectangle about ½ inch thick. Wrap and chill the dough until it is firm—about an hour.

3. While the dough is chilling, make the filling. Combine the cream, butter, and corn syrup in a saucepan and bring to a boil over low heat. Remove from heat and add both chocolates. Shake the pan gently to submerge chocolate in the hot liquid. Let stand 5 minutes, then whisk smooth and scrape filling into a bowl. Let stand at room temperature or in the refrigerator until of spreading consistency.

4. To bake the cookie bases, set racks in the upper and lower thirds of the oven and preheat to 350 degrees.

5. If the dough is very hard, pound it gently with the rolling pin to soften it so that it rolls out more easily. Divide dough in half and, on a floured surface, roll one half about 3/16 inch thick. Use a fluted, round 2-inch cutter to cut the dough into cookies. Place them on prepared pans as they are cut, leaving about an inch between the cookies. Repeat with remaining dough. Save all the scraps. Reroll scraps and cut more cookies.

6. Bake the cookies 12 to 15 minutes, until they are firm and slightly colored. Cool the cookies in the pans on racks.

7. When cookies and filling have cooled, arrange half the cookies, flat side up. Place a dab of filling on them and cover with the remaining cookies, flat sides together. Dust cookies very lightly with confectioners' sugar before serving.

LEMON-SCENTED WHITE CAKE WITH MILK CHOCOLATE FROSTING

• • •

Makes one 9-inch 2-layer cake,
about 12 servings

LEMONY WHITE CAKE

2¼ cups cake flour

3 teaspoons baking powder

½ teaspoon salt

8 tablespoons (1 stick) unsalted
butter, softened

1½ cups sugar

2 teaspoons finely grated lemon zest

½ teaspoon lemon extract

½ cup egg whites (from about 4
large eggs)

1¼ cups milk

MILK CHOCOLATE GANACHE

Zest of 2 lemons removed in long
strips with a vegetable peeler

2 cups heavy whipping cream

4 tablespoons (½ stick) unsalted
butter, softened

20 ounces milk chocolate, cut into
¼-inch pieces

4 ounces bittersweet chocolate, cut
into ¼-inch pieces

Two 9-inch round pans, 1½ to 2
inches deep, buttered and lined
with buttered parchment or wax
paper

The unusual flavoring for this cake is lemon zest. It is used in both the light, moist cake and the milk chocolate ganache and it delicately perfumes and complements both. It works because the lemon zest, which is rich in the essential oil of lemon, transmits a lemon perfume without any of the acidity of lemon juice, which would mar the chocolate flavor.

1. Set a rack at the middle level of the oven and preheat to 350 degrees.

2. Sift the cake flour, baking powder, and salt onto a piece of parchment or wax paper and set aside.

3. Use an electric mixer set at medium speed to beat the butter and sugar until light, about 3 minutes. Beat in the lemon zest and extract.

4. In a bowl, whisk together the egg whites and milk.

5. Add a third of the flour mixture to the butter and sugar mixture and beat until smooth. Scrape down bowl and beater(s). Beat in half the milk and egg white mixture until incorporated, then beat in another third of the flour mixture. Scrape bowl and beater(s). Beat in remaining liquid until absorbed, followed by remaining flour mixture. Scrape well after each addition.

6. Divide batter between prepared pans and smooth tops evenly. Bake for about 30 to 35 minutes, until well risen and a toothpick inserted in the center emerges clean. Cool layers in pans for 5 minutes, then invert to racks to cool. Peel off paper. If prepared in advance, double-wrap layers in plastic wrap and chill for up to several days or freeze.

7. To make the ganache, place the pieces of zest in a saucepan and add the cream. Place over low heat and bring to a simmer. Remove from heat and allow to steep about 5 minutes. Remove zests from cream with a slotted spoon and discard them. Add butter to the cream and bring to a boil over low heat. Remove from heat and add chocolates. Shake pan to submerge chocolate and allow to stand 5 minutes. Whisk smooth, then cool to room temperature. Ganache will thicken to spreading consistency.

8. To finish, put one layer right side up on a platter or cardboard. Place ganache in mixer bowl and beat until light, about 20 seconds. Using an offset spatula, spread the layer with a little more than a third of the ganache. Place the other cake layer upside down on the ganache, so that the smooth bottom of the cake layer is uppermost. Spread the top and sides of the cake evenly with most of the remaining ganache.

SERVING: This rich cake needs no accompaniment.

STORAGE: Keep the cake at a cool room temperature before serving. Keep leftovers under a cake dome at a cool room temperature or covered with plastic wrap in the refrigerator.

beautiful desserts,
one step at a time

author

Pastry pro Jacques Torres, executive pastry chef of Le Cirque 2000 and Dean of Pastry Arts at the French Culinary Institute, both in New York City

why he wrote it

"Pastry is really very logical. Once you learn the basic building blocks, you can use them to create simple designs or spectacular creations. With this book, I hope to demystify pastry and encourage you to develop your own creations."

why it made our list

No need to wonder which of the pastries in this book is right for your level of skill. Each one is rated, on a scale of one diamond—recipes an inexperienced cook can prepare easily—to three diamonds—recipes an inexperienced cook might like to look at pictures of. No, actually, Torres believes that, by learning the basics and then slowly working up to more ambitious projects, anyone can make the dazzling three-diamond desserts that are his signature dishes at Le Cirque 2000. We're not so sure, but practicing would certainly be delicious fun.

chapters

Getting Started: Equipment, Ingredients, and Terms • The Basics • Pastries and Puff Pastries • Cookies and Petit Fours • I Love Chocolate • Crème de la Crème • Fruity Delights • Signature Desserts • Frozen Finales • For the Truly Adventurous

other books

Torres is a coauthor of another of this year's *Best of the Best* honorees, *The French Culinary Institute's Salute to Healthy Cooking* (page 158).

specifics

352 pages, 91 recipes, 83 color photographs, 115 black-and-white photographs, $28. Published by William Morrow and Company, Inc.

from the book

"Sometimes it can be more interesting to make a fruit tart than an elaborate dessert. In a simple recipe, each flavor and technique is transparent, meaning that there is nothing to hide behind, so you work harder to enhance the recipe and develop all of the flavors."

JACQUES TORRES

Dessert Circus

Extraordinary

Desserts You Can Make at Home

Companion to the National Public Television Series

Chocolate Fondants

14 FONDANTS

*T*his is one of the most requested desserts at Le Cirque. Once you have tasted it, you will know why it is a chocolate lover's fantasy. Although it is often compared to a flourless chocolate cake, it really is a cross between a chocolate mousse and a chocolate soufflé. To make them even more decadent, I cover the baked Fondants with chocolate sauce and decorate them with candied orange or grapefruit peels. Since the peels and sauce take a while to make, you may want to prepare them a day in advance.

It is very important to use the best-quality chocolate for this recipe. I like to use Callebaut from Belgium. Fondants can be prepared in about thirty minutes. Make a double batch and keep half of them in the freezer for a tasty last-minute treat.

For the Fondants

Unsalted butter, cubed	1 cup + 2½ tablespoons	9.4 ounces	260 grams
Bittersweet chocolate, chopped		17.7 ounces	500 grams
Unsweetened Dutch-processed cocoa powder	⅓ cup + 1½ tablespoons	1.6 ounces	50 grams
Pinch of salt			
8 large egg whites			
Meringue powder (optional)	⅓ cup	1 ounce	25 grams
Granulated sugar	½ cup	3.5 ounces	100 grams

For the garnish

Heavy cream, whipped to stiff peaks	Scant 1 cup	8 ounces	220 grams
Candied orange or grapefruit peels (page 261)			
Chocolate Sauce (page 263)			

Preheat the oven to 400°F (200°C). Use a pastry brush to evenly coat the inside of 14 individual 3-ounce molds (I use disposable aluminum molds) with softened butter. Fill each mold with granulated sugar; then pour out the excess. If you have properly

buttered the molds, the sugar will stick to the sides and bottoms of them. The butter and sugar will keep the Fondants from sticking to the sides of the molds and allow them to rise evenly. The sugar will also give the Fondants a crunchy crust, which I think makes a great contrast to the soft interior. It will be easier to move the molds in and out of the oven if you place them on a baking sheet.

Prepare the Fondants: Melt the butter in a 2-quart heavy-bottomed saucepan over medium-high heat. Remove from the heat. Add the chopped chocolate, cocoa powder, and salt and stir until well combined and all the chocolate has melted. The cocoa powder and salt accentuate the taste of the chocolate.

continued

Place the egg whites in a large mixing bowl and whip with an electric mixer on medium speed until foamy. If using the meringue powder, combine it with the sugar in a small bowl. The meringue powder contains a high quantity of albumin, which will add strength and allow for a stiffer meringue. Increase the mixer speed to medium-high and make a French meringue by adding the sugar mixture, or the sugar, 1 tablespoon at a time and whipping the egg whites to stiff but not dry peaks.

Gently but quickly fold the warm chocolate mixture into the meringue until combined. Be careful not to deflate the mixture, or your baked Fondants will be flat and heavy. The mixture should be homogenous in color. However, if you can still see streaks of meringue in it, that's okay.

Place the batter in a large pastry bag with a large opening (no tip). The pastry bag will be easier to handle if you fill it only half full; you will probably need to refill the bag two or three times to use all of the batter. Pipe the molds three quarters full with batter. (At this stage, the molded Fondants can be stored in the freezer for up to 2 weeks, well wrapped in plastic wrap. Thaw in the refrigerator for 2 hours before baking.)

Bake the Fondants until they have risen about $1/2$ inch over the top of the mold, 7 to 10 minutes.

Meanwhile, place the whipped cream in a pastry bag fitted with a star tip and pipe rosettes onto each serving plate. Garnish with candied orange or grapefruit peels. Remove the Fondants from the oven and immediately invert each one over the center of a plate. Lightly tap the bottom and shake slightly to allow the Fondant to gently drop from the mold. Cover the Fondants with the chocolate sauce and serve. When you cut into the Fondant, the center should still be somewhat liquid.

Variation: Sometimes I like to make an orange sauce to accompany the Fondants. Combine 2 cups (16 ounces; 458 grams) orange juice, a scant $1/2$ cup (2.5 ounces; 75 grams) Sure-Jell, and $3/4$ cup (5.3 ounces; 150 grams) granulated sugar in a nonreactive 1-quart heavy-bottomed saucepan and bring to a boil over medium heat. Cook until the mixture has reduced about one third in volume. Place in an ice bath to cool. This will make $1\frac{1}{2}$ to 2 cups sauce.

Candied Grapefruit Peels

ABOUT 180 PIECES

*I*f you eat a lot of grapefruit and have ever wondered what to do with the peels, this is the recipe for you. I usually wait until I have the peels of at least four grapefruit. It is easy to make a large batch of these and keep them in the refrigerator. They make great petits fours and can be given away as gifts. I especially like the contrast of sweet and citrus after dinner.

The candied peels can be served three ways, depending on personal taste: rolled in granulated sugar, partially dipped in dark chocolate, or au natural.

I prefer to use grapefruit for this recipe, but you can also use orange, lemon, or lime peels.

4 grapefruit			
Granulated sugar	2¹/₂ cups	17.5 ounces	500 grams
For the final presentation			
Granulated sugar (optional)	1 cup	7 ounces	200 grams
Bittersweet chocolate, tempered (optional)		26.3 ounces	750 grams

Use a sharp knife to cut each grapefruit into quarters. Remove the fruit from the peel, leaving the white membrane or pith attached to the peel. Save the fruit for another use. Slice each quarter peel on a diagonal into strips about ¹/₂ inch wide. If you cut them evenly, they will look nicer when displayed.

Place the sliced grapefruit peels in a nonreactive 4-quart heavy-bottomed saucepan and add enough water to cover the peels by about 1 inch. Place over high heat and bring to a rolling boil. (A rolling boil is one that cannot be stirred down.) Remove from the heat and drain. Return only the peels to the saucepan, cover again with fresh water, and repeat the boiling and draining process three more times. It is really important to change the water, because it retains the bitterness of the peel.

After the fourth boil, return the drained peels to the saucepan. Add the sugar and enough water to cover the peels by 1 inch. Place over low heat and let simmer for

continued

2 hours. During this time, the sugar will sweeten and preserve the natural flavor of the peels. After 2 hours, they will be soft and translucent and the syrup will be thick. Let the peels cool in the syrup and keep them stored in the syrup, refrigerated, in an airtight container until you are ready to serve. They will keep this way for up to three weeks.

When ready to use, allow the peels to drain on a wire rack for a few hours to remove the excess syrup. I put my rack over a baking sheet so the syrup does not drip all over the table. Once the peels are fully drained, you have three options for serving: First, you can serve them as they are. Second, you can place the peels in a medium-size bowl filled with granulated sugar and roll the peels around in the sugar until they are well coated.

Third, you can dip the sugared peels in a bowl of tempered chocolate. Personally, I love the contrast between the bittersweet chocolate and the acidity of grapefruit. Dip two thirds of each sugared peel into the tempered chocolate. Gently wipe the excess chocolate from the end of each peel before placing on parchment paper. The chocolate should set in a few minutes if the kitchen is not too hot.

Whatever variation you choose, present the peels on a plate, in a small bowl, or, as I do at the restaurant, in petits fours cups.

Once the peels have been sugared and dipped in chocolate, they can be stored in an airtight container at room temperature for up to three days.

Chocolate Sauce

2⅔ CUPS (23.5 OUNCES; 675 GRAMS)

Everyone loves chocolate sauce and it is easy to please with this recipe. Taste is its most important aspect, so it is imperative to use the best-quality bittersweet chocolate. I usually use a European bittersweet chocolate like Callebaut from Belgium. A lesser-quality chocolate will produce a sauce with inferior flavor.

The deep chocolate flavor of this sauce will satisfy even the toughest chocoholic. It is great to make in batches to give away as gifts, and it makes a wonderful hot fudge sauce that hardens to a chewy texture when poured over ice cream. Make this sauce a staple in your refrigerator.

Whole milk	Generous 1 cup	8.8 ounces	250 grams
Bittersweet chocolate, chopped		10.5 ounces	300 grams
Heavy cream	Generous ½ cup	4.4 ounces	125 grams
Unsalted butter	2 tablespoons	1 ounce	30 grams
Granulated sugar	¼ cup + 2 tablespoons	2.5 ounces	75 grams

Pour the milk into a 2-quart heavy-bottomed saucepan, place over medium-high heat, and bring to a boil. When the milk boils, remove it from the heat and make a ganache by adding the chopped chocolate. Whisk well, stirring into the edge of the saucepan to combine. The ganache should be homogenous and smooth. Set the ganache aside.

In a 1-quart heavy-bottomed saucepan, combine the heavy cream, butter, and sugar. Place the saucepan over medium-high heat and bring to a boil, stirring occasionally. The butter should be completely melted and the sugar completely dissolved. Once the mixture has come to a boil, pour the cream into the warm ganache.

Place the sauce over medium-high heat and bring to a boil, stirring constantly with a whisk. As the chocolate sauce cooks, it will begin to thicken slightly. When it reaches a boil, remove it from the heat and pour it into a clean, dry bowl. Cover by placing plastic wrap directly on top of the sauce to prevent a skin from forming. Let the chocolate sauce cool to room temperature before storing in the refrigerator. When cold, the chocolate sauce will become thick enough to be scooped with a spoon.

continued

One of the wonderful qualities of this sauce is that it can be reheated whenever needed. If using a microwave, simply place the chocolate sauce in a microwaveable bowl and heat it at medium-high power in 30-second intervals until it becomes liquid. On the stovetop, place it in a heavy-bottomed saucepan over medium heat and stir occasionally until it becomes liquid. If you store it in a squeeze bottle, you can easily drizzle it over a dessert or decorate a plate. It will keep in the refrigerator for up to three weeks. It can also be frozen for up to two months if stored in an airtight container, to be kept on hand for a last-minute dinner party. Thaw in the refrigerator and heat as described above until liquid.

Linda's Red Raspberry Jam

SEVEN 8-OUNCE JARS

My sister-in-law Linda's raspberry jam is legendary. If you have ever been given a jar, you know why. This recipe was passed to Linda and Kris by their grandmother. Linda tells me "Gram" used to take the girls berry picking every summer. The ritual meant getting up early on a July day, driving to the berry farm to pick the fruit, and returning home by noon to make the jam. Of all the jams and jellies Linda creates, this is the one I love and use the most. Now, when I visit her in the summer, she shares with me the time-honored tradition of making red raspberry jam.

Fresh raspberries	*5 cups*	*25.6 ounces*	*684 grams*
Powdered pectin	*1 box*	*1.75 ounces*	*49 grams*
Granulated sugar	*6 ¾ cups*	*47.8 ounces*	*1350 grams*
Unsalted butter	*1½ tablespoons*	*0.75 ounce*	*21 grams*

Carefully wash the berries and pat dry. Set aside. Wash and rinse seven 8-ounce glass canning jars. Keep the jars warm until ready to fill by leaving them in a sink filled with hot water. Fill a small saucepan with water and place over medium heat. Place the washed and rinsed canning lids and metal bands in the pan and bring to a simmer. Remove from the heat and set aside, leaving the lids and bands in the hot water until ready to use.

Place enough of the berries in an 8- to 10-quart heavy-bottomed enamel or stainless steel pot or kettle to cover the bottom. It is important to use a large pot so the jam will have enough room to rise in the pot when it boils. Use a potato masher to gently crush the berries. Add another layer of berries and crush them; repeat until all of the berries are in the pot. Add the pectin and bring to a full boil over high heat, stirring constantly with a wooden spoon. Add the sugar and butter and stir thoroughly. Bring the mixture to a full, rolling boil. (A rolling boil is one that cannot be stirred down.) At this stage, boil hard for 1 full minute, stirring constantly. Remove from the heat. Use a large spoon to skim and discard the foam that has formed.

Remove a hot jar, lid and band from the hot water. Use a sterilized jar funnel to fill the jar with the hot jam to 1/4 inch from the top. Carefully clean the rim of the jar with a clean damp cloth. Place the lid and band on the jar and twist the band just until the lid is firmly secured—do not twist tightly at this stage. Fill each of the remaining jars in the same way. Set aside.

Sealing the jars using a water bath is optional. Be sure to read the back of the box of pectin for canning instructions. Modern techniques instruct you to simply invert the jars and when cool, turn them upright and they'll seal. Linda uses a water bath because it was the way she learned from her Gram.

To make a water bath: Use either the pot you used for the jam (clean it first) or a water bath canner. Fill the pot with about 6 inches of water and place over high heat until the water boils. It will be easiest if you set the jars in a canning rack and place the rack in the boiling water. If you do not have a canning rack, you will need to use a jar lifter to carefully place the jars upright on the bottom of the pot. The water should cover the jars by at least 1 inch. Cover the pot and allow the water to boil for 10 minutes. Remove from the heat. Carefully remove the jars from the water. Linda usually sets the jars on top of a folded dish towel on the counter. As the jars cool, a tight vacuum seal is formed. You will hear the lids make a dull "ping" noise and see that each lid has indented slightly. If you have a jar that was not filled at least 1/4 inch from the top or if the rim of a jar was not completely clean, it may not seal. In that case, store the jar in the refrigerator and use within two months. The sealed canned jam can be stored at room temperature in a cool, dark place for up to one year. Refrigerate it once opened.

Dame Blanche

ABOUT 26 SANDWICHED COOKIES

One of my earliest memories is making these cookies with my mom. It was an all-day affair, since she made the jam from scratch. Now I see my mom only once a year. To let her know she is always on my mind, I make a big batch of these and send them to her on Mother's Day. My dad really loves that!

The texture of these cookies is like shortbread and the jam adds sweetness and moisture. Displayed on a platter, they make a simple and elegant finish to any meal.

For the dough

Cold unsalted butter, cubed	¾ cup + 2 tablespoons	7 ounces	200 grams
Almond flour	½ cup	1.7 ounces	50 grams
Powdered sugar	¾ cup + 2 tablespoons	3.5 ounces	100 grams
2 large eggs			
1 vanilla bean			
Pastry flour	1 cup	4.4 ounces	125 grams
All-purpose flour	1 cup	4.4 ounces	125 grams
Pinch of salt			

To finish the cookies

Linda's Red Raspberry Jam (page 264)	½ cup	5.4 ounces	153 grams
Powdered sugar	¼ cup	1 ounce	32 grams

Prepare the dough: Place the butter, almond flour, sugar, and eggs in a large mixing bowl. Mix with an electric mixer on medium speed until the mixture looks like scrambled eggs. Use a sharp knife to slice the vanilla bean in half lengthwise. Separate the seeds from the skin by scraping the blade of the knife along the inside of the bean. Add the vanilla bean seeds, pastry flour, all-purpose flour, and salt and mix on medium speed just until everything is incorporated, about 1 minute. If you overwork the dough, it will become tough and elastic. Remove the dough from the bowl and pat it into a rectangle. Wrap it in plastic wrap and place in the refrigerator for 30 minutes to allow the dough to stiffen. (You can make the dough a day in advance and let it rest overnight.)

Preheat the oven to 350°F (175°C). Remove the dough from the refrigerator, place on a lightly floured work surface, and roll out into a ⅛-inch-thick rectangle. If the dough sticks to the work surface or rolling pin, lightly dust each with flour. The thinner you roll it, the stickier it is likely to become. I like to use a 2½-inch-wide heart-shaped cookie cutter to form the cookies, but you can use any shape and size you like; a fluted cutter makes a more decorative cookie. Cut as many cookies from the dough as you can and place them about 1 inch apart on a parchment paper–covered baking sheet. Pat together any leftover dough, gently roll it out, and use it for more cookies.

Use the top of a 1-inch plain decorating tip to cut the centers from half of the cookies on the baking sheet. Bake the cookies until they are light brown, about 10 minutes. Remove the baking sheet from the oven, place on a wire rack, and let cool completely.

To finish the cookies: Spread the raspberry jam to ¼ inch from the edge of each whole cookie and set aside. Place the powdered sugar in a fine-mesh sieve and liberally sprinkle the surfaces of the cut-out cookies. Now all you have to do is sandwich the cut-out tops and the bottoms together. These cookies will keep for four to five days if stored in an airtight container at room temperature.

sublime sweets from a celebrated pastry chef

authors

France's Pierre Hermé, dubbed the Picasso of pastry and the Dior of desserts, in collaboration with cookbook writer Dorie Greenspan

why they wrote it

To bring his exceptional recipes, previously published only in France, to an American audience. Those recipes have been translated, adapted, and tested so that, writes Greenspan, "none of the recipes is beyond the capabilities of an average home baker, although some, because they take a while to prepare, require above-average patience. What the recipes demand is attention to detail. Pay attention, and you'll always be rewarded with a sensational dessert—you'll usually learn something, too."

why it made our list

Since Hermé is arguably the most famous pastry chef in the world, we were eager to sample his renowned repertoire . . . and a little concerned that the recipes might be off-puttingly complex. We worried for nothing: Some of these recipes are quite simple indeed, and they're as extraordinarily flavored as the trickier dishes. Hermé is known for employing novel combinations of ingredients—basmati rice and Rice Krispies, black pepper and chocolate mousse, bananas and chiles—to create unexpected flavors. "Technique is not so significant," says Hermé. "Anyone can make my recipes. But it's important to understand the taste." The taste, of course, is divine.

chapters

Basic Recipes • Fruits, Creams, and Cookies • Tarts and Tartlets • Cakes

previous books

Hermé's four French collections include the *Larousse of Desserts*. Greenspan's last book was *Baking with Julia*, written with Julia Child.

specifics

304 pages, 80 recipes, 50 color photographs, $35. Published by Little, Brown and Company.

from the book

"People think buttercream is heavy, but when it's properly made, when the butter is blended into the mixture very well, it's light on the palate. And of course, buttercream must have butter—nothing else works."

DESSERTS BY
Pierre Hermé

WRITTEN BY
Dorie Greenspan
Author of *Baking with Julia*

philadelphia ALMOND
CAKE

Cream cheese, the star of American cheesecakes, rarely makes even a cameo appearance in French bakers' spectaculars, and when it does, it's billed as "Philadelphia," a name derived from Kraft's well-known Philadelphia Brand Cream Cheese. In this recipe, Pierre, who's always looking for new foods or ways to make familiar foods seem new, uses the "Philadelphia" in a most un-American but dazzlingly delicious way — it forms a thick layer of extra-creamy mousse interlaced with griottes, small, tart cherries. The mousse is smoothed across a soft, chewy, brown sugar–sweetened almond cake and topped with a crunchy almond streusel so good it deserves a "best-of-class" blue ribbon. The cake is not formal, but it is very chic, and as right for a dinner party as for a midafternoon nibble. ("Breakfast too," says Pierre.) You can even vary it: Try it with some fresh raspberries standing in for the griottes (see page 275 for instructions).

Once the griottes are macerated (best done a day ahead), you can make this cake in one fell swoop, but you don't have to. If you get all the components prepared ahead, you'll have only the mousse as an *à la minute* must-do.

《 *This cake is full of sensations: It's smooth, creamy, and moist, but there's also a little crunch from the streusel. I love it when a cake has these kinds of contrasts.* **》** — P. H .

Makes 8 to 10 servings

the griottes

- 2 cups drained bottled or thawed frozen griottes (available in specialty stores; or see Variation, page 275)
- ¾ cup water
- ¾ cup sugar

I. Turn the griottes into a medium bowl or refrigerator container; set aside. Bring the water and sugar to a boil in a medium saucepan. Pour this syrup over the griottes, stir to moisten all of the cherries, and cool to room temperature. When the mixture is cool, cover and refrigerate 24 hours. *(The cherries can be kept under refrigeration for 1 week.)*

2. Two hours before you need them, put the cherries in a colander to drain. Gently pat off any excess moisture before layering them with the mousse.

the cake

- ⅔ cup ground blanched almonds (see page 279), plus 1 tablespoon blanched almonds, toasted (see page 279) and coarsely chopped
- ½ cup confectioner's sugar, sifted
- 2½ tablespoons all-purpose flour
- 3 large egg whites
- ¼ cup (packed) light brown sugar, pushed through a strainer

I. Center a rack in the oven and preheat the oven to 350°F. Line a baking sheet with parchment paper and place an 8¾-inch/22-cm dessert ring on the sheet; set aside.

2. In a medium mixing bowl, stir the ground almonds, chopped almonds, confectioner's sugar, and flour together just to combine. Place the egg whites in an impeccably clean, dry mixing bowl, preferably the bowl of a mixer fitted with the whisk attachment, and beat on medium-high speed just until the whites form soft peaks. Mixing all the while, add the brown sugar a little at a time. Increase the speed to high and beat until the whites form firm, glossy peaks.

3. Working with a large flexible rubber spatula, gently fold the almond mixture into the meringue in three additions, taking care to maintain as much of the meringue's volume as possible. Turn the mixture into the dessert ring and use the spatula to smooth the top.

4. Slip the baking sheet into the oven and, as you're closing the oven door, insert the handle of a wooden spoon into the oven so that the door remains slightly ajar. Bake the cake for 24 to 26 minutes, or until the top, which will look dry, is springy to the touch and honey brown. Transfer the baking sheet to a cooling rack and allow the cake to cool to room temperature. When the cake is absolutely cool, run a thin knife between it and the ring and lift off the ring.

(Don't be concerned if, after you remove the ring, the cake shrinks a little — it's inevitable.) Wash and dry the ring — you'll need it to construct the finished cake. *(Wrapped airtight in plastic, the cake can be kept at room temperature for 4 days or frozen for a month.)*

the mousse

The mousse needs to be molded as soon as it is made, so, before you begin preparation, make certain to drain the griottes and check that the cake layer is cool.

- 1 cup heavy cream
- 6 ounces cream cheese
- 1 tablespoon confectioner's sugar
- 3 large egg yolks
- 4½ tablespoons sugar
- 3 tablespoons cold water
- 1½ teaspoons gelatin

1. In a medium bowl, whip the heavy cream until it holds medium-firm peaks. Cover the bowl with plastic wrap and refrigerate until needed.

2. Place the cream cheese in a metal bowl over a pan of simmering water and heat to melt, stirring occasionally with a rubber spatula. Whisk in the confectioner's sugar and continue to whisk until the mixture is smooth. Remove the bowl from the saucepan and set the cream cheese aside to cool while you prepare the rest of the ingredients for the mousse.

3. Bring a couple of inches of water to a simmer in a saucepan. Put the yolks in a metal bowl that can fit into the saucepan and serve as the top of a double boiler; reserve. Bring the sugar and 1 tablespoon of the water to the boil in a small saucepan or a microwave oven. Whisking the yolks constantly, scrape the sugar syrup onto the yolks and whisk to blend. Set the bowl over the pan of simmering water and heat, whisking lightly, until the mixture is very foamy and slightly thickened, about 5 to 7 minutes. Remove the bowl to a counter and allow the yolks to cool, stirring occasionally, until they reach 77°F, as measured on an instant-read thermometer. (The yolks will continue to thicken as they cool.)

4. While the yolks are cooling, sprinkle the gelatin over the remaining 2 tablespoons cold water and allow it to rest until softened. Heat the gelatin in the microwave oven for about 15 seconds, or cook over low heat, until the gelatin dissolves.

5. Working with a large rubber spatula, stir the gelatin into the cream cheese mixture. Fold in the cooled yolks and, finally, the reserved whipped cream.

to assemble

Center the 8¾-inch/22-cm dessert ring on a cardboard cake round and set the almond cake in the ring. Spoon about one third of the mousse over the cake, smoothing the layer with an offset spatula. Cover the mousse with a single, even layer of the well-drained griottes, then spoon on the rest of the mousse and smooth the top. Freeze the cake for at least 2 hours to set the mousse. *(Once frozen, the cake can be wrapped airtight, still in the dessert ring, and frozen for up to 2 weeks.)*

the streusel

- 3 tablespoons plus 1 teaspoon unsalted butter, softened
- 3½ tablespoons sugar
- 6 tablespoons ground blanched almonds (see page 279)
- Pinch of salt
- 6 tablespoons all-purpose flour

1. Working in a medium bowl, beat the butter with a large rubber spatula until creamy. Add the remaining ingredients one by one, blending each ingredient into the mixture before adding the next. Cover the bowl and refrigerate the mixture until it is thoroughly chilled, about 45 minutes.

2. Center a rack in the oven and preheat the oven to 325°F. Line a baking sheet with parchment paper and set it aside.

3. Remove the bowl from the refrigerator and, using your fingers, break the streusel into clumps of varying sizes (the unevenness of the pieces will add textural interest to the finished cake). Spread the streusel out on the lined baking sheet and bake for 10 minutes. Using a metal spatula, break up any streusel that may have formed large pieces, stir and turn the streusel, and continue to bake until well browned, another 5 to 10 minutes. Transfer the streusel, still on the parchment paper, from the pan to a rack and cool to room temperature. *(The streusel can be made a day or two ahead and kept at room temperature in an airtight container.)*

to finish

- Confectioner's sugar

1. Thirty minutes to an hour before serving, remove the cake from the freezer. Transfer the cake to a serving platter and remove the dessert ring (see page 279). Allow the cake to defrost at room temperature. (If your cake has been in the freezer long enough for it to

freeze solid, you'll need more than an hour to defrost it. Long-frozen cakes are best defrosted by giving them an overnight stay in the refrigerator.) When the mousse is defrosted but the cake is still cool, top with the streusel, using your fingers to lightly press it in an even layer on top of the mousse.

2. Cut two bands of parchment or wax paper, each about 1 inch wide and at least 9 inches long. Place the bands across the cake on a bias and dust the top of the cake with confectioner's sugar; remove the bands. Serve immediately.

VARIATION

If you'd like, you can omit the griottes and substitute about 2 cups of fresh raspberries for the griottes, placing them in an even layer between the two layers of mousse. If you're using raspberries, there's no need to macerate them.

Keeping

Without the streusel, the cake can be wrapped airtight and kept frozen for 2 weeks. Once topped with streusel, the cake can be kept covered in the refrigerator for up to 2 days. Apply the confectioner's sugar decoration right before serving.

chocolate-caramel MOUSSE

with

CARAMEL PEARS

Chocolate and caramel, a celestial combination, are blended to cosmic perfection in this mousse. To get the just-right blend, make sure you cook the sugar to a deep color — one between dark amber and light mahogany. The caramel should not be bitter (as it would be if you let it get too dark), but it must be powerful enough to hold its own against the mousse's chocolate and whipped cream. Delicious as is, it is most special paired with slices of ripe, juicy pears cooked in a rich caramel sauce.

≪*Once the sugar is caramelized for the mousse, it is blended with salted butter and whipped cream. I often add salt to caramel as well as to chocolate because it intensifies the best qualities of both flavors. And adding whipped cream rather than liquid cream is a* truc *that keeps the caramelized sugar from bubbling over the pan.* ≫ — P. H .

the mousse

- 1½ cups heavy cream
- 3¾ ounces bittersweet chocolate (preferably Valrhona Noir Gastronomie), coarsely chopped
- 1 (scant) cup sugar
- 2½ tablespoons salted butter

I. Whip the cream until it holds soft-to-medium peaks. Spoon out a rounded ½ cup — you'll use this to liquefy the caramel — and keep both portions of whipped cream covered in the refrigerator until needed.

Makes 4 servings

2. Melt the chocolate in a microwave oven or in a bowl over simmering water. Set the chocolate aside to cool to 114°F, as measured on an instant-read thermometer.

3. Rinse a bowl with warm water, dry it well, and keep it in a warm place while you prepare the caramel. (You want the bowl to be warm so that when you pour in the caramel, it doesn't chill quickly and harden around the edges. Should it harden, it's not fatal — you can rewarm it over low heat.)

4. Working in a large heavy-bottomed skillet, preferably nonstick, caramelize the sugar bit by bit: Heat the pan over medium-high heat and then sprinkle about 2 tablespoons of the sugar into the center of the pan. Start stirring the sugar with a wooden spoon or spatula as soon as it begins to melt. When it is completely melted, bubbly, and caramelized, add 2 tablespoons more of the sugar, and cook, stirring constantly, until it, too, caramelizes. Repeat until all of the sugar has been caramelized and is a deep amber color; test the color by dropping a bit on a white plate. Reduce the heat to medium and, still stirring, add the butter and the reserved ½ cup whipped cream. Take care — even though you've whipped the cream, the mixture will still bubble. It also may seize and clump — just keep heating and stirring and it will even out. Bring the mixture to a boil again, then turn it into the warm bowl to cool to 114°F.

5. When the caramel and melted chocolate are both 114°F, delicately stir the chocolate into the caramel. Gradually and gently fold the remaining whipped cream into the mixture. (Start with about a quarter of the cream so its cold doesn't shock the caramel and chocolate.) Cover the bowl and refrigerate until the mousse is thoroughly chilled, about 2 hours. *(The mousse can be made up to 2 days ahead and kept covered and chilled.)*

the pears

- 4 ripe pears, cut into eighths and cored (peeling is optional)
- 1 tablespoon freshly squeezed lemon juice
- ¼ cup sugar
- 1½ tablespoons salted butter
- 2 tablespoons heavy cream
- Freshly ground black pepper

1. Toss the pears with the lemon juice to keep them from discoloring; reserve.

2. Working in a large heavy-bottomed skillet, preferably nonstick, caramelize the sugar bit by bit, as you did for the mousse. When the sugar is a deep amber, stir in the butter and then the cream. Let the caramel return to the boil before adding the pear slices. Cook the pears in the caramel for about 7 to 8 minutes, stirring frequently but gently, until the pears are caramel-coated and can be pierced with the tip of a knife. Remove the pan from the heat and pepper the pears lightly. The pears are ready to serve.

3. To serve, arrange eight slices of pear in a fan shape on each dessert plate and drizzle with caramel sauce, if any remains. Center three scoops of mousse on each plate and serve immediately. (You may have mousse left over.) If you want to shape the mousse into quenelles, dip two soup spoons into cold water, shake off the excess water, and dip one into the mousse to scoop up a generous spoonful; use the second spoon to smooth and round the top of the mousse in the first spoon and then to scrape it out of the spoon.

Keeping

The mousse can be kept covered in the refrigerator for about 2 days. While the caramelized pears are best served when they're just made, they can be prepared a day or two in advance, cooled to room temperature, covered, and refrigerated. When ready to serve, warm the pears and their sauce in a microwave oven at medium power. Take care not to overheat them — these are not meant to be served steaming hot.

from

A DICTIONARY OF TERMS, TECHNIQUES, EQUIPMENT, AND INGREDIENTS

Dessert or cake rings

The majority of Pierre's cakes are constructed (and some are baked) in dessert or cake rings, known as *cercles d'entremets,* bottomless stainless steel bands that are 1½ inches/4 centimeters high. Most cakes are assembled in 8¾-inch/22-centimeter rings and a few in 10¼-inch/26-centimeter rings. (Actually, Pierre prefers 9¾-inch/25-centimeter rings, but these are, for all practical purposes, unavailable in the United States.) With a dessert ring as the "mold" in which you build a cake, you'll get a straight-sided, polished, professional-looking cake every time. Using a ring is easier (and neater) than filling and stacking layers freehand, and if you've never used one, the first time you lift it off and get a look at your layers of cake and cream, mousse, or fruit, stacked up with military precision, you'll be thrilled.

Since dessert or cake rings (and tart or flan rings) are essentially pieces of European and/or professional equipment, the measurements are given in centimeters as well as in inches. Indeed, in many stores you'll find only the metric measurements listed and, in fact, you'll do best to purchase the rings by their metric sizes if you can.

Rings cost about $10 to $15 and it's worth having two of the 8¾-inch/22-centimeter rings, especially if you're planning to serve more than one cake at a time. Don't be seduced by those adjustable rings that can be sized from very small to larger-than-you'll-probably-need. The band that makes these rings adjustable also makes a dent in the side of your cake. Also, don't buy a ring in black metal — it can turn whipped creams and fillings an unpleasant color and give an off taste to anything acidic, such as lemon cream.

If you do not have a dessert ring, you can substitute the ring of an appropriately sized springform pan, but you'll never get the perfectly smooth side that's a hallmark of the dessert ring.

To remove dessert rings, heat is the key. Since most desserts constructed in rings are chilled or frozen, you need to apply heat so that the dessert softens sufficiently to allow you to lift off the ring without damaging what's inside. A hair dryer is what makes this delicate operation quick, easy, and foolproof: Just blow hot air around the ring and presto — you've achieved liftoff. If you don't have a hair dryer, you can remove dessert rings by soaking a kitchen towel in hot water, wringing it out, and then wrapping it around the ring, although it may take a couple of soaks to warm things up. Similarly, you can use a sponge that's been dipped in hot water. Finally, if all you've got is a knife at your disposal, run it between the ring and the dessert, but be forewarned — the side of your dessert might suffer (only a minor problem if you can dust it with nuts or chocolate shavings).

Nuts

Nuts add incomparable flavor and texture to desserts, but they must be treated with care. The oils that make nuts delicious can also make them rancid, so taste before you buy (if that's possible) and then taste again before you bake. To keep fresh nuts fresh, it's best to wrap them airtight and store them in the freezer, where they'll keep for a few months. There's no need to thaw frozen nuts before you use them.

To toast nuts, place them in a single layer on a baking sheet or in a jelly-roll pan and either bake them in a 350°F oven for 10 to 12 minutes or do as Pierre does: Toast them in a 300°F to 325°F oven for 18 to 20 minutes. Toasting them at a lower temperature for a longer time ensures that the nuts are toasted evenly all the way through. (Long slow toasting also means nuts are less likely to scorch.)

To grind nuts, place the nuts in the work bowl of a food processor and pulse until the nuts are finely and evenly ground. Don't process the nuts continuously, and do check their progress regularly — if you go overboard, you'll end up with nut paste, not powder. To be on the safe side, grind the nuts with a spoonful of sugar (you can use some of the sugar from the recipe).

artful medleys of flavors and textures

author

Charlie Trotter, chef/owner of Charlie Trotter's in Chicago

why he wrote it

"As far as I'm concerned, a meal is not complete without a sweet thing or two at the end. Maybe it's simply a perfect fig or a bowl of luscious berries, or maybe it's a bittersweet burnt crème caramel, or a fraise des bois linzertorte or a jasmine rice pudding or tamarind soup with vanilla yogurt sorbet, or deep-dish apple pie with aged Cheddar cheese, or chocolate-cherry cake with cherry-cognac ice cream, or . . . . "

why it made our list

With desserts this beautiful, it's hard not to want to forego the rest of the meal and skip straight to the sweets. Trotter's style is imaginative, the results impressive. Each dessert has several components which, when combined, yield a unique creation with a medley of interesting flavors and textures. Of course, if you want to serve the elements individually, or make your own combinations, that's fine by Trotter. "Keep in mind when preparing these recipes, or any recipes for that matter, they are often meant to be used as a guide," he writes. "And therein lies the beauty of all food—it is easy to change, adjust, and adapt as the foodstuffs dictate or your mood changes."

chapters

Soups and Sorbets • Citrus Fruits • Berries • Tropical Fruits • Tree Fruits • Vegetables and Grains • Custards • Nuts • Spices • Chocolate • Chateau d'Yquem

previous books

Trotter's other cookbooks include *Charlie Trotter's* and *Charlie Trotter's Seafood*.

specifics

240 pages, more than 70 recipes, 72 color photographs, 147 black-and-white photographs, $50. Published by Ten Speed Press.

from the book

"As for mistakes . . . don't worry! I have made plenty, but I always learn from my failures. In fact, I would say I have learned more from my failures than from my successes. James Joyce once remarked, 'A person's errors are his portals of discovery.' This is utterly true with regard to cuisine."

CHARLIE TROTTER'S

DESSERTS

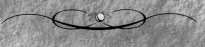

CHICAGO

Strawberry-Almond Shortcake with Basil

Everyone loves the classic strawberry shortcake, but sometimes a more refined presentation is welcome. This dish is easy to prepare and truly emphasizes the glorious flavor of the strawberries, or any berry, in the height of their season. The components of this dish can be prepared well in advance and assembled at the last moment. This dessert stands alone nicely as the sole finishing point of a meal, or it makes a wonderful introduction to something more substantial like chocolate. The serving size is easily adjusted to suit any occasion. For a variation, try substituting chopped candied ginger or ground praline for the vanilla in the crème fraîche.

Serves 6

1 cup unsalted butter

½ cup plus 2 tablespoons sugar

1 cup whole toasted almonds, skin on

2 cups flour

Pinch of salt

2 tablespoons sliced almonds, skin on, lightly toasted

2 cups strawberries, cut into wedges

¼ cup Simple Syrup (recipe follows)

1 teaspoon lime zest

½ cup crème fraîche

1 cup heavy cream

Pulp of ½ vanilla bean

2 tablespoons aged balsamic vinegar

Basil Syrup (recipe follows)

2 tablespoons tiny fresh basil leaves

METHOD To make the shortcake: Cream the butter and 6 tablespoons of the sugar until light, fluffy, and almost white. Purée the whole almonds for 2 minutes, or until very fine, and add to the butter mixture along with the flour and salt. Mix until just combined. Roll out the dough between 2 sheets of plastic wrap until ⅛ inch thick. Lay the sheet of shortcake dough on a sheet pan, still covered in the plastic wrap, and refrigerate for 30 minutes. Remove the plastic wrap, place the dough on a cutting board, and cut into at least thirty 1½ by 2-inch rectangles. Place on a parchment-lined sheet pan and lightly press 2 or 3 almond slices into each rectangle. Bake at 350 degrees for 15 to 20 minutes, or until golden brown.

To prepare the strawberries: Toss the strawberry wedges with the Simple Syrup and lime zest.

To make the cream: Whisk the crème fraîche, heavy cream, the remaining ¼ cup of sugar, and the vanilla pulp until soft peaks form.

ASSEMBLY Spoon some of the strawberry wedges in the center of each plate and drizzle with the balsamic vinegar and the Basil Syrup. Layer the almond squares with the cream mixture until there are 6 separate stacks of 5 almond squares. Set the stacks sideways on top of the strawberries and sprinkle with the basil leaves.

Simple Syrup

Yield: approximately 3 cups

2 cups water

2 cups sugar

METHOD Bring the water and sugar to a boil, remove from the heat, and let cool.

Basil Syrup

Yield: ½ cup

½ cup fresh basil leaves

¼ cup fresh spinach leaves

¼ cup Simple Syrup (recipe above)

METHOD Blanch the basil and spinach in boiling water for 10 seconds. Remove from the pan and immediately shock in ice water. Squeeze any excess water from the leaves and coarsely chop. Purée with the Simple Syrup for 3 minutes, or until bright green. Strain through a fine-mesh sieve. Store in the refrigerator until ready to use.

Ginger-Molasses Spice Cake with Mascarpone Cream and Clear Lady Apple Chips

This fragrant spice cake is perfect as a light ending to a substantial meal or as an early course in a dessert progression. The cake can even be served as part of a breakfast menu because it is not very sweet. This is a great make-ahead preparation; the cake does not suffer in any way from being baked the day before.

Serves 9

½ cup finely chopped peeled ginger

¼ cup freshly squeezed orange juice

½ cup milk (approximately)

2 tablespoons brandy

1½ teaspoons rice wine vinegar

½ cup unsalted butter

2⅓ cups plus 2 tablespoons granulated sugar

2 eggs

¼ cup light molasses

2 cups flour

1½ teaspoons baking soda

¼ teaspoon salt

1 teaspoon ground cinnamon

⅛ teaspoon ground cloves

½ cup water

3 apples, peeled, halved, cored, and cut into ⅛-inch slices

1 cup mascarpone

½ cup heavy cream

Confectioners' sugar, for dusting

Clear Lady Apple Chips (recipe follows)

METHOD To make the cake: Cook ¼ cup of the ginger in the orange juice over low heat for 3 minutes, or until the juice is warm. Remove from the heat, cover, and steep for 30 minutes. Strain through a fine-mesh sieve and discard the ginger. Add enough milk to the orange juice to total ¾ cup of liquid, then add the brandy and vinegar. Cream the butter and ⅓ cup of the granulated sugar until light and fluffy. Add the eggs and continue beating until they are fully incorporated. Add the molasses and beat until well mixed. Sift together the flour, baking soda, salt, cinnamon, and cloves. Alternately add the dry ingredients and the orange juice mixture to the batter, mixing well after each addition. Pour the batter into a greased, floured, parchment-lined 9 by 9-inch pan and bake at 350 degrees for 25 to 30 minutes, or until a toothpick inserted in the center of the cake comes out clean. When cooled, cut the cake into 2½-inch squares and use a round cutter to cut a 1-inch hole in the center of each piece.

To make the apples and apple-ginger sauce: Cook 2 cups of the granulated sugar and the water in a medium, heavy-bottomed sauté pan over medium heat for 10 minutes, or until golden brown and caramelized. Add the apple slices and simmer gently for 3 minutes. Remove the apples, set aside, and add the remaining ¼ cup ginger to the pan. Cook for 10 minutes, or until reduced by half. Strain through a fine-mesh sieve and discard the ginger.

To make the filling: Whip the mascarpone, cream, and the remaining 2 tablespoons granulated sugar until stiff peaks form.

ASSEMBLY Lightly dust each plate with confectioners' sugar and set a piece of cake in the center. Fill the hole in the cake with the mascarpone mixture and top with some of the warmed apples. Spoon some of the mascarpone on top of the apples and stand 2 Clear Lady Apple Chips in the mascarpone. Drizzle the ginger-apple sauce around the plate.

Clear Lady Apple Chips

Yield: 20 to 25 chips

2 cups water

1 cup sugar

¼ cup freshly squeezed lemon juice

20 to 25 thin slices lady apples

METHOD Bring the water, sugar, and lemon juice to a simmer, add the apple slices, and simmer for 10 minutes, or until the slices are translucent. Remove the apple slices from the liquid and lay them flat on a Silpat-lined sheet pan. Bake at 225 degrees for 1 hour, or until the apples are thoroughly dry. Carefully transfer the chips to a cooling rack. Store in an airtight container at room temperature until ready to use.

the definitive guide
to perfect pastry

author

Baking expert Rose Levy Beranbaum, a frequent contributor to *The New York Times*

why she wrote it

"I adore pastry because of its multiplicity of textures and prevalence of juicy, flavorful fruit. I have had the pleasure of developing the recipes in this book for more than ten years. All were enjoyable, but I have included only those I personally would want to have again and again. My fondest wish is that everyone will know the goodness of making and eating wonderful pastry. Then they will walk down the street with a secret little smile on their faces—like mine."

why it made our list

Everything you ever wanted to know about making pastry can be found in this painstakingly thorough guide. This is not the easiest book to use, due to the complexity of its cross-referencing, but it offers recipes for just about anything made with dough, along with a huge variety of filling recipes, problem-solving tips, and extensive decorating instructions. "There is nothing more empowering than the thrill of achieving good pastry," writes Beranbaum. And thanks to this informative book, many home cooks will know that feeling.

chapters

Crusts • Fruit Pies • Chiffon Pies • Meringue Pies and Tarts • Custard Pies and Tarts • Ice Cream Pies and Ice Creams • Tarts and Tartlets • Savory Tarts and Pies—and Quiche • Biscuits and Scones • Fillo • Strudel • Puff Pastry and Croissant • Danish Pastry • Brioche • Cream Puff Pastry • Fillings and Toppings • Sauces and Glazes • Techniques • Ingredients • Equipment

previous books

Beranbaum is the author of *The Cake Bible*, *A Passion for Chocolate*, and *Rose's Christmas Cookies*.

specifics

704 pages, more than 235 recipes, 70 color photographs, $35. Published by Scribner.

from the book

"Even with the clearest directions, making pie crust is a craft, and one must develop a feel for the dough. The more you make dough, the better you get. The French have a saying for this: *Il faut mettre la main à la pâte*, which means, 'It is necessary to put your hand to the dough'—or, to paraphrase, *hands-on experience is everything.*"

ROSE LEVY BERANBAUM

THE PIE AND PASTRY BIBLE

CHOCOLATE PEANUT BUTTER
MOUSSE SEVEN-TIER TART

There are many people who would be thrilled to find this exquisitely delicious tiered tart in place of the traditional wedding cake. And it is very practical to make it, as it freezes perfectly for up to 3 months. There are three luscious layers to each tier of this tart: a quarter-inch-deep peanut butter cookie crust, a five-eighths-inch deep peanut butter mousse, and a just under one-eighth-inch-thick milk chocolate ganache. It is delicious both chilled and at room temperature, making it perfect for a presentation piece. The special acrylic stand (page 294) makes it appear to be levitating in air.

The recipe here is given for all seven layers, but if you prefer not to make all the layers, the components are broken down in amounts for each individual size in the chart on page 290.

SERVES: 55 AS A DESSERT, 80 AS A WEDDING TART

INGREDIENTS	MEASURE	WEIGHT	
	VOLUME	OUNCES	GRAMS
6 recipes Sweet Peanut Butter Cookie Tart Crust (page 290), prebaked in 7 tart pans	8½ cups + 2 tablespoons (1 cup dough = 8.8 ounces/252 grams)	76.2 ounces	2 kg 178 grams
Peanut Butter Mousse	(17½ cups)	(7 pounds)	(3 kg 223 grams)
cream cheese, softened	3½ cups	2 pounds	904 grams
peanut butter (at room temperature), preferably Jif	4 cups	36.75 ounces	1 kg 64 grams
sugar	2 cups	14 ounces	400 grams
pure vanilla extract	2 tablespoons + 2 teaspoons	approx. 1 ounce	32 grams
heavy cream, softly whipped	6 liquid cups (1½ quarts)	48 ounces	1 kg 392 grams
Milk Chocolate Ganache Topping	(7½ cups)	(45 ounces)	(1 kg 272 grams)
milk chocolate	six 3-ounce bars	18 ounces	510 grams
bittersweet chocolate	four 3-ounce bars	12 ounces	342 grams
heavy cream	2 liquid cups	16.2 ounces	462 grams
pure vanilla extract	¾ teaspoon	•	•

EQUIPMENT

Seven fluted tart pans with removable bottoms (see page 293: 4¾-inch, 5½-inch, 7¾-inch, 9½-inch, 10-inch, 11-inch, and 12½-inch) and Pie in the Sky acrylic tiered stand (see page 294)

Make the dough (page 290). Roll, shape (see page 293), and prebake it, starting with the largest tart (see chart, page 290). Add scraps to the dough for each subsequent tart as you proceed, ending with the smallest. Let cool. Leftover dough can be frozen or made into cookies.

MAKE THE PEANUT BUTTER MOUSSE

In a mixer bowl, preferably with the whisk beater, beat the cream cheese, peanut butter, and sugar until uniform in color. On low speed, beat in the vanilla. Beat in 2 cups of the whipped cream just until incorporated. With a large rubber spatula, fold in the rest of the whipped cream until well blended. Scrape the mousse into the prepared shells, filling them to ⅛ to ¼ inch below the top of the crusts, and smooth the surface of each so that it is level. Refrigerate the tarts while preparing the ganache.

MAKE THE GANACHE TOPPING

Break the chocolates into small pieces into the bowl of a food processor with the metal blade. Process until the chocolate is very finely ground.

In a heatproof glass measure, if using a microwave oven, or in a small saucepan, bring the cream to a boil. With the motor running, immediately pour it through the feed tube onto the chocolate mixture. Process until smooth, about 15 seconds, scraping the sides of the bowl once or twice. Add the vanilla and pulse a few times to incorporate it. Pour it into a bowl. Let cool to room temperature.

Pour the ganache over the peanut butter mousse in each tart in a circular motion, so that it does not land too heavily in any one spot and cause a depression. If the ganache becomes too firm to pour, spread it instead or reheat it slightly, stirring very gently, in a microwave or double boiler. With a small metal spatula, start by spreading the ganache to the edges of the pastry. Then spread it evenly to cover the entire surface of each tart; make a thin layer, a little under ⅛ inch. Make a spiral pattern by lightly pressing the spatula against the surface and running it from the outside to the center.

Refrigerate the tarts for at least 2 hours to set.

ASSEMBLE THE TART

Unmold the tart (see page 294) and set each layer on its base. Place the center post firmly into the base of the stand. Slide the first acrylic spacer onto the post. Cut out a 1¾-inch hole in the center for the center post in all of the tiers except the top one.

Slide each tier onto the post, placing an acrylic spacer in between each one. To serve, cut with a sharp thin-bladed knife, preferably dipped in hot water between each slice.

STORE
Room temperature, up to 1 day; refrigerated, up to 5 days; frozen, up to 3 months.

NOTE
If the dough is rolled to the exact thickness specified, the filling and ganache amounts will be exact. If the dough is rolled a little thicker, there will be a little leftover filling and ganache.

TART SIZE	DOUGH CIRCLE DIAMETER	APPROXIMATE BAKING TIME AT 375°F.
4¾ inches/12 cm	6 inches	8 min.
5½ inches/14 cm	7¾ inches	10 min.
7¾ inches/19½ cm	9½ inches	10 min.
9½ inches/24 cm	11½ inches	10 to 12 min.
10 inches/25½ cm	12½ inches	10 to 12 min.
11 inches/28 cm	13 inches	12 to 14 min.
12½ inches/32 cm	14½ inches	14 min.

SWEET PEANUT BUTTER COOKIE TART CRUST

If you love peanut butter cookies, this is your crust. It is actually my peanut butter cookie baked in a tart pan. It makes a sensational crust for the Chocolate Peanut Butter Mousse Seven-Tier Tart (page 288).

PREPARING THE PAN
See page 292.

FOOD PROCESSOR METHOD
Into a small bowl, sift together the flour, baking soda, and salt, then whisk to mix evenly.

In a food processor with the metal blade, process the sugars for several minutes

INGREDIENTS	MEASURE	WEIGHT	
	VOLUME	OUNCES	GRAMS
bleached all-purpose flour	½ cup (dip and sweep method)	2.5 ounces	71 grams
baking soda	½ teaspoon	•	2.5 grams
salt	¹⁄₁₆ teaspoon	•	•
light brown sugar	¼ cup, packed	approx. 2 ounces	54 grams
sugar, preferably superfine	2 tablespoons	0.8 ounce	25 grams
unsalted butter, cold, cut into 1-inch cubes	4 tablespoons	2 ounces	57 grams
smooth peanut butter, preferably Jif, at room temperature	½ cup	4.6 ounces	133 grams
½ large egg (beat before measuring)	1½ tablespoons	0.8 ounce (weighed without the shell)	25 grams
pure vanilla extract	¼ teaspoon	•	•

or until very fine. With the motor running, add the butter cubes. Add the peanut butter and process until smooth and creamy, about 10 seconds. With the motor running, add the egg and vanilla extract and process until incorporated. Scrape the sides of the bowl. Add the flour mixture and pulse just until incorporated.

ELECTRIC MIXER METHOD
Soften the butter.

Into a small bowl, sift together the flour, baking soda, and salt. Whisk to combine well.

In a mixing bowl, beat the sugars until well mixed. Add the butter and peanut butter and beat for several minutes or until very smooth and creamy. Add the egg and vanilla extract and beat until incorporated, scraping the sides of the bowl. At low speed, gradually beat in the flour mixture just until incorporated.

FOR BOTH METHODS
Scrape the dough into a bowl and refrigerate for at least 1 hour, or overnight.

Press the dough evenly into the tart pan. (It is a little more challenging, but faster and neater, to roll it out between sheets of plastic wrap to about 11½ inches in diameter for a 9½-inch tart*; for the seven-tier tart, see the diameters on page 290. Remove one piece of plastic, invert the dough into the pan, easing the border into the sides of the pan so that the sharp top surface does not cut it off, and use the remaining plastic wrap to press it evenly into the pan, pressing it well against the sides. If the dough softens, refrigerate it until the plastic wrap can be removed easily. If it tears, simply press it together or use the scraps to press into any empty areas.) Cover it with plastic wrap and refrigerate for at least 1 hour. If using a 9½-inch tart pan, I usually have about 2 tablespoons (1 ounce/30 grams) of excess dough, which can be baked as cookies.

Bake the tart shell, without weights, in a preheated 375°F. oven for 10 to 12 minutes or until golden (for a 9½- or 10-inch tart; for the seven-tier tart, see cooking times on page 290). It will puff at first and then settle down toward the end of baking. The sides will be soft but spring back when touched gently with a finger. Cool it on a wire rack.

STORE
Unbaked: refrigerated, up to 1 week; frozen, about 1 year.

UNDERSTANDING
The baking soda is used to impart a golden brown color to the dough. Decreasing it will not lessen the puff.

PREPARING THE PAN
For cookie tart crusts like Sweet Peanut Butter Cookie Tart Crust, the pan does not need greasing or flouring unless it is being used for the first time. For all other crusts, Baker's Joy is easier to apply than grease and flour because tart pans with removable bottoms can't be turned upside down to knock out excess flour. Small flan rings do not require greasing or flouring no matter what the dough.

THE ROLLING SURFACE
A cool surface, such as marble, is preferable to keep the dough from softening too quickly. A piece of marble 16 inches by 20 inches by ¾ inch (available in gourmet stores or from a marble supply store) is a good size that is small enough to slip into your refrigerator to chill on hot summer days. (A bag of ice applied to a marble counter or a large piece also works to chill it.)

The dough should be floured on both sides and rolled between sheets of plastic wrap, overlapped if not large enough.

*The dough will be between 1/16 and 1/8 inch thick and rise to 1/4 inch thick during baking.

ROLLING, SHAPING, AND PREBAKING SWEET COOKIE CRUST FOR 9½- AND 10-INCH TARTS

Spray the pan with Baker's Joy or grease and flour it.

ROLL AND SHAPE THE DOUGH OR PRESS THE DOUGH INTO THE PAN   If the dough has been refrigerated for more than 30 minutes, it will be too cold to roll or press without cracking. It will take at least 40 minutes at room temperature to become malleable. But if you prefer not to wait, use the coarse side of a box grater to disperse the dough evenly into the pan and then press it into place.

Otherwise, let the dough sit until is is malleable, then roll it ⅛ inch thick and large enough to cut an 11-inch circle, for a 9½-inch tart pan, or 11½ inches for a 10-inch tart pan (for the seven-tier tart, see the diameters on page 290) and fit it into the pan, or press the dough into the pan.

When the tart pan has been lined, the dough should come to about ⅛ inch above the rim of the pan, as it always falls a little during baking. If necessary, push it up using your fingers.

BAKE THE DOUGH (FREEZE OR BLIND BAKE) If the dough is frozen for at least 2 hours or refrigerated for at least 6 hours before baking, it is not necessary to use weights. Make sure that there isn't any dough on the outside of the tart pan to ensure that it will unmold well.

TART PANS

Two-piece removable-bottom tart pans are essential for ease in unmolding. The smallest two-piece tart pans at the present time are 4 inches in diameter.

As with pie pans, dark metal produces a better crust than shiny metal. My favorite fluted tart pans are produced by Gobel. They are dark metal and have an excellent nonstick surface that is slightly rough so that the pastry develops a nice texture. They also produce plain fluted tart pans that are shiny metal with a plain finish. The 2-inch-deep pans are not available in the dark nonstick finish. Gobel pans are carried by J. B. Prince (in large quantities only; 36 East 31st Street, 11th floor, New York, NY 10016; 212-683-3553) and La Cuisine (323 Cameron Street, Alexandria, VA 22314; 800-521-1176). La Cuisine carries all sizes necessary for the seven-tier tart.

SIZES AND VOLUME   Tart pans are made in Europe, according to metric measure in centimeters. In converting to the inch measurement, I have rounded off to the nearest ½ inch. For ordering purposes, I also list the centimeter measurement where needed.

Gobel dark nonstick tart pans are currently available in the following sizes, measured in centimeters across the top: 12, 14, 20, 22, 24, 26, 28, 30, 32. Gobel plain metal two-piece fluted tart pans are available in the following sizes, measured across the top in centimeters (from 4 inches to 12½ inches in ¾-inch/2-centimeter increments): 10, 12, 14, 16, 18, 20, 22, 24, 26, 28, 30, 32. All are 2½-cm/1-inch deep except for the 10- and 12-cm ones, which are just under 2 cm/¾ inches deep. The 10-cm/4-inch tartlet pan is my favorite size for tartlets and is now available in two-piece.

Gobel also makes the extra-deep 4-cm/1½-inch tart pans in 15-cm/6-inch, 20-cm/8-inch, and 23-cm/9-inch sizes, and 5-cm/2-inch deep pans in 25-cm/almost-10-inch and 28-cm/11-inch sizes.

To unmold a tart or tartlet baked in a two-piece tart pan, generally it is best to leave the crust in the pan until it is filled and baked, or chilled, as the pan gives the crust support. When ready to unmold the tart, place it on top of a canister that is smaller than the opening of the tart pan rim. A flaky crust unmolds easily, but a sweet cookie crust unmolds most neatly when heated slightly. Wet a towel with hot water and wring it out well. Apply it to the bottom and sides of the tart pan. Press firmly down on both sides of the tart ring. It should slip away easily. If not, apply more heat. Slip a large pancake turner between the bottom crust and the pan and slide the tart onto a serving plate.

PRESENTATION PLATES

When I ordered a special acrylic tiered stand from the Van Horn–Hayward company in Texas (P.O. Box 903, Bellaire, TX 77402; 713-782-8532) and told them my plan for it, they titled it the "Pie in the Sky" stand. The magic of this acrylic stand is that it all but disappears from sight, giving the tarts the illusion of floating in air. These stands can be custom-ordered in whatever size or shape one desires. The sizes needed for the Chocolate Peanut Butter Mousse Seven-Tier Tart are: 4⅜ inches, 5 inches, 7⅜ inches, 8⅞ inches, 9¾ inches, 10½ inches, and 12⅛ inches. (This is the measurement of the bottom of each tart pan.) The spacers are 2¾ inches high.

credits

1 restaurant chefs

pages 10 – 23

Reprinted with the permission of Scribner, a division of Simon & Schuster, from *Lobster at Home* by Jasper White. Text copyright © 1998 by Jasper White. Photographs copyright © 1998 by Thibault Jeanson.

photographs Thibault Jeanson
illustrations Glenn Wolff
design Margery Cantor

pages 24 – 35

From *Le Bernardin Cookbook: Four-Star Simplicity* by Maguy Le Coze and Eric Ripert. Copyright © 1998 by Maguy Le Coze and Eric Ripert. Used by permission of Doubleday, a division of Random House, Inc.

photographs Francois Portman
illustrations Richard Waxberg
book design Deborah Kerner
jacket design Calvin Chu
jacket photograph Wyatt Counts

pages 36 – 43

From *Jean-Georges: Cooking at Home with a Four-Star Chef* by Jean-Georges Vongerichten and Mark Bittman. Copyright © 1998 by Jean-Georges Vongerichten and Mark Bittman. Used by permission of Broadway Books, a division of Random House, Inc.

photographs Quentin Bacon
book design Vertigo Design
jacket design Roberto de Vicq de Cumptich

pages 44 – 51

From *The Cafe Cook Book: Italian Recipes from London's River Cafe* by Rose Gray and Ruth Rogers. Copyright © 1998 by Rose Gray and Ruth Rogers. Used by permission of Broadway Books, a division of Random House, Inc.

food photographs Martyn Thompson
black-and-white photographs Jean Pigozzi
design The Senate

pages 52 – 61

Reprinted with the permission of Simon & Schuster from *The Figs Table: More than 100 Recipes for Pizzas, Pastas, Salads, and Desserts* by Todd English and Sally Sampson. Copyright © 1998 by Todd English and Sally Sampson.

photographs Carl Tremblay
book design Deborah Kerner
jacket design Timothy Hsu

pages 62 – 71

From *Simple Menus for the Bento Box* by Ellen Greaves and Wayne Nish. Copyright © 1998 by Ellen Greaves and Wayne Nish. Photographs copyright © 1998 by Wayne Nish. Used by permission of William Morrow and Company, Inc.

photographs Wayne Nish
design Richard Oriolo

pages 72 – 79

From *Bobby Flay's From My Kitchen to Your Table* by Bobby Flay and Joan Schwartz. Copyright © 1998 by Boy Meets Grill, Inc. Photographs copyright © 1998 by Tom Eckerle. Reprinted by permission of Clarkson N. Potter Publishers, a division of Crown Publishers, Inc.

photographs Tom Eckerle
design Alexander Isley Inc.

3 general interest

4 special subjects

pages 186 – 193

From *Seductions of Rice: A Cookbook* by Jeffrey Alford and Naomi Duguid. Copyright © 1998 by Jeffrey Alford and Naomi Duguid. Used by permission of Artisan, a division of Workman Publishing Company, Inc.

photographs Jeffrey Alford and Naomi Duguid
food photograph (page 189) Colin Faulkner
book design Vertigo Design
jacket design Alexandra Maldonado
jacket photographs Beatriz Da Costa (*top*), Jeffrey Alford and Naomi Duguid (*all others*)

pages 194 – 203

From *Quick from Scratch: Herbs and Spices* edited by Judith Hill. Copyright © 1998 by American Express Publishing Corporation. Reprinted by permission of FOOD & WINE Books, a division of American Express Publishing Corporation.

photographs Melanie Acevedo
design Nina Scerbo

pages 204 – 209

From *Vegetables* by James Peterson. Copyright © 1998 by James Peterson. Used by permission of William Morrow and Company, Inc.

photographs James Peterson
book design Deborah Kerner
jacket design Deborah Kerner and Richard L. Aquan

pages 210 – 219

From *The Complete Meat Cookbook: A Juicy and Authoritative Guide to Selecting, Seasoning, and Cooking Today's Beef, Pork, Lamb, and Veal* by Bruce Aidells and Denis Kelly. Copyright © 1998 by Bruce Aidells and Denis Kelly. Photographs copyright © 1998 by Beatriz Da Costa. Illustrations copyright © 1998 by Mary DePalma. Reprinted by permission of Houghton Mifflin Company.

photographs Beatriz Da Costa
illustrations Mary DePalma
design Susan McClellan

pages 220 – 227

From *Soup: A Way of Life* by Barbara Kafka. Copyright © 1998 by Barbara Kafka. Photographs copyright © 1998 by Gentl & Hyers. Used by permission of Artisan, a division of Workman Publishing Company, Inc.

photographs Gentl & Hyers
book design Vertigo Design
jacket design Susi Oberhelman

pages 228 – 233

From *The Barbecue! Bible* by Steven Raichlen. Copyright © 1998 by Steven Raichlen. Illustrations copyright © 1998 by Margaret Chodos-Irvine. Used by permission of Workman Publishing Company, Inc.

illustrations Margaret Chodos-Irvine
book design Lisa Hollander
jacket design Paul Hanson
jacket photographs Anthony Loew (*author*), Greg Schneider (*chicken, grilled vegetable plate*), StockFood America/Conrad (*red chile pepper*), StockFood America/Bumann (*bell peppers*), Louis Wallach (*all others*)

pages 234 – 239

From *Born to Grill: An American Celebration* by Cheryl Alters Jamison and Bill Jamison. Copyright © 1998 by Cheryl Alters Jamison and Bill Jamison. Illustrations copyright © 1998 by Sara Love. Used by permission of The Harvard Common Press.

illustrations Sara Love
design Kathy Herlihy-Paoli, Inkstone Design
jacket illustration Nancy Stahl

 desserts

pages 242 – 249

From *My Mother's Southern Desserts* by James Villas with Martha Pearl Villas. Text copyright © 1998 by James Villas. Photographs © 1998 by Dennis Gottlieb. Used by permission of William Morrow and Company, Inc.

photographs Dennis Gottlieb
book design Jeannette Jacobs
jacket design Susan Newman Design, Inc.
jacket photograph Amos Chan

pages 250 – 255

From *Chocolate: From Simple Cookies to Extravagant Showstoppers* by Nick Malgieri. Copyright © 1998 by Nick Malgieri. Reprinted by permission of HarperCollins Publishers, Inc.

photographs Tom Eckerle
design Joel Avirom and Jason Snyder

pages 256 – 267

From *Dessert Circus: Extraordinary Desserts You Can Make at Home* by Jacques Torres. Text copyright © 1998 by Team Torres. Dessert photographs copyright © 1998 by John Uher. Used by permission of William Morrow and Company, Inc.

dessert photographs John Uher
design Richard Oriolo
jacket photographs John Uher (*dessert*), Lou Manna (*author*)

pages 268 – 279

From *Desserts by Pierre Hermé* by Pierre Hermé and Dorie Greenspan. Copyright © 1998 by SOCREPA and Dorie Greenspan. Used by permission of Little, Brown and Company.

photographs Hartmut Kiefer
book design Julia Sedykh
jacket design Amy Goldfarb

pages 280 – 285

Reprinted with the permission of Ten Speed Press from *Charlie Trotter's Desserts* by Charlie Trotter. Copyright © 1998 by Charlie Trotter. Color photographs © 1998 by Tim Turner.

color photographs Tim Turner
design Elizabeth Nelson and Adam Kallish

pages 286 – 295

Reprinted with the permission of Scribner, a division of Simon & Schuster, from *The Pie and Pastry Bible* by Rose Levy Beranbaum. Text copyright © 1998 by Cordon Rose, Inc. Illustrations copyright © 1998 by Laura Hartman Maestro. Photographs copyright © 1998 by Gentl & Hyers/Edge.

photographs Gentl & Hyers
Illustrations Laura Hartman Maestro
book design Margery Cantor
jacket design John Fontana

guide to publishers

Artisan (a division of Workman Publishing Company, Inc.)

708 Broadway
New York, NY 10003
(212) 254-5900
www.workman.com

- *Seductions of Rice: A Cookbook* by Jeffrey Alford and Naomi Duguid; ISBN 1-57965-113-5
- *Soup: A Way of Life* by Barbara Kafka; ISBN 1-57965-125-9

Bay Books and Tapes, Inc.

555 De Haro Street, No. 220
San Francisco, CA 94107
(415) 252-4350

- *Jacques Pépin's Kitchen: Encore with Claudine* by Jacques Pépin; ISBN 0-912333-86-3

Broadway Books (a division of Random House, Inc.)

1540 Broadway
New York, NY 10036
(212) 354-6500
www.broadwaybooks.com

- *The Cafe Cook Book: Italian Recipes from London's River Cafe* by Rose Gray and Ruth Rogers; ISBN 0-7679-0213-0
- *Flavors of Tuscany: Traditional Recipes from the Tuscan Countryside* by Nancy Harmon Jenkins; ISBN 0-7679-0144-4
- *Jean-Georges: Cooking at Home with a Four-Star Chef* by Jean-Georges Vongerichten and Mark Bittman; ISBN 0-7679-0155-X

Clarkson N. Potter Publishers

(a division of Crown Publishers, Inc.)

201 East 50th Street
New York, NY 10022
(212) 751-2600
www.clarksonpotter.com

- *Bobby Flay's From My Kitchen to Your Table* by Bobby Flay and Joan Schwartz; ISBN 0-517-70729-2
- *My Mexico: A Culinary Odyssey with More than 300 Recipes* by Diana Kennedy; ISBN 0-609-60247-0
- *The Two Fat Ladies Ride Again* by Clarissa Dickson Wright and Jennifer Paterson; ISBN 0-609-60379-5

Doubleday (a division of Random House, Inc.)

1540 Broadway
New York, NY 10036
(212) 782-9000
www.doublecay.com

- *Le Bernardin Cookbook: Four-Star Simplicity* by Maguy Le Coze and Eric Ripert; ISBN 0-385-48841-6

Food & Wine Books

(a division of American Express Publishing Corporation)

1120 Avenue of the Americas
New York, NY 10036
(212) 382-5618
www.amexpub.com

- *Quick From Scratch: Herbs and Spices* edited by Judith Hill; ISBN 0-916103-45-5

HarperCollins Publishers, Inc.

10 East 53rd Street
New York, NY 10022
(212) 207-7000
www.harpercollins.com

- *Chocolate: From Simple Cookies to Extravagant Showstoppers* by Nick Malgieri; ISBN 0-06-018711-5
- *Mediterranean Grains and Greens: A Book of Savory, Sun-Drenched Recipes* by Paula Wolfert; ISBN 0-06-017251-7

The Harvard Common Press

535 Albany Street
Boston, MA 02118
(617) 423-5303

- *Born to Grill: An American Celebration* by Cheryl Alters Jamison and Bill Jamison; ISBN 1-55832-111-X

Houghton Mifflin Company

222 Berkeley Street
Boston, MA 02116
(617) 351-5000
www.hmco.com/trade

- *The Complete Meat Cookbook: A Juicy and Authoritative Guide to Selecting, Seasoning, and Cooking Today's Beef, Pork, Lamb, and Veal* by Bruce Aidells and Denis Kelly; ISBN 0-395-90492-7
- *The Perfect Recipe: Getting It Right Every Time—Making Our Favorite Dishes the Absolute Best They Can Be* by Pam Anderson; ISBN 0-395-89403-4

Little, Brown and Company

1271 Avenue of the Americas
New York, NY 10020
(212) 522-8700
www.littlebrown.com

- *Desserts by Pierre Hermé* by Pierre Hermé and Dorie Greenspan; ISBN 0-316-35720-0
- *The Yellow Farmhouse Cookbook* by Christopher Kimball; ISBN 0-316-49699-5

Macmillan General Reference USA

(a division Ahsuog, Inc.)

1633 Broadway
New York, NY 10019
(212) 654-8500
www.macmillanusa.com

- *How to Cook Everything: Simple Recipes for Great Food* by Mark Bittman; ISBN 0-02-861010-5

Random House, Inc.

1540 Broadway
New York, NY 10036
(212) 782-9000
www.randomhouse.com

- *Rao's Cookbook: Over 100 Years of Italian Home Cooking* by Frank Pellegrino; ISBN 0-679-45749-6
- *Taste: One Palate's Journey Through the World's Favorite Dishes* by David Rosengarten; ISBN 0-375-50011-1

Rodale Press, Inc.

33 East Minor Street
Emmaus, PA 18098
(610) 967-5171
www.rodale.com

- *The French Culinary Institute's Salute to Healthy Cooking: From America's Foremost French Chefs* by Alain Sailhac, Jacques Pépin, André Soltner, Jacques Torres, and the faculty of the French Culinary Institute; ISBN 0-87586-440-0

Scribner (a division of Simon & Schuster)

1230 Avenue of the Americas
New York, NY 10020
(212) 698-7000
www.simonsays.com

- *Lobster at Home* by Jasper White; ISBN 0-684-80077-2
- *The Pie and Pastry Bible* by Rose Levy Beranbaum; ISBN 0-684-81348-3

Simon & Schuster

1230 Avenue of the Americas
New York, NY 10020
(212) 698-7000
www.simonsays.com

- *The Figs Table: More than 100 Recipes for Pizzas, Pastas, Salads, and Desserts* by Todd English and Sally Sampson; ISBN 0-684-85264-0
- *Newman's Own Cookbook* by Paul Newman and A. E. Hotchner; ISBN 0-684-84832-5

Ten Speed Press

P.O. Box 7123
Berkeley, CA 94707
(510) 559-1600
www.tenspeedpress.com

- *Charlie Trotter's Desserts* by Charlie Trotter; ISBN 0-89815-815-X

William Morrow and Company, Inc.

1350 Avenue of the Americas
New York, NY 10019
(212) 261-6500
www.williammorrow.com

- *Bugialli's Italy: Traditional Recipes from the Regions of Italy* by Giuliano Bugialli; ISBN 0-688-15864-1
- *Dessert Circus: Extraordinary Desserts You Can Make at Home* by Jacques Torres; ISBN 0-688-15654-1
- *Emeril's TV Dinners* by Emeril Lagasse with Marcelle Bienvenu and Felicia Willett; ISBN 0-688-16378-5
- *Lidia's Italian Table* by Lidia Matticchio Bastianich; ISBN 0-688-15410-7
- *My Mother's Southern Desserts* by James Villas with Martha Pearl Villas; ISBN 0-688-15695-9
- *Simple Menus from the Bento Box* by Ellen Greaves and Wayne Nish; ISBN 0-688-14204-4
- *Vegetables* by James Peterson; ISBN 0-688-14658-9

Workman Publishing Company, Inc.

708 Broadway
New York, NY 10003
(212) 254-5900
www.workman.com

- *The Barbecue! Bible* by Steven Raichlen; ISBN 0-7611-1317-7

recipes by course

hors d'oeuvres and first courses

main dishes

index

Page numbers in **boldface** indicate photographs